SACRED AMBITIONS

Pursuing Jesus & Church Planting
—— *in the Regions Beyond* ——

DICK BROGDEN

Published by Abide Publishers
1600 N. Boonville, Suite B&C, Springfield, MO 65803

Cover design, typesetting, and interior design by Lucent Digital
(www.lucentdigital.co).

Cover artwork created by R. N. Hereth.

ISBN-13: 978-1-952562-99-0

Printed in the United States of America

For my big sons and little brothers

Table of Contents

FOREWORD

I can't remember who first told me that there are still billions of people living with little or no access to the knowledge that Jesus loves them, but ever since, this fact has become increasingly unacceptable to me. Similarly, I can't remember when I first learned that approximately forty-two percent of the world has not yet heard the gospel of Jesus Christ, but once again, as I became aware of this sobering reality, I wanted to do so much more than I was currently doing for the unreached.

When I personalize the forty-two percent, the need becomes increasingly urgent. When I imagine my own children as a part of the forty-two percent, lost without access to a church, a missionary, and in some cases no Scripture in a language they understand, I desperately want to engage anyone and everyone to do something, anything, everything to help me find my lost children.

To God, the forty-two percent still unreached are not just a number or percentage. He loves each one in that number very personally. His level of urgency towards them is described in many ways and places throughout Scripture, but none greater than in the ultimate sacrifice of His Son, Jesus. God wants us to do something, anything, everything to find His lost children. We know this because Jesus' last command found in all four Gospels and in Acts was to go into all the world and preach this gospel to all creation, even to the ends of the earth.

Surprisingly, surveys show that very few Christians today are even aware there are still unreached people groups, let alone nearly 7,000 of them. Perhaps even more surprisingly, less than one percent of current church resources are even being used to find the lost children living with little or no access to the gospel.

We need the pendulum of both human and financial resources to swing towards the unreached. It is my prayer that this book would educate and inspire many more to join in Jesus' last command and God's Great Commission of bringing the gospel of Jesus Christ to those still waiting to hear of His love for the very first time.

Personally, my understanding and passion for those living without access to the gospel of Jesus Christ grows every time I read one of Dick's writings, and I hope the same happens for you as you read this book. I hope your passion becomes similar to that of the Apostle Paul when he said: "I have made it my aim to preach the gospel, not where Christ was named, lest I should build on another man's foundation" (Rom. 15:20).

JUSTIN MACK
Project 42 // Access for the Unreached
www.project42partners.org

INTRODUCTION

This book is a day-by-day record of the first months of our church planting journey in a new pioneer field, a record of what I learned, what I did, what I did wrong, and what God did despite me. Each day has a reflection from Scripture and a thought about church planting. Interspersed are thematic thoughts and articles I have written on church planting, leadership, character, and ministry. The intention is to provide a practical reference on what to do and what to avoid. My hope is that the combination of reflections will be of benefit to new church planters who are fired up to represent Jesus among the unreached but wonder where to start.

For the safety of those mentioned, I have changed names and called this wonderful land Narnia. Entering Narnia, we did have a modest level of Arabic, twenty-five years of experience in the Arab world, and the benefit of landing in the house of some friends and renting their car while they were away. What follows assumes the church planters have some of the local language and culture under their belt and are settled in context as they turn their attention and energy towards the work of church planting.

PROLOGUE

We have said our goodbyes and are in the air to our new home. My heart is full of wonder that Jesus allows us the privilege of glorifying His name among the nations. That we, at this point in history in this most critical part of the world, are allowed to go and live for Him joyfully among Narnians is a delight and honor. Jennifer and I know we have nothing in our natural selves to offer, but we are thrilled to be channels of Jesus' love, truth, and power as He sees fit.

Over the last few days trusted friends have shared dreams, pictures, and thoughts with us that are sobering. One was that my sons and I were killed by a crocodile we did not see lurking as we fought off the crocodile we could see. Another friend had a vision of dead flowers, a casket, and cascading pearls—and then later, Muslim women joyfully removing their Islamic veils. Other friends have had dreams and impressions. Jennifer and I have talked about these images, prayed about them, and are at peace. We know that our God is able to deliver us, but if not, we are undismayed.

It was May of 1940. The dreaded German Panzar Division had swept across Europe and had the British Army pinned down at Dunkirk. The British and French generals thought that the narrow twisting roads and paths through the Ardennes Forest were too small to allow the mass movement of the large German tanks and machinery. However, German General Heinz Guderian managed to maneuver the large tank force through the Ardennes and was ready to strike. The British commander was able to get a communiqué back to Britain that consisted of just three words, "but if not!" Those three words sparked a surge of courage, determination and downright grit throughout the British military and the entire civilian population. Those three words brought about the bravest, most unorthodox successful rescue of any army in the pages of history.[1]

I wrote in *Missionary God, Missionary Bible*:

Those same three words [but if not] to a constituency biblically literate enough to know they originated in Daniel also galvanized a nation to pray, with King George calling for prayer from all his citizens. And pray they did. God delivered on the beaches of Dunkirk just as He did at the fiery furnace and the lion's den. Yet, the declaration 'but if not' transcends deliverance; it is a stake in the ground, the contention that as long as God is glorified, we will be satisfied whether by life or death.

Missionaries are not guaranteed safety among the peoples of earth, but we are guaranteed the presence of Jesus. We know God is able to deliver us, but if not, we still won't bow. What's the worst that can happen? We go to our heavenly home and God uses what seems gory for His glory among the people He sent us to love, warn, and woo. After all, martyrdom is God's idea, not the devil's. God is the one who sent His only Son to die for the ransom of all peoples. The devil is astute enough to know with Tertullian that "the blood of the martyrs is indeed the seed of the church," so he distracts, divides, seduces, confuses, and pesters us enough to remove our attention from God's mission. The devil tends to revert to making martyrs when his bloodlust overcomes his senses. Those that die for Jesus are neither fools nor heroes—how can they be when God is the One who choses that death? "But if not!" is the cry of the missionary. It is the joy that whether by life or by death God will be glorified among the nations.[2]

I am not sure what Narnia holds, and in one way I don't really care. Our God is able to deliver us, but if not, all that matters is that He is glorified.

Already the spiritual intensity has been ratcheting up. Our sleep is disturbed with difficult dreams. Jennifer senses more anxiety. We feel a sapping of energy in our physical bodies. The enemy is trying to get us crossways with leaders and friends. At church this week as I was speaking on missions, a new, excellent sound system began to act up—dials moving of their own accord, things happening that the sound crew was sure were demonic. Checking into the airport today,

Jennifer's boarding pass was processed, and while the agents worked on mine, an electrical surge shut all computers down. Lights flickered for about forty-five minutes and an eerie quiet filled the terminal.

None of these things alarm or dissuade us, but they do sober us. We are not naïve; we realize that as Samuel Zwemer said, all wars cost blood and treasure. I spent yesterday writing letters for Jennifer, my sons, my family, and my colleagues in case I miss the significant events in their life. God knows, and I am content to let Him decide. What we do know is that Jesus is worth it. Jesus is worth everything. We are His currency; He will spend us as He sees fit. If my life can be used to glorify Jesus, so be it. If my death can be used to glorify Jesus, so be it. To live is Christ, to die is gain. I do not know what He will choose for me, but this I know, to be with Jesus is *far* better.

In the meantime, for as long as Jesus wants me to represent Him on earth, I want to do so simply. I want to have a single eye on His beauty and a simple devotion to loving Him, loving the church, and loving the lost. I am asking Him to use Jennifer and me to bring joy to Him by making disciples and planting churches among Muslims. We have been at it for twenty-seven years and made many mistakes, seen a little fruit, and are hungrier than ever to see book of Acts-like salvations and multiplication—all in the power of the Holy Spirit.

Thankful for this gift of returning to the ground level for basic cross-cultural evangelism in a pioneer setting, we have been encouraged to record the step-by-step process. I'll try to do it as transparently and practically as possible. The hope is that future pioneers can glean from the ups and downs, successes and failures, joys and pains. Each day I want to write about how we looked to Jesus and pursued Him, and how we pursued our mandate to plant His church.

PURSUING JESUS:

My security is in a person, not in a place. My stronghold is God Himself (Psalm 59:16). We are indeed bulletproof until God's wisdom decides otherwise. There are moments when I think of what could go wrong in Narnia and I shudder, but then I remember my refuge is God Himself and no power of hell or agent of man can hurt me outside of God's loving will and purpose. I choose to trust that God is my defense, to fight against the fear that rises in my heart, to live boldly, and to proclaim joyfully that Jesus saves. Fearless testimony is itself a witness when given from the right heart, a humble heart. Jesus, I want to represent You with courage. Help me; I am not naturally brave.

It seems that the big asks in Luke 11 are for the Kingdom to come (v. 2) (which I understand to be the maranatha cry, "Come back, King Jesus!") and to be re-filled with the Holy Spirit (v. 13). For Narnia, then, I pray these two things: Come, King Jesus, come in power and glory. Certainly, come physically to restore all things, and in the meantime reveal Yourself to Narnians and ransom millions to Yourself. Come to me, Holy Spirit. Fill and possess me. Control and illumine me. Flow through me and out of me. Fill me with *Yourself* so that I live and move and have my being in Your unending strength, wisdom, and creativity. I need You, Lord Jesus, fill me afresh with Your Spirit. Let my eye be single and clear (v. 34) and let there be no darkness in me (v. 36). Let me speak as You lead me, insulting as necessary (v. 45), giving the key of knowledge (v. 52), not taking it away, entering in myself and modeling to others how to follow You. If I will live above reproach (1 Tim. 3:2) and with dignity (v. 8), it can give others great confidence in the faith that is in Christ Jesus (v. 13). Help me, Lord, help me live in such a way that my life and my words are consistent, a unified invitation to the Narnia Muslim to join the household of faith, the church (v. 15).

PURSUING CHURCH PLANTING:

Over this last year Jennifer and I have been reviewing what we have learned about church planting and praying about what we would like to do when we arrive in Narnia. We wanted to have a clear, simple strategy that our team members could follow and adopt, one that addressed the stages of entry, evangelism, disciple making, church formation, and leadership development. Loosely based on the four fields understanding, here is what we came up with:

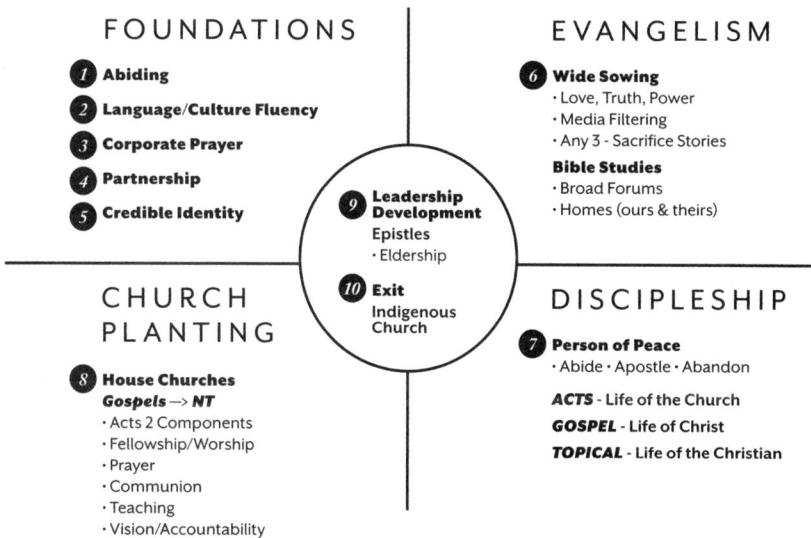

FOUNDATIONS

1. **Abiding**
2. **Language/Culture Fluency**
3. **Corporate Prayer**
4. **Partnership**
5. **Credible Identity**

EVANGELISM

6. **Wide Sowing**
   - Love, Truth, Power
   - Media Filtering
   - Any 3 - Sacrifice Stories

Bible Studies
   - Broad Forums
   - Homes (ours & theirs)

9. **Leadership Development**
   Epistles
   - Eldership

10. **Exit**
    Indigenous Church

CHURCH PLANTING

8. **House Churches**
   Gospels —> NT
   - Acts 2 Components
   - Fellowship/Worship
   - Prayer
   - Communion
   - Teaching
   - Vision/Accountability

DISCIPLESHIP

7. **Person of Peace**
   - Abide · Apostle · Abandon

ACTS - Life of the Church
GOSPEL - Life of Christ
TOPICAL - Life of the Christian

Our first year will be dedicated to the entry stage, Foundations (see graph above). Of course, we do want to be evangelizing during this time, but these are our five priorities for our first year.

The Lord has the sovereign right to change whatever He will, to accelerate the evangelism, discipleship, and church planting phases, but that is up to Him. What we feel led to do is to spend extravagant time abiding with Jesus; working on the local dialect of Arabic; praying more with others and in private intercession (different from personal abiding); learning from other workers and MBBs (Muslim background believers) in the country so we can see what God is already doing and where we can add value (without duplicating, competing, or undermining what God's team is already doing); and setting up a viable identity that will allow long-term visas for ourselves and many others. The identity piece must be robust professionally (legitimate business), culturally (language and local customs and behaviors within biblical parameters), and most important spiritually. We must clearly establish that we are Jesus/Bible people from the beginning.

We are looking at four possible tracks for visas:

1. Step Global: We will begin with this business, opening a branch in the city focusing on intercultural training. I would like to find a way to bring Chi Alpha (university ministry) and church-based teams to Narnia, running all finances through our business. We also want to facilitate Narnians going to the U.S. for education or medical services and while there, link them to Christians for hospitality and witness. This, too, would be monetized.

2. Assemblies of God Narnia Arabia (LLC): Rather than hiding our global AG connections, I want to leverage them. We have university presidents, global leaders, professors, coaches, men and women of the highest leadership caliber. I would like to create an adjunct faculty that can come and coach for a fee in all sectors of Narnian society.

3. All Nations: This is a shared workspace idea that would be building based, housing office space, childcare facilities, meeting rooms, conference halls, etc. It would be rented out to the community all week and provide a space for Step Global training and international churches.

4. We have started a discussion with the U.S. State Department for them to approach Narnian authorities with the request to have the Assemblies of God church registered in Narnia. We are asking for 300 clergy visas and the right to own property. There are thirty-three million people living in Narnia (2019) and ten million of which are expatriate. We would like clergy visas to pastor those expatriates who are Christians, be able to meet with them legally, and train them all to be missionaries who start house churches among their Narnian friends (off the radar).

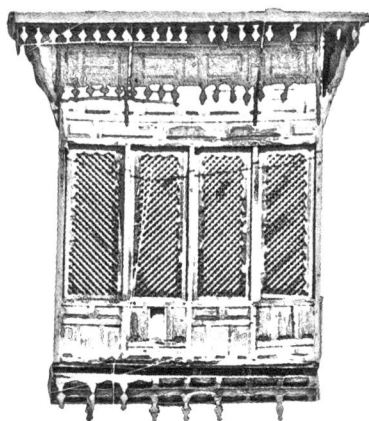

TO BE KNOWN

In every human heart there is a desire at some level to be seen, to be known, to be loved. We were created to love and be loved. Thus, when we feel unloved, we seek love in a continuum of ways. We are wired to think that if we are known, we will be loved, so we search for love by seeking to be known. The desire to be known has a range of motivations, some seemingly better than others, but all broken. We attempt to be known....

1. For Being Terrible

Sometimes we seek to be known for being powerful or for causing fear, for being dangerous or notorious for some egregious or outlandish behavior. Sometimes it's subtler. We seek to be known for being shocking, for being contrary, for being hard to please. When we seek attention by flirting, by crudity, by exaggeration, or by bragging, these all are permutations of what is wicked, and we are seeking to be known for being terrible.

2. For Being Known

Sometimes we seek to be known for being beautiful, strong, glamorous, rich, witty, charming, adventurous, courageous, or erudite. We buy into the lie that any attention is good attention, and we crave the eyes, respect, and admiration of others, no matter what it costs our body, soul, or relationships. It's the celebrity syndrome. We just want attention, and we do anything (with diminishing returns) to get it.

3. For Being Different

Sometimes we seek to be known by being unique. Our identity is that we are other, opposed to whatever anyone says, for we find people notice us when we object. We can be that negative voice that always finds fault, for our critical orientation makes others pay attention to us, makes others try to please us—and this feeds our vanity. We feel better about ourselves when we find fault in others. We find value in non-conformity, not based on principle but based on attention.

4. For Being Inclusive

Sometimes we seek to be known by being generous of heart, pluralistic, broad-minded, accommodating, pleasing to all. When inclusivity at heart is from a desire to be affirmed, it leads to the dilution of truth and a reverse bigotry that accepts all, except those who are themselves principled. When inclusion is the goal, perversion is the result.

5. For Knowing

Sometimes we seek to be known by being the expert in the field. Our self-value is drawn when we think we know more than others or when others laud us as the leading light in a particular arena. We put great effort into our specialty, for it brings us praise, which we mistake for love.

6. For Being Good

Sometimes we seek to be known for being wise, kind, and generous. We want to be known for being a good spouse, a good parent, a good team member, or a good leader. We draw affirmation for being humanitarians, liberal, for doing the right thing, for behavior that society finds refreshing and empowering of others. Our value comes from the commendation we receive when our good deeds are recognized by others. We love others because we want desperately to be loved.

7. For Being Holy

Sometimes, both in the circle of faith and by the watching world, we want to be known for being righteous, spiritual, prayerful, or anointed. Our identity and worth are drawn from people's respect of our "godliness." We make it our ambition to be known for being biblical, pure, and devout. This desire can be all the more twisted as it has a great appearance of virtue.

8. For Being Fruitful

Sometimes we seek to be known for being effective in ministry. We take our pride and energy from having a large church, from having a broad ministry, from influencing many and making many disciples, from having a spiritual tree that is the envy of our peers. We work, labor, and dedicate ourselves in spiritual service so that we will be known as the one with the most significant ministry impact.

9. For Being Faithful

Sometimes we scorn our colleagues who take pride in being known for numbers and make the equal and opposite error of wanting to be known for being faithful. We shun the spotlight but secretly revel in how many years we have been laboring in obscure places with scant attention. We still secretly want attention, but we want it because we have built a reputation of faithfulness.

10. For Being Unknown

Sometimes all the above motivations repel us, and we frame our desire to be known through the curious twist of wanting to be unknown. This desire can be the most complex as it does indeed recognize the danger of the desire to be known, yet deep down there is still a longing for recognition. Similar to being proud for being humble, this desire can be the most convoluted of them all.

11. For Making Him Known

Sometimes we seek attention by being the outspoken one for Jesus. We seek apostolic fame by being the one who pioneers, the one who is bold, the one who risks all for Christ, the one who endures hardship, isolation, danger, persecution, scorn, and the loss of all things. Our value is drawn by being recognized for being zealous for the glory of God. Like all these latter motivations there is a subtle something not quite plumb, a pursuit of noble and priceless goals that is colored yet by that incessant desire to be known, known for what is right.

12. For Knowing Him

Sometimes we realize that being known for our actions, even our actions for Him, is suspect and we simply desire to know Him. We desire others to see that the central aspect of our being is that we long to know Jesus. While this may be the purest of the desires to be known, it is still broken, as are all the desires to be known.

This continuum of reasons to be known are all marred, some worse than others. They are marred because at their root is the desire to be known, rather than the desire to know. Paul did not say, "I want to be known for knowing Christ." He just wanted to know Christ. The purest motivation of heart is the simple desire to know Jesus and the laying down of wanting to be known. We Christians long to be known with all men; we just tend to spiritualize what is, at its core, a broken self-love. Only in laying down the desire to be known and taking up the raging desire to know Christ can we truly be pure in heart.

I confess that all twelve of these desires to be known have flickered or raged in my heart, and still do. Jesus, forgive me. Jesus, may my ambition truly be not to be known, not even for good things. Let my one fire be to know Christ. For when we simply, purely, wholly long to know Jesus, we realize we are already known. He sees us, He knows us, and He loves us. Secure in the knowledge that our Creator loves us, knows us, and sees us, we no longer need to be seen or known by man. We then do what is good, true, and holy for His sake, not for the sake of being known, and we glow from the inside out with the security of the love of God.

PURSUING JESUS:

Banners of truth need to be displayed (Psalm 60:4). May Jesus help me wave His truth fearlessly in Narnia. He chooses what kind of vessel we are, honorable or not (vv. 7–8); it is our joy to be used. At the end of the day, we do valiantly *through God*, for He is the One who treads down (vv. 11–12). There is only One whom I should fear (Luke 12:5) and disobedience will be punished with greater severity for those with greater understanding of His will (vv. 47–48). Much has been given to me (spiritual heritage); now much is required. Though there is pressure to it, I must live a transparent and disciplined life (1 Tim. 4:8,15), taking pains, being absorbed to live as an example (v. 12). I must persevere in the things (teaching!) that Jesus has asked me to do (v. 16) as it will have eternal consequence both for me and for those who hear me.

PURSUING CHURCH PLANTING:

Teaching is a critical part of church planting, despite some who say otherwise. Yes, the Spirit will teach us (Luke 12:12), but we must also be devoted to teaching others (1 Tim. 4:16). We must take pains, be absorbed, and persevere in teaching. It is critical.

On this first morning in Narnia, I took my Bible to Starbucks and have been reading it openly. I did not do this to be seen by others or to get "boldness" credit, but as a statement to myself, that I would be a Jesus and Bible person from the beginning, ever and always. I sat next to a Narnian man and we had a good conversation. He asked me about my profession and I told him about Step Global and how we train expatriates coming to Narnia and Narnians going abroad. He loved the idea as he was a student himself in America and would have appreciated such training. I was very open with him that I am a pastor sent by the church and he had no objections. We exchanged numbers and he has offered to help me as he can. I want to be intentional about a robust and legitimate identity—one that is clearly Jesus, Bible, and church-related while at the same time being professionally and culturally robust.

One way I have considered describing myself is as a *murshid mesiihi*. This means a Christian guide, with connotations of being a spiritual advisor. I am not sure how the term "pastor" is understood in Narnia, but I will experiment with it and see.

DAY 3

PURSUING JESUS:

Jesus leads us to refuge, strength, answers, and security (Psalm 61:1–4) and appoints to us lovingkindness and truth (v. 7). Jesus can keep me safe and make me loving and truthful. For this I pray. It's interesting that Jesus was not above humiliating those who opposed Him (Luke 13:17 NASB). It's also noteworthy that Jesus was ever a teacher, never stopped being a rabbi, teaching as He proceeded (v. 22). It is always the establishment that kills prophets (v. 33).

As a faithful minister of the gospel, I must work hard at preaching and teaching (1 Tim. 5:17). I must also be ruthless against sin in my own life. Some sins are evident, some catch up with you later (v. 24), but all sin catches up with you and with the body. Whether with myself or with those I lead, sin must be dealt with firmly. But I can only deal with sin in others if I have been flayed open by others and the Spirit, received correction, repented, and walked in holiness. Nothing is as stinky as the sinner who pretends to be a saint. It is a puzzle, then, how the Lord uses anyone to correct anyone as we are all sinful. The true bearing of anyone the Lord would use to call to holiness must be a deep and sincere humility. For this I ask, Lord Jesus, true holiness and true humility, for any hypocrisy at all sullies what the Spirit wants to do. Lord, teach me the balance of working hard at teaching, preaching, and holiness *while* I recognize that I am completely dependent on You. Without the Spirit I can do nothing.

Pursuing Church Planting:

Today, we are attending the Weekly Meal, which is where the missionaries and like-minded (businesspeople who want to share their faith) gather for fellowship. On the continuum of missionaries some are more security conscious than others; some do not use the word "missionary" even around their children. I understand their concern (as the word is misunderstood in Muslim society and is inflammatory), while my concern is that it *is* understood in society and so we back away from the truth that we are conversionary cross-cultural evangelists, commissioned to preach and teach.

I am on the other far end of the security continuum, believing it is better to be more transparent and open, finding ways to explain that we are ministers of the gospel, sent by the church, with the goal of seeing Narnians saved from sin, becoming followers of Christ openly and part of His global and historic body. Because of my more open position (and public profile), it is likely that I make some nervous and they prefer not to engage or interact with me. I understand this and bear no ill will. Going to the meeting today (and building relationships moving forward), we don't want to walk in arrogantly. We want to come in lowly, even as we hold to our own convictions, learning from others who have been here longer and understand the context well. There is room in our hearts for others who see things differently. We want to be learners, slow to speak, quick to listen. We want to be prayerful and patient, waiting for the Lord to show us what to do here, how to partner well, where we can add value, where we should adjust, and where we need to stand on our convictions.

The principle is that partnership is beautiful and necessary, and that others have wisdom and insight we need to glean from. No one person, entity, or approach is perfect. The body needs diversity and mission work requires partnership wherever possible without the gospel being compromised. So, the goal for this first year is to build relationship with other missionaries, learn from them, bless them, stay lowly, and see where we can partner and add value to what is already in place. It may be that there are convictions which lead us to do some things outside of what is already being done, but those are later decisions. On the front end we need to listen, learn, and partner where we can.

God always has people in the city. His Spirit has ever been at work. Jesus, let there be no presumption or pride in me. Help me come down. Help me stay a learner and a blesser.

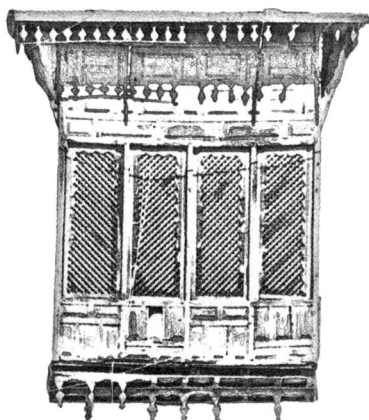

THE BEST (AND HARDEST) JOB IN ALL THE WORLD

Jennifer and I took some time to rest, renew, read, and refresh. As part of the process, I decided to re-read C. S. Lewis' *The Chronicles of Narnia* and re-watch J. R. R. Tolkien's *The Lord of The Rings*. From the plethora of rich material, one common theme reached out and smacked me: the allure of power—ostensibly to do good—and its inevitable corrupting influence.

This is the major theme in *The Lord of the Rings*, of course, where men, dwarves, elves, and hobbits are all tempted with varying results. The same idea is found in *The Last Battle* when Shift, the ape, convinces Puzzle, the ass, to don a lion's skin and pretend to be Aslan so that "everyone would do whatever you told them."

"But I don't want to tell them anything," said Puzzle.

"But think of all the good we could do!" said Shift. "You'd have me to advise you, you know. I'd think of sensible orders for you to give. And everyone would have to obey us, even the King himself. We would set everything right in Narnia."

And so it ever starts in our twisted human hearts. We survey the landscape and in judgment see what we think is wrong. We reflect on what we would do if we had the power to change things. Ambition creeps in and we tell ourselves that we'll only wear the ring or the lion skin to do good. Ever so slowly and steadily our eyes shift from our current assignment to the one we wish we had so that we could "serve the greater good."

I have fallen prey to this confusion over the last several years. With one eye on my present assignment and the other on the possibilities if only I had "the power," I became cross-eyed and lost focus on what is the best job in the world.

The best job in all the world is making disciples where there are none.

The best job in all the world is planting churches where there are none.

The best job in all the world is being a pioneer missionary on the frontier.

The best job in all the world is proclaiming Jesus where He is not known.

The best and hardest job in all the world is fighting for the lost where Satan has his throne.

Why do we want to do anything else?

In Isaiah 28:5–6, it is written: "In that day the Lord of hosts will be for a crown of glory and a diadem of beauty, to the remnant of His people, for a spirit of justice to him who sits in judgment, and for strength to those who turn back the battle at the gate."

I think back to all those city- and castle-storming scenes in *The Lord of the Rings*. The vital action was the desperate fights at ground level where the hoards of orcs and other demonic beings swarmed towards the gates. That's where I really want to be—in the thick of it all.

We are privileged to be assigned to turn back the battle at the gate. Our station is at the edge of hell. Our call is to those who have not heard in the most dangerous, difficult, and volatile places of earth. Who in their right mind and spirit would want to be anywhere else? Fighting at the gate is where our beauty and strength is found.

Let's keep both eyes on the prize: "Lift up your heads, O ye gates. And be ye lifted up ye everlasting doors that the King of Glory shall come in" (Psalm 24:9).

PURSUING JESUS:

Ohne key way we pursue Jesus is by silent waiting (Psalm 62:1). Lord, help me to be patient here in Narnia, not to launch out and then ask you to bless. Let me have the discipline to wait for you. Position is vanity and a lie, lighter than breath (v. 9), for all power belongs to God (v. 11). Jesus learned/knew how to deal with the pressure of being watched. He didn't back down from doing what was right, robustly "taking hold to heal" (Luke 14:1, 4).

God still has room at His table, though man continually rejects the invitation (Luke 14:16–24). It's not a universalist free-for-all (v. 15), but anyone left out is left out due to their own stubborn and insulting refusals. Heaven has space yet, and God still invites. Hell is crowded because of man's badness, not God's.

We have to carry our own cross (v. 27). Jesus carried His, not ours. In comparison to our obedient love for Jesus, all other loves must seem like hate (v. 26). We simply can't be a disciple if we don't give up all our possessions (v. 33). We are most salty (v. 34) when we have nothing of ourselves, clutch nothing, own nothing, and steward everything. We will take nothing from this world; thus, our contentment should be with godliness, which is great gain, and the only thing we carry with us to eternity (1 Tim. 6:6–7).

Godly men are called to be both gentle and to fight the good fight of faith without being argumentative with those who twist the knowledge of God (v. 11–12, 20). What we need to focus on is *the blessed and only Sovereign, the King of kings and Lord of lords, who alone possesses immortality and dwells in unapproachable light, whom no man has seen or can see.* (vv. 15–16). The ***awesomesomeness*** of Jesus (no man has seen or can see!) in all His glory is what I want to fight, advocate, announce, and live for.

Pursuing Church Planting:

Waiting for the King who will come in His due time (1 Tim. 6:15) is an essential and difficult component of church planting. I have many ideas in my head about business platforms, ministry opportunities, partnership roles, evangelistic outreaches, and church formation. As I think of them, I note that anxiety and doubt creep in: anxiety about how to accomplish them with the practical and spiritual forces that resist gospel advance, and doubt as to whether they are good ideas, God ideas, or just plans of the flesh. For both anxiety and doubt, my church planting solution is to wait (in prayer) for Jesus to come. Jesus can open doors I haven't even thought of; Jesus can give peace where the enemy sows anxiety; and Jesus can assure my doubts and confirm what I'm thinking—if I will but wait for Him. In the waiting, He can also correct my thinking if it's errant, amend or tweak it if needed, or simply remove that passion and replace it with His zeal and energy in a different direction.

Waiting on God is a critical tool for church planting. There is much to do, and night comes when no man can work, but we cannot let this reality rush us into an equal and opposite error of launching out without the blessing of God. Waiting is a gift. It protects, calms, and assures.

PURSUING JESUS:

Jesus, I want to seek You, yearn, thirst for You. I want to remember, meditate, cling. I want to praise, sing, bless, lift up Your name (Psalm 63). Help me be intentional about pursuing You all day long. With the same intensity, let me "go after…until," search carefully, and with compassion run to the lost (Luke 15:4, 8, 20). Let me ask to be filled with power because I was baptized and re-baptized in the Holy Spirit, refusing to move on until the Lord has endued with power (Acts 1:4–8). Let me kindle afresh what You have given and bestowed (2 Tim. 1:6), taking responsibility to pursue what God has granted. Jesus, today I recommit to seeking You, pursuing You, waiting for You, and longing for You with intensity. Jesus, help me likewise have intensity in seeking the lost that You love.

PURSUING CHURCH PLANTING:

We had a lovely breakfast on the water with colleagues yesterday and talked about team life. We need one another, and we need to base all we do on prayer. Our team is small right now (two couples and two children), and small fosters intimacy. I pray that we can create a culture together of simple devotion to Jesus and the lost. After breakfast we went to the old town area of the city and saw a historic house under renovation. The guard, named David, was from Yemen, and he said that Noah's son Shem was the "founder" of the Yemeni nation. I asked him if he had ever read David's psalms found in the Bible. He replied he had only read the Qur'an. I was trying to find a way to get him interested in the Bible, but it did not result. I would like to carry Scriptures with me so that I have something to put in their hands if possible. Oh, that Jehovah would dwell again in the tents of Shem, in Yemeni hearts!

We moved into our apartment today, and I was pleased to meet the Sudanese house guard named Mohammad. He is very kind and has invited me to tea in his one room living quarters. I plan to take him up on it. I also met the landlord Abdullah (who lives in the flat across the hall) and his son Samir (who lives in the flat below us) and works at the ministry of health. They were assisting us getting our gas line turned on. After working with Mohammad for twenty minutes and chatting in Arabic, Samir asked me, "How long have you been in Narnia?" I answered, "Three days." He stepped back wide-eyed in astonishment and exclaimed, "Three days?! And you can speak Arabic like that?" I laughed and explained that we have been in the Arab world for 27 years. It made me thankful for the Arabic I have and hungry to learn this dialect well so I can evangelize and disciple.

It is evident that the missionary couple that live in this house (we are sub-renting it for six months while they are in America, giving us time to find a place) have been wise and intentional. The Narnians know they are Christians and love them. Their house is prudently and contextually arranged, allowing for both a sitting room (*majlis*) for Narnian visitors and a private, comfortable space for the family upstairs. The home is a simple but practical church planting tool, and to set it up in a way conducive for hospitality and as a haven is a subtle but important skill. This family has done it well. I respect them for it.

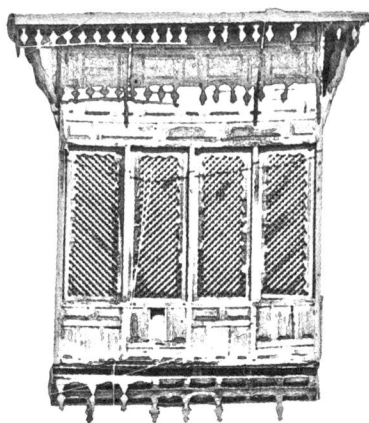

IN LINE, OUT OF STEP

My father likes to tell the anecdote of the proud parent watching a parade: "Look at that!" a mother exclaimed. "All those boys are out of step, except my son."

We the church (the called-out ones) are in this world, but not to be of it. We are to live in society as salt, light, and a prophetic voice while completely allegiant to King Jesus. We are to obey authorities and live in harmony wherever that command and chorus is not dissonant with the heavenly Word. We are to march in the parade, united with it—yet gloriously out of step.

The followers of the Lord Jesus Christ are to live in faith, not fear. We are to serve, not self-preserve. We are to risk, not retreat. We are not to confuse caution with cowardice. We are to go when others stay, and we are to stay when others leave. We are to stand with the poor, the suffering, the sick, the weak, and the lost, and die so that others might live. Followers of Jesus live in the slums, touch the lepers, and embed among the unreached. Followers of Jesus open their mouths and speak what is unpopular. Followers of Jesus take up crosses and lay down lives. Followers of Jesus shine brightest when the world is darkest.

Because of a hidden, unseen virus the world recoils in fear. This is an unprecedented opportunity for the glory of Christ to be evident among the nations through His church. Let's joyfully march in the parade out of step. Let's be the ones who risk. Let's be the ones who serve. Let's be the ones who touch. Let's be the ones who bless. Let's be the ones who mingle. Let's be the ones who give. Let's be the ones who travel across the street and to the uttermost, the unengaged, and the underserved. Let's be the ones who whistle with cheer. Let's be the ones who show no fear.

Let these days of worry be the very days where the church marches in the parade obviously and wonderfully out of step with the world. May the Father above look down in pride upon the earth and exclaim: "Well, will you look at that! All the earth is out of step—except my sons."

PURSUING JESUS:

God deals violently with those who oppose Him by opposing His children (Psalm 64:7). He is the defender who makes the playground bullies quake in fear (v. 9). The Kingdom is entered forcefully, and ultimately hell is violently real with no escape from torment, agony, and flame (Luke 16:19–30). The Holy Spirit came with a mighty rushing wind (Acts 2:2). And the Lord has promised to pour out (in a torrent, not a dribble) His Spirit (vv. 17–18). No soldier in active service entangles himself in the affairs of everyday life, so that he may please the one who enlisted him as a soldier (2 Tim. 2:4).

There is nothing passive about Almighty God. He forcefully intervenes on our behalf; He causes our enemies to quake. He literally punishes the wicked with eternal hell (and would not be good if He did not). He powerfully fills with His Spirit. The Kingdom advances violently (passionately, actively, purposefully, militantly in the Spirit), and I must have a soldier mentality, focused on fighting for the glory of God to the exclusion of all else. Jesus, help me be focused on one thing: Your glory. Better said, let me be focused on *You*! Let me be consumed on fighting to be with You, to know You, to obey Your orders. Let me push the cares, daily worries, and busyness to the side and contend to obey You, to fight to know You, to fight to help others know You. There are many things that call for my attention—many good things and many useless things. Oh, Jesus, fill me violently, forcefully with Your Spirit that I can think of nothing else than obeying Your orders and making You smile.

PURSUING CHURCH PLANTING:

Yesterday was a mix of the normal and the sublime, as is usual in missionary life. Still suffering from jet lag, I woke up around 3 a.m. and enjoyed a wonderful time of reading the Bible and abiding in Jesus. When dawn came, I went for a walk along the wadi (stream bed) that has pleasant walking paths and an exercise station. Returning home, I did my usual writing (currently working through the book of Proverbs and the *Missionary God, Missionary Bible* devotional) followed by email correspondence, then reading while the air conditioning maintenance workers came. A pretty staid, stay-at-home morning and early afternoon. Staid, but stirred as I'm reading E. Stanley Jones' *Christ of the Indian Road*. I'm struck with the elegant simplicity of lectures for the upper classes focusing on Jesus in a way that avoids the baggage of Western Christianity while being absolutely faithful to Christ. Reading his description of the lecture series and the content he would deliver stirred me to do something similar here in Narnia. I would love to give a series of lectures on Jesus that is open to the Muslim community, respectful but uncompromising as Jones so adroitly models.

At 4 p.m. I went to meet with Thomas, a young (31) Narnian entrepreneur. He is an energy bunny and connected me to government officials, lawyers, and businesses by phone. We spent four hours together, went out for tea and cake, and visited his coffeehouse business and his shared workspace locations. He introduced me to influential Narnians including an interior designer who said she would be delighted to meet Jennifer. The lawyer was very informative about business registrations and investment details. It was a helpful if slightly discouraging meeting. The government wants more and more Narnians to work, so it's becoming harder to register foreign entities unless you can prove they don't take jobs from Narnians. They also regulate the sectors for investment.

I realized I am sensing mounting pressure to figure out how to get visas for other team members. On the visa I currently have, I cannot purchase a car in my own name, rent an apartment in my own name, or open a bank account.

The pressure I sense could lead to rush and worry. I was reminded in my abiding time today to trust Jesus and to take one thing at a time. I do have the multi-year visa and we do have the opportunity to learn language without extra duties. I should not squander that opportunity. The first step is to figure out in the short term how to get needed funds into the country. The second step is to slowly investigate how to get the residence visa (whether by setting up our own business or finding a company who will issue it to me as part of a cooperative association, where on the books I am their employee but in reality, my U.S. company pays me through them).

I was able to ask Thomas if he ever read the Bible; he said no. I asked if he would read it if I gave it to him; he said yes. I asked if we could meet to discuss what he reads; he said yes. I gave him the Bible and he calmly held it as other Narnians joined us in the elevator. When we got into his car, he put it in his glove compartment and said with a smile, "This book is a little dangerous here." At the end of the evening I had the chance to clearly share the gospel for about twenty minutes. I felt the Lord's passion, presence, and power as I shared. Thomas asked great questions, and at the end, we embraced. He is working out details with his mother for when we can visit his house. Providentially, they live near our apartment.

I am reminded of 2 Timothy 2:4 which says, "No soldier in active service entangles himself in the affairs of everyday life…." Thomas is a whirlwind of activity. He knows so many influential people. He is starting multiple businesses. He very well could be a person of peace. He also could drag me into a thousand intoxicating possibilities that are not quite my assignment. I have noticed the allure of power and charming connections. Narnia from the outside is so intimidating and forbidding, but on the inside, we are meeting charming and engaging people, surprisingly women as much as men, in the marketplace. There is an allure to be cool, connected, busy, engaged in community, moving among the progressive and intelligent, amused and enchanted by connecting with the new Narnian culture. I feel there is a subtle possibility of diversion there.

Jesus, help me stay centered on church planting. Help me not to give into the anxious thoughts of how money, cars, apartments, bank accounts, visas, and everything else will all work out, to not be distracted by them so that I don't do my soldier work of church planting: abiding in You, language and culture, building Kingdom partnerships, prayer. And then slowly and calmly, one by one working out the details of identity and longevity. I have the gift of the multi-year visa and the opportunity to learn language before things get busy. I have the gift to build a schedule oriented around abiding and prayer. Jesus, let me not through impatience (or the temptation to run with the cool Narnian crowd) squander that opportunity. Give me discernment to take little steps in wise ways. I am an active service soldier. Let me not be entangled in the affairs of everyday life, so that I may please the One who enlisted me.

DAY 7

PURSUING JESUS:

The overflow of God is such that man and nature cannot contain Him. His paths drip with bounty and fatness (Psalm 65:11–12). Jesus fills to overflowing. To meet Him is to be overwhelmed with joy, enough to share and pass on. The cure for being an underwhelming presence on earth is to be overwhelmed with our heavenly God. God does so much for us, and our obedient service is our expression of thankfulness; hence, we do not need to be thanked for being thankful (Luke 17:10). God does not exist to thank or glorify us. We exist to make much of Him for the magnificent wonders He has done for us, even as we wait for the restoration of all things when King Jesus comes with a flash to shine (v. 24). There is no greater blessing than being turned to Jesus by Jesus (Acts 3:26). We will be persecuted and rescued, and in all things the Bible is able to give us wisdom to teach, reprove, correct, train, and make us adequate (2 Tim. 3:11–12, 15–17). Oh, hallelujah! Jesus, I am overwhelmed and inadequate, but, *You*, Lord of heaven and earth, are overwhelming and overflowing, and You have given us Your sacred Scripture and Spirit to make us adequate.

PURSUING CHURCH PLANTING:

Language school began yesterday. It was comforting to realize how much we have retained and how transferrable our Sudanese Arabic is to Narnian. It was sobering to realize how much we have yet to learn. There are many Narnians who speak English and all understand our Arabic, yet it is critical that we press in and learn to speak the heart language of the precious Narnians we are called to evangelize.

Herbert A. Simon said: "The great enemy of foreign language learning is a sense of shame, an inability or unwillingness to become like a child again and let one's inadequacies show."[3] When we first studied Arabic, we were in a classic language school and studied Modern Standard Arabic first. I am grateful for this and would not change it, for we learned the grammar and can speak anywhere in the Arab world. This time we are doing GPA (guided participatory approach) which begins with the focus on hearing. In principle the concept is that you learn your second language as you did your first—listening before speaking. There are some flaws or limitations in the concept, but the heart is right: lowliness.

Language learning, as my friend Timothy says, is indeed sanctification. We must swallow our pride and our desire to look intelligent and sound inspiring and have the simplicity of a child, sitting at the feet of cultural nurturers and coaches. There are many reasons to truncate language learning or to settle for less than fluency (the primary reasons being the difficulty and required time), but a subtler reason is pride. We don't want to be tutored long; rather, we long to have the prestige of being the teacher. Language learning is a long, humble road with no exit ramp. The lessons may become milder, but a good missionary must always be learning, and the first steps in raising up local leaders is by following them.

Lao Tzu (some debate the origin) said: "Go to the people. Live with them. Learn from them. Love them. Start with what they know. Build with what they have. But with the best leaders, when the work is done, the task accomplished, the people will say, 'We have done this ourselves.'" Whether Lao Tzu or not, the principle is real: We must ever be learners if we would aspire to teach. We must follow first before we lead.

Another enemy to linguistic and cultural fluency is the friendship we must pursue with evangelism. A sense of urgency propels us to proclaim the gospel, for all around us the lost perish. After all we were commissioned to make disciples (the end goal), not learn language (the means). We must not allow church planting and language learning to become enemies in our emotions or thoughts. We must see them as a married couple, ever destined to work together. We must also recognize the seasonal nature of prioritizing language learning early on so that we can prioritize church planting skillfully for the long haul. Essentially, we do both all the time, but in different ratios. In the beginning of our missionary career we must put long hours into language learning (while taking the opportunity to evangelize in the language we do know). After we gain a base level of language capacity, we spend the majority of our time ministering in the heart language while taking the opportunity to refine our language aptitude along the way. As in any marriage, there will be times of tension and compromise, but the union must never be questioned or undermined. Let us be so committed to planting churches among the unreached that we are completely dedicated to linguistic and cultural fluency.

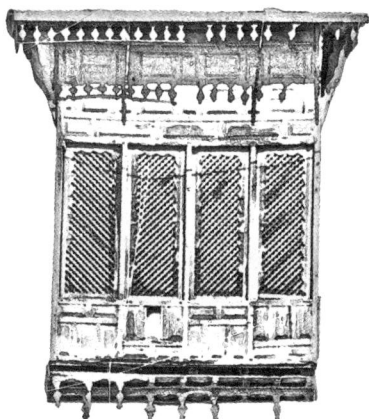

DEALING WITH DISAPPOINTMENT

In missions, ministry, marriage, and life, we will deal with disappointment in others and with ourselves. Here are some ways to deal with the inevitable disappointment that arises from being fallen humans living and working with fallen humans.

1. Keep your eyes on Jesus.

There is only One who never fails. Parents, friends, children, colleagues, leaders, disciples, mentors, heroes will eventually fail you. Only Jesus is enduringly faithful and ever available. All others stumble or leave. Discouragement, in effect, is a transfer of our eyes and thoughts away from the perfect One to the imperfect ones.

The devil constantly tries to manipulate our disappointment with one another into broader disillusionment. Relational hurts quickly snowball into grievances against the team, the body of Christ, the church, the denomination, the missions agency, or the ultimate aim of the devil's messing with us—disappointment with God.

When we are disappointed in ourselves or others, the first thing we need to do is keep our eyes on Jesus. Jesus never fails.

2. Keep your mind on Scripture.

When dealing with disappointment, we need to read more Scripture, not less. The tendency is to fill our head with grievances (real or imagined), and we lay awake at night replaying conversations and interactions, building angst not calm. What we need to do is read the Bible (often out loud). We need to stand on the promises of God. We need to shift our thoughts away from a fixation on relational difficulties, which are passing, to a fixation on the timeless truths of God's character as revealed in the Word. Focusing on the macro-workings of God in history and the world helps in dealing with the disappointments of our micro-experience. The big picture is not about us and what happens to us. The big picture is about God and what He is doing across time and space. Rather than navel gazing, Scripture helps lift our eyes to the eternal One.

When our eyes are on God's global glory, we do not fixate on the bumps and bruises inevitable in daily life (often from friends and colleagues). When you play a game of rugby, you have to absorb some hits—some from well-meaning teammates who inadvertently crash into you or who, in truth, sometimes intentionally squash you in order to push back the enemy. Sometimes their cleats must accidentally or unfortunately rake your back to hold ground against the opposition. In such times, to stop playing the game in a huff in order to concentrate on your hurts is counterproductive to the overall goal of the team. You absorb the pain, seeing it for its minor status in the big scheme of things, and you play on with eyes fixed on the prize. Even so, we deal with disappointment by getting over ourselves and our minor complaints and by concentrating on what God is doing in all the earth. Focus on who God is as Scripture reveals Him, not on your petty injuries. And if indeed your injuries are so debilitating that you have to step off the field for a season, stand on the sidelines and cheer.

3. Keep asking to be filled with the Spirit.

When we are disappointed, our spirits are swimming in a multitude of emotions and essences—anger, hurt, loneliness, frustration, impatience, selfishness, carnality, misunderstanding, miscommunication, and fatigue. All of these are in us as well as others. We need to be intentional that the overriding spirit of what we do and say, think and react, is not ours but the Spirit of God. When disappointed, we need to avoid the imprecatory psalms ("Break their teeth in their mouth, O God!") and focus on the Spirit of Jesus ("Father, forgive them. Forgive me. We do not know what we do."). When dealing with disappointment, we should repeatedly pray: "Father, fill me anew and afresh with Your Spirit. Control my emotions and my tongue. Speak through me. Let me represent Your heart and Your Spirit, not a spirit of the world, the flesh, or the devil."

4. Keep praying the mercy prayer.

The mercy prayer is not a formula or magic spell to be repeated mindlessly. It is a prayer that enters into the viewpoint of Jesus for the other. In essence the prayer is:

> Lord, fill the one I am thinking of (disappointed in) with FLOODS of Your fulfilling mercy. Meet their every need as You see it, not as I see it. Draw them to Yourself, make Jesus real to them, and fill them with Your Holy Spirit.

The essence of the prayer, not the strict repetition of it, is the critical thing. As we pray mercy on the other, two things usually happen, one of them always happens (if we have prayed in good faith and prayed through until victory). What always happens is that our heart softens and changes toward the other. What usually or often happens is that they sense our compassionate heart towards them and their heart softens towards us. This mutual softening paves the way for understanding, reconciliation, and restoration.

When we keep forgiving and blessing others, especially those who have hurt us, God forgives, blesses, and restores us. Job 42:10 reminds us that God restores our losses when we pray for our friends, even the friends who gave bad counsel, made bad decisions, accused us falsely, or said hurtful things.

5. Keep your eyes on the lost.

When missionaries, ministers, married couples, and Christians fight, the lost always suffer. Any energy spent fighting each other is energy taken away from fighting for lost souls. When we fight each other, the devil pulls up a chair, cackles in glee, and enjoys the fireworks. He is delighted because behind his back and ours, who are so consumed with petty annoyances, the lost are perishing and going to hell.

Don't let disappointment distract you from your primary calling of making disciples. There are so many organizational, structural, leadership, philosophy, vision, position, and authority issues over which we can disagree. Let us be diligent that nothing will distract us from widely sowing the gospel, discipling the found, planting churches among the unreached, training up indigenous leaders, and focusing on the harvest. If the harvesting sickle of your neighbor swings so close it scratches your pride, don't stop swinging your sickle in order to sulk or shout and don't start swinging your sickle at him or her. Just take three steps sideways and focus on the grain to be harvested in front of you. There is enough harvest spoiling in the field to attend to. Let's keep our eyes on the lost.

6. Keep doing your job.

It is very rare that disappointment restricts us from the assignment in front of us. Yes, it can slow things down, but hardly ever does it stop us from fulfilling our assignment. Continue to focus on what you can control. Put your primary energy into the task you've been given. Let the things that concern or irritate you be marginal to your attention and emotional energy. Let your influence be unforced and natural and flow from the working model to which you diligently apply yourself. When disappointed, don't divert energy from your assignment. Focus on your job and let some of these other issues be addressed by God, time, and the maturation of all involved.

Time is always on the side of the right. If you are in the right, you are probably not going to prove it by arguing or protesting. Time will prove it by the fruit of the decision, whether good or bad. There are very few hills to die on, and most ministries can recover from the effects of bad decisions if they are judgment calls, not moral rebellions. If you are not the authority, submit and trust the Lord and time to work it out. Outlast and outlive your critics. I do not mean in a manipulative way, I mean in a faithful endurance. Do your job and the verification will be in the fruit of your ministry. It is possible that others will be proved right (and you wrong) in the course of time. If that happens, be humble enough to admit it. It happens to all of us!

7. Keep perspective on how many joyful relationships you currently have.

When we are disappointed with someone near, we tend to let that disappointment consume our emotions and thinking. In that fixation we do a disservice to the many other relationships around us that are either fulfilling or needing our emotional investment. As the old hymn says, "we are to count our blessings," but in our hurt we prefer to count our curses (which is how we view the ones who disappoint us). Don't let one person or situation dominate your internal reflection or external action. Remember the many others around you that bring great joy to your life and/or need your positive input in their lives. At any given time, there are more life-giving relationships around us than life-taking. We just have to not let the life-taking relationships dominate. That is on us. We must determine to give attention to the numerous joyful relationships around us.

Here, too, the devil loves to cloud our thinking. When we have a major or ongoing relational disappointment, the enemy puts his slimy finger into that hurt and presses. He begins to hum: "Nobody likes me. Everybody hates me. I think I'll go eat worms." If we are not vigilant to rebuke that lie, we start humming it with him. The next sinister whisper in our ear is: "I alone of all the prophets of God am the only one left." We start thinking that no one understands, no one endures what we endure, no one appreciates us or our difficulty, and everyone else has it better than we do. We take on a deluded martyr mentality. This, too, is self-deception and self-pity. There is always someone else who has it worse than we do, and our bad is not as bad as we make it out in our own mind. We need to take a deep breath, step back, and start praising God for all the wonderful people and opportunities in our life.

8. Keep your own frailties in mind.

When we are disappointed with others or going through a season of disappointment, we need to get up every morning, look in the mirror, and say, "I could be wrong today." I do not mean we live in a crisis of self-confidence. I mean we live humbly and recognize that we too are fallen. We too disappoint others. We too make and are making mistakes. We do not have a corner on righteousness, wisdom, or clear thinking. Charles Spurgeon said (my paraphrase): "However bad others think of you, be encouraged that you are probably much, much worse." When you are disappointed in others, leaven that with the sober realization that they are probably a little bit disappointed in you and they probably have good reason to be.

9. Keep believing the best.

In disappointment we need to retain our loyalties to those we work with and love. Trust is both earned and conferred; it is then both lost and withdrawn. We need to be very slow to remove trust. We need to continue to believe the best and assign the best possible meaning to every word, email, phone call, conversation, and communication. When we are disappointed, we tend to default to the worst possible meaning or motive of the other. We build a case in our mind by interpreting their words and actions in the worst possible way. We all are neither as good as we are made out to be (in the new, fresh, good times), nor are we as bad as we are made out to be (in the tense, long-term, tough times). Disappointment tends to make us vilify others. This is especially true if we have lionized someone or placed them on a pedestal. The higher in our esteem we place others, the more painful it is when they fall off that pedestal, or frankly when we throw them off. In the tough times, we need to keep believing the best about others.

Critical to believing the best is the pursuance of Matthew 18 principles of conflict resolution. When disappointed, a huge, common error is to start talking about someone rather than talking to them. Keep taking your concerns to the person that disappoints you. Follow the recourse given in Matthew 18 if that dialogue breaks down. Follow the Golden Rule and treat others as you want to be treated. In disappointment with others, keep believing the best about them.

10. Keep dying to self.

The reality is, we can't self-crucify. It is physically and spiritually impossible. God hands the hammer to those who are near, which is part of the indignity. When we are disappointed in others, it is part of the dying-to-self process. Don't wiggle off the cross. Don't grab the hammer and start smiting the ones God has appointed to crucify you. There are probably forces and purposes at play far larger than the specific decision or circumstance. The Lord of glory is hammering you into His image. Grin and bear it. Keep dying to self.

11. Keep your eyes on the eastern sky.

One day Jesus will come. Soon and very soon. What seems like a prison is only a phase. You will get through it. If you try to escape it, you will be sorely disappointed, as half the problem in this disappointment is your own flesh. You can't escape your flesh until Jesus comes. And on that day, that glorious day, in a moment, in a twinkling *we shall be changed!* Oh, thank you, Jesus. On that day, all disappointment will both be healed and cease. On that day we will never again be disappointed. We look forward to that day with joy.

DAY 8

PURSUING JESUS:

We are prophets, priests, and proclaimers—not pragmatists. We don't stand at the foot of the cross shaking our heads saying, "Well, that didn't work!" We gaze up in wonder at the crucified Son saying, "Behold, the Lamb of God who takes away the sins of the world." This is why we are to make His praise glorious (Psalm 66:2). This is why we are to pray at all times and not lose heart (Luke 18:1). This is why we are to cry out to Him day and night (v. 7), so that when the Son of Man comes, He finds the faithful on the earth, not pragmatists. We have to see God clearly if we are going to see ourselves rightly (v. 13). We must continue to cry out for His help, and following Him we must glorify (vv. 39, 43). We cannot stop speaking about the things we have seen and heard so that all will glorify God (Acts 4:20–21). We must give testimony to the resurrection of Jesus with great power (v. 2). We must preach the word in all seasons with great patience (2 Tim. 4:2) and with fight (v.7), for the Lord will stand with us and strengthen us so that through us the proclamation might be fully accomplished that all the Gentiles might hear (v. 17). And the Lord will rescue me from every evil deed (v. 18).

I was praying early this morning about meeting the ruler of the country. In that prayer I was wondering what might happen if that meeting was favored. He could grant churches permission to meet. He could allow clergy visas for pastors and ministers. He could provide protection from police or vigilante radicals. He could really open the door as a person of the greatest influence in the land. As I thought about this—the great things that the crown prince could do if only I could meet him and have favor—I was convicted. I have an open invitation into the presence of the King of Kings every day, every moment! King Jesus has all authority in heaven and earth! The Lord Jesus rules in the kingdoms of men appointing over them whom He wills, and He is able to do immeasurably above all I could think or ask an earthly king. Let me not desire an audience with a limited human when I have been granted a divine one daily with the Lord of Lords. Jesus, forgive me for seeking the favor of lesser powers. I will run to You today. You can turn the heart of kings. If You want to use an earthly king for Your glory, You surely can. Jesus, *You* are my King. I will seek You.

PURSUING CHURCH PLANTING:

During the break in our language school lesson yesterday, our tutor went into another room to pray. It was fascinating that as she emerged from her Muslim prayers, she sat down at the table and bluntly asked us, "So why do you really want to study Narnian Arabic?" We frankly stated our great passion to be able to talk to Narnians about Jesus in their heart language because we desperately want to see Narnians in heaven. Our teacher is really sweet, but she came out of her Islamic prayer time a little edgy. The Lord used it to open a door for a short discussion about faith. We are ever in a battle, and even if we don't recognize it, the principalities do. Something was troubling this sweet woman's spirit in her interaction with us, and her Islamic prayers exacerbated that sentiment. As always, the Spirit is not without response, and her somewhat edgy question did indeed allow us to talk about Jesus, and as we shared I sensed His peace. In fact, the conversation allowed me to share a Bible verse and show her how she could access the YouVersion app on her phone which has the Bible in Arabic. An antagonistic question (or at least an edgy one) led to opportunity, and now she cannot "un-know" how to access the Scripture on the privacy of her phone.

Two days ago, my landlord was driving by me as I began my early morning prayer walk (he was returning from morning prayers), and he pulled over to greet me. I told him I would love to have a cup of tea with him. Yesterday he called and invited me to the roof where he has a large, furnished, air-conditioned, carpeted, tranquil room with Arab couches (cushions that circle the room). He came directly at me with an invitation to become a Muslim. He was direct, frank, articulate, charming, and insistent. He told me I was a *kaffir* (unbeliever) and that I was going to hell. He begged me to consider Islam, listen to Allah, and come into the true path. All of this he did with both persistence and respect. I responded in kind. He allowed me time to answer and explain my perspective, and I thanked him for his directness and marveled at how similar we were, for I too was grieved that he is on the road to hell and I begged him to consider the claims of Christ and to turn to Jesus as his Savior. We went back and forth in Arabic on all the usual points of contention (divinity of Jesus, alleged corruption of Scripture, necessity of atonement, etc.). It was a profound if direct conversation and I have to admit I really liked him. He had pointed questions that were fair, and he was a good listener. Above all, he had zeal for my conversion. Oh, that Muslims would see in us the zeal I saw in this man. Oh, that we would have passion for their conversion and be unashamed to invite them to turn to Jesus as Savior and Lord. It will be for them as it was for me last night—they may disagree completely, but they will be moved by the passion and compassion in the invitation.

There was another element at work beyond the relational. As this man talked, I sensed the presence of evil, kind as he was, and I realized I was without a wingman. What I needed in that moment was a brother with me, praying quietly, praying steadily, chiming in when the Spirit gave him some illumination. It is so much better to have prayer support right there, in the moment, while conversations of eternal import are happening. I regretted that I was there without prayer support and resolved to marshal it whenever possible.

Last night I wrote an email to the Government Investment Authority about the businesses we want to start. I had spoken with their representative in the capital city about receiving the permission to pursue registration, and he asked for a summary of our business idea. I was intentionally candid about being supported by churches and being a minister with the Assemblies of God church. I prayed about the decision and felt a peace to be candid, fully realizing it could backfire and be a conversation stopper. I am trusting that in this current climate of liberalization God will instead use the candor as a positive distinction, somehow appealing to the largess that is latent in these reforms. I now wait with expectation to see if there is a way forward, or better said, I wait to see how God leads us onward.

DAY 9

PURSUING JESUS:

What a joy to my spirit to be reminded again from Your word that You will bless us, grace us, and shine upon us, so that Your way will be made known on earth and Your salvation among all nations, so that the peoples will praise You, so that the nations will be glad, so that the ends of the earth will fear You (Psalm 67). To live a missionary life is not a personal choice, but a joy, a privilege, a joining in with the heart of God. Thank you, Lord, that we are not making "this" (missions) up. We are just bending our will, energy, and lives to conform to Your great passions.

Thank you also that You are to be feared. The Bible has such a high view of God and is unapologetic of who He is and who we are. "Well done, good slave," says the master with no need for pleasantries (Luke 19:17 NASB). He is an exacting Master (v. 21), and He will slay His enemies in His presence (v. 27). There should be no discomfort in the reality that we are slaves, donkeys to be loosed when the Lord has need of us (v. 31). We must be content to be tied up and to be loosed without explanation, to be ridden in obscurity as Jesus is acclaimed, to be led gently or prodded in urgency. Let us remember that to dishonor God by living any kind of lie is to risk immediate death (Acts 5:5). Let us live as a church in great fear of the Lord (v. 11). Let us keep on teaching a high view of God, teaching and preaching, filling our city with teaching (vv. 21, 25, 28, 42). Lord, I am Your donkey. Leave me tied in obscurity. Ride me in such a fashion that every eye is on You. Let me preach and teach the gospel, living and exhorting a high view of God and an honest view of man, die, and be forgotten. Remove from me, Lord, the self-imposed pressure of wanting to excel, and let me revel in the freedom of being Your donkey whom You bind and loose at Your good pleasure. Let me rejoice in "well done, good donkey." Let there be no rebellious, evil talk or deception from me that is sordid and must be silenced (Titus 1:10–11).

PURSUING CHURCH PLANTING:

Still working through jetlag, I awoke yesterday at 3:30 a.m. and after some abiding time sent my landlord a text message, following up on our meeting. I let him know that I was praying he would have a dream about Jesus. He is so set in his opinions that I think he needs something to shake his falsely based confidence. We do see that love (relationship and service), truth (Bible testimony and reading), and power (signs, wonders, miracles, dreams) all interact in evangelism to Muslims. He had insisted that we believe God is three, so I sent him Deuteronomy 6:4–5 as well. I wanted him to see that the Bible says God is one. But I also wanted him to have access to the Bible on his phone, so I copied the verses from YouVersion into the text message with a link to access them on the app. He had told me he has no desire to read the Bible as it is corrupted, but I am praying that hunger and curiosity will draw him by the Spirit to the Scripture. He responded, saying that he is praying God will explain things to "my chest" and lead me to Islam. I love his candor. He then sent me the Qur'anic verse: "If anyone desires a religion other than Islam, never will it be accepted of him…." So while I grieve that he is so confidently lost, I respect that he is so enthusiastically devoted. Men like this—when

Jesus saves them—can stand against the tide of persecution that inevitably follows. May Jesus ransom him from the lies of Islam and bring him into the glorious liberty of the sons of God.

I spoke with an official in the capital city about our business registration. In the application I was candid about being an AG minister supported by the church. This man works in the private sector to help businesses register. I know this information might be a deal breaker in the wrong hands, but I felt a peace and conviction about being open and leaving the results in God's hand. As I mentioned this openness to this man, he was appreciative and told me, "Just today I was registering my kids for school and had to check a box that was not true. I had no one to talk to and so lost my moral compass." It was a frank admission for this Muslim man. We are trusting that Jesus will turn this open approach into an advantage and grant favor. We are trusting that no matter what happens, He will receive glory.

I constantly have to fight back a self-imposed pressure to succeed. That success might be in language, BAM set-up, partnership, evangelism, team leading, or fruitfulness. This is pride and wickedness. I constantly need to force myself away from a desire to be recognized and to be thought well of to a posture of Jesus being recognized and thought well of. In this approach (open reference to the church in BAM application), I do feel a conviction to be transparent *and* I also see where pride and hubris can be mixed into my motives: a spirit of showing off because I was more open or "bolder" than others. Part of the church planting pursuit is a consistent parsing of motives as we carry both pure and perverted motives intertwined in our hearts—at least I do. Lord Jesus Christ, Son of David, have mercy on me.

Language study went well, then I answered email, worked on our BAM website and some other registration details, wrote a little for Proverbs and *Missionary God* books, and then went to team meeting. Currently, we are only two couples, which is so different from the larger teams we've had for the last twenty years. There is a completely different feel. It's much lower key, relational, and simple. We discussed a few things, prayed, fellowshipped, and did some simple brainstorming. Our team will have two layers: full team members directly under our authority and associate team members who belong to other organizations and have other mentors and responsibilities. There is a sweetness and intimacy in being small again. We will have to figure out going forward how intentional we can and should be about missiology, and how much liberty we give associate members in their church planting approach. Right now, while we are small (and new), we will err on the side of liberty. When we add full team members, we will add a little more structure and teaching.

We also have an unplanned house guest for the next two weeks: a young man, fellow missionary, who is in between opportunities. Due to a miscommunication he showed up at the door two days ago with his boxes. He is intelligent and gracious, but it does make rhythms of life a little trickier. He comes along with me for my one-hour prayer walk, and we have been mutually encouraged. At first, I resented the intrusion, but I see the Lord's hand in it now and we want to bless him however we can. He is very teachable and I am also learning from him.

DAY 10

PURSUING JESUS:

Let God arise. Let His enemies be scattered. Let the righteous be glad, exult before God, rejoice with gladness, and sing praises (Psalm 68:1, 3–4). Lift up a song for Him who rides through deserts, whose name is the LORD, and exalt before Him. Jesus, ride through the deserts of Narnia! Jesus, who is our mighty God, owes us no explanations, and I should not put Him in the dock (Luke 20:2–3, 20). If we are foolish enough to pick a fight with God, we will find ourselves giving up just when He is getting started (vv. 40–41). If we should not poke a sleeping bear, we should certainly not provoke a slow-to-anger and merciful yet terrifying God.

Jesus, help me to devote myself to prayer and the ministry of the Word (Acts 6:4). Help me see and believe that in so doing the word of God will keep spreading, the number of disciples will be increased, and a great many of the religious leaders (princes and imams!) will be obedient to the faith. Help me empower many Stephens who will be full of grace and power, incessantly speaking (vv. 8, 13). As for me, let me speak the things fitting for sound doctrine, being sound in faith, love, and perseverance, adorning the doctrine of God in every respect, looking for the blessed hope of Christ's appearing (Titus 2:1–2, 13).

Jesus, before You come physically in power and glory (which we long for!), come in revival fire and awaken the dead peoples of Narnia, that they may welcome You on that great and terrible day when our hopes are blessed and fulfilled.

PURSUING CHURCH PLANTING:

As part of our orientation to Narnia, we are intentionally meeting with other workers and like-minded men and women of God. We want to learn what is going on, what God is doing, and what yet needs to be done. Last night we met with a European couple who are tentmakers and who host a weekly lunch and house church. They were gracious to answer our questions and to share freely of what they are involved in. After a lovely meal we had a time of prayer with another single man who has worked as a tentmaker for twenty years in Narnia.

When it was my turn to share prayer requests, to my shame, I did so proudly. I dropped a few names of important people we had met. I shared how I boldly given a Bible to someone publicly and quick to push back against false belief about Jesus. I wrapped these "look at me" incidents in the language of asking for prayer. I realize again how much filthy pride is in me. I want recognition. I want others to think I am brave. I want to be respected. I want to teach others. How twisted are my motives regarding church planting! How depraved my heart is! Lord, have mercy on me. I fight, scheme, and think about how to win others to *me*, rather than fighting to see Jesus praised, respected, and adored. So many of my conversations and behaviors are motivated by winning others to myself, not to *Himself* alone. Lord, have mercy on me. Lord, grant me the motive in all I do of winning people to *Jesus*! Lord, I am a proud fool. Lord, I am even proud of seeing that I am a fool. Lord Jesus Christ, Son of God, have mercy on me.

If we are to plant churches, we must continually repent of pride, mixed motives, and the desire to be seen, recognized, and lauded. Instead of jumping up and down like spiritual infants yelling, "Look at me! Look at me! Like me! Pick me! Praise me!", let's jump up and down and yell, sing, pray, preach, and invite everyone, saved and lost, to look at Jesus.

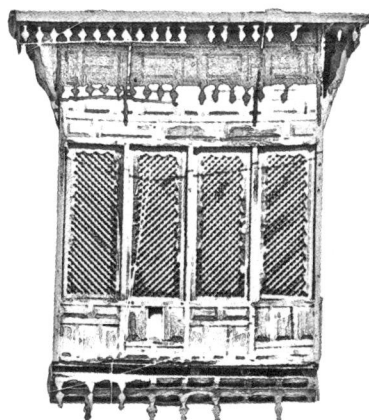

BUILDING AND PRESERVING TEAM CULTURE

FORMING TEAM CULTURE

There are pastoral, theological, and legal components of framing culture. Even before you meet, the team leader needs to articulate and establish in print what those components are so that those joining can be clear about expectations. Pastoral aspects are covenantal. Theological elements are doctrinal or a statement of faith. Legal portions are structure and MOU-related (what to do in times of discipline or disagreement). In one way all these charters (articulated in print) are living documents. We do not govern by them, but all incoming team members need to read them and agree to them, and then they are used as recourse in times of tension. They only handle the obvious divergences, not the nuanced or interpretive ones. These charters are the starting place.

Team culture has to be lived, not taught, modeled not demanded. In other words, the team leader (TL) has to be consistently on the ground for long uninterrupted times before an absence. If the TL has great theory about team culture but has frequent travel absences, you in effect will have a culture in your head but not in reality. There has to be a long enough and sustained time with the TL on the ground that the culture is indeed adopted at the heart level of the team, not just agreed to academically. This DNA spread is slow and concentric. It starts with the TLs, and then goes to their closest team members, and then spreads out to the periphery. This implies that not all your team members will have equal buy in or influence. This is obvious if you contrast long-term workers and short-term workers, but it is also true for long-term and long-term. It's actually biblical to have levels of influence: Jesus with the 3, 12, 70, 500, etc. Within team, culture starts forming at the core and moves outward. Not everyone buys in equally, not everyone has equal wisdom, and not everyone should be given equal influence or authority, but you start with the center and radiate out. This takes time, this takes trust, and this takes determination.

Time and determination mean concretely that you employ repetition. You come back to simple concepts (vision and values, maxims and truisms) over and over and over again. You never get tired of repeating old truths. You intentionally keep it simple. You repeat and revise and repeat again. You know you are getting there when your team members start making jokes about it, when your vision and values seep into your humor and banter. You find fresh ways to present the same, simple non-negotiables. You resist constant sea change even as you constantly adjust and grow. This means that you always focus on CP, UPGs, and teams, and abide, apostle, and abandon, even as you tweak consistently.

You intentionally marginalize the bad apples. There are some in teams whose attitude and perspective are not where they should be. You are careful (both when present or when absent) to not allow those voices to have influence. You don't give them leadership or vocal opportunities. You correct and address waywardness quickly (attitude, thinking, missiology, perspective, spirit), and you do that both privately and publicly when necessary. By publicly, I mean that if someone says something out of alignment with team culture publicly, you don't let it slide, but graciously steer the "feel" back to center. When you travel, you do not give them a place, even if they are older; it's an indirect way to tell the others who to listen to (and who not to listen to).

You publicly encourage team members. Often you should praise others in front of others. You teach through encouragement. You laud the behavior that you cherish, and you speak it into being—not just in the one who did well, but in the observers. They see what behavior is rewarded and they strive to align with that behavior. You do this realizing that gifts vary and so you intentionally spread praise and laud everyone for something they do well.

You deal with things that are not plumb quickly and transparently. People lose their way if they lose their why. Explain your decisions, process with people as a team, keep short accounts, and move on. Create a climate where team members can feel free to disagree respectfully, question honorably, and season your decisions. Don't let things fester. Model how to deal with conflict and disagreement and how to move on.

Be clear that there are three types of decisions and that they vary in how much input team members have. When an issue is on the table, let everyone know what type of decision it is. Type 1 are top-down decisions. Whether from you, the area director, or the organization, it's not up for debate. Questions can be asked, but the decision has been made. As a team the decision must be owned and implemented. After questions are asked (if necessary), we salute and like it. Obviously, there may be more of these types of decisions at the beginning, but it is not wise to have many of these. Type 2 are decisions that have been made (the "yes" or "no" is not up for debate), but the team discusses the details (how, when, where, who) and you lead a collaborative process (giving the why) to reach a consensus. Type 3 decisions are possibilities, and anyone can bring these to the table. You discuss as a team if you should do it, and if so, how, when, who, where, what, etc. Nothing is as frustrating for team members than to think a decision is type 3 and it's actually type 2, or to think it's a type 2 when it's a type 1. Be clear. Most can handle the leader being clear about the boundaries. No one wants to waste time on what has already been decided. If it is a type 1, tell me. I will salute, obey, and when I leave the team room, I'll smile, own, and like it.

You balance the main components of team (church planting strategy and missiology, intercessory prayer, fellowship centered on Jesus) in both time and maturity. Time refers to the regular touch points during the course of the week—often enough to guide and spread out enough to keep team members with the lost and dependent on Jesus. You want your people to want to be in team meetings. Maturity means you treat the mature differently than the immature. Weak team leadership treats everyone the same, while strong team leadership makes accommodations according to the person and situation.

Give the team the tools to handle conflict and peacemaking. Some essentials are:

- Familiarity with the five dysfunctions of a team and how to avoid them
- Familiarity with the book *Crucial Conversations* and how to have them
- Commitment to Matthew 18 principles
- Create a culture intolerant of gossip, dissent, criticism, and division
- Dedication to the Golden Rule
- Understanding the paths of recourse: When things are going south, what third party can be brought in?
- Peacemaking guidelines: skills in how to pour water, not gasoline, on conflict
- Steadiness in praying the mercy prayer (and living it out): "Lord, flood the one I am thinking about with Your fulfilling mercies. Meet their every need as You see it.

Fill them with the Holy Spirit. Make Jesus real to them and draw them close to Yourself." When we pray this prayer (every two hours, two days, two months, two years, however long) and mean it, one thing always happens, and another sometimes happens. What always happens is that our heart changes towards the other. What sometimes happens is the other senses a change in us—a love, a warmth, an acceptance—and their heart softens toward us. The challenge may remain, but at least we can talk about it and find a way forward without baggage.

Consistent fun. Game nights, quarterly retreats, activity days. Camaraderie built over meals or WhatsApp groups, and other means of interaction. Play together and laugh. Keep it balanced and tempered, but fun bonding is critical.

KEEPING TEAM CULTURE

If the set-up phase has been done well, this is easier. If the above things have been done poorly, it is an uphill battle. The real energy then goes into education (which is so much easier than re-education) and prevention (which is so much easier than cure).

Have a transition process before the leader leaves. The whole M.A.W.L (Model, Assist, Watch, Leave) pattern. If the transfer has happened six months before the leader has left, there are these advantages: (a) The departing leader has time to observe blind spots of the transitional or new leader and to correct them. The incoming leader has time to encounter issues and to have the old leader nearby to work through them. (b) The ongoing followers have time to identify concerns and to deal with them in an open way with the new leader, and if that stalls with the departing leader. (c) The leader has time to demonstrate his trust in the new leader to the followers and to the new leader.

When the leader leaves, leave. Don't interfere. Don't undermine the guy on the ground. Don't make decisions from afar. Don't solicit or encourage negative reports from the field. Enforce all the things above that you have taught by insisting they work through them biblically. Be comfortable that some things will be done differently, even poorly, and some things better. Prepare the team for this reality before you go and assure them it is okay. Before you leave, establish publicly with the new leader and the team what things can be tweaked and changed and what things are inviolable. Let it be clear what needs to remain and grow, and what areas can be adjusted. Inevitably culture of a team is shaped by the personality of the leader. Nothing wrong with this. Accept it and exhort the team to accept it.

Be intentional that the person left in charge is a collaborative leader or a leader that is expected to lead collaboratively. If you are gone for six months or a year, there is protection for all in a less authoritarian style (if the group culture is well understood). If the group culture is not well understood, the temporary leader may need the protective empowerment of bit more authorization so that the errant majority cannot lead the whole astray.

DEFENDING TEAM CULTURE FROM EXTERNAL ATTACKS

These are actually easier than internal division. When under threat from authorities or radicals, stay calm and don't over react. Trust Jesus. He is Sovereign. Stay theological and don't get emotional. Suffering is normal. We were appointed to this, and this has been granted to us on behalf of Christ. Model well to the MBBs and live up to what the Bible says and to what you ask them to do. Call the team together and pray. Mobilize your prayer partners. Review contingency plans but stay in country if you can. If you need to send short-termers or families out, that is fine. (If the husband/father has been abducted or being held, it helps him to know his wife and kids are safely out of the country; then any lies about his family he can discount and concentrate on being a witness in his duress.) I think we should stay even if that means prison or death. How can we teach MBBs to shine for Jesus in persecution if we flee the country every time there is trouble? Remember you are being watched by many sets of eyes.

Consult with your leaders outside the country. Consult with local and ministry partners. Don't isolate. Keep meeting together and keep being who you are. Stay intentionally unified. Often the best thing to do is to meet more often, even if for short periods. For example, meet every morning at 8 a.m. for thirty minutes (briefing and prayer). The biggest mistake is to stop or reduce team time due to fear of your visa or security. Overcommunicate to your team and leaders. Send daily summaries. Look for the opportunity in the challenge—everything is a witnessing opportunity, a God-glorifying opportunity. Don't neglect the practical things: eat well, exercise, and sleep. Don't live under a bondage of tension. Diffuse and settle those around you by being normal: laugh, smile, worship, rejoice, praise the Lord. Fight it spiritually first and practical wisdom will follow. Be wise and brave. Ask the Lord to keep you safe and to make you dangerous.

DEFENDING TEAM CULTURE FROM INTERNAL ATTACKS AND DIVISION

These attacks are harder to deal with. Bring everything into the light. Deal with things quickly. Have come-to-Jesus meetings, or broker them. Determine not to let the enemy win. Absorb, absorb, and swallow the wrath. Don't make things more complicated by reacting in the flesh. Be extra prayerful. Have a spouse or trusted colleague vet your answers. Don't deal with anything by email; rather, meet face to face. Make sure that stress doesn't lead you to break your own moral principles. Be slow to speak and become angry; once words are out, you can't get them back. Determine to forgive, forgive, forgive; in fact, pre-forgive. Take the high road of being lowly: repent, diffuse, be humble, and listen. Pour water, not gasoline, on every hot conversation. Let Jesus and time defend you. Don't be vindictive or pray for God to vindicate you; pray that you will become more like Jesus. Talk to your leaders and mentors, or someone safe outside your team, for advice.

Don't fixate on the problem. Keep abiding, and praise more than you ponder. Remind Jesus: "This is *Your* problem. What are *You* going to do about it? Here I am available. Use me as You will."

Be gracious and don't hold against people what they do or say when they are stressed and angry. Be strong enough to be patient. If you need to, remove the toxic person(s). Make the painful decisions in the short term. Short-term pain is better than long-term problems. Grow your compartmentalization muscle. Learn to have portions of your mind and spirit that you lock the painful issue in. Bring it out (open the door) when you need to deal with it, then lock it away. There is much to do CP-wise, so others need your best self—don't let the person or the issue rule your thoughts. My regional director Omar Beiler says, "Don't give people free rent in your head." Recognize that the devil uses some people, but this does not mean they are demonic. Ask yourself if it matters ten years from now; then don't spend too much energy on what no one will remember a decade from now. Very few issues have 10-year ramifications so identify those that do and hone in on them.

DAY 11

PURSUING JESUS:

Jesus, I want zeal for Your house (name, honor, reputation, character) to consume me (Psalm 69:9). I will praise the name of God with song and magnify Him with thanksgiving, and it will please the Lord (v. 30). Jesus is coming in power and great glory, so straighten up and lift up your heads because your redemption draws near (Luke 21:27–28). The time of the promise is approaching (Acts 7:17), but Jesus, don't let me blow it by being in the flesh. Moses, a man of power in words and deed approaching the age of 40, had something enter his mind. He supposed that his brethren understood (vv. 22–25) but was pushed away ("Who made you judge?" v. 27). And at this remark Moses fled and became an alien in Narnia (v. 29).

Jesus, here I am in Narnia. Let it not be because in the "approaching" of the promise, I acted in the flesh full of pride, either puffing up or shrinking back. Jesus, grant a fresh revelation to me of the God of Abraham to the extent that I will shake with fear in Your presence as Moses did on holy ground (vv. 32–33). Thank you that *You* have seen, heard, and will come down to rescue (v. 34). Let me simply be full of the Holy Spirit and see only Jesus, no matter what happens to me (v. 55). Then may I speak confidently about the core aspects of the gospel: mercy, spirit regeneration, justification by grace, heirs of eternal life, belief in God, and care to engage in good works (Titus 3:5–8).

PURSUING CHURCH PLANTING:

Yesterday we took some Sabbath rest, or tried to, learning some lessons about what is not helpful or best for us. After a gentle morning of reading and writing, we went to a beach north of the city reserved for non-Narnians (or at least those with non-Narnian passports). Most of the people there were wealthy Arabs and a few expatriates. The snorkeling was lovely. Jennifer saw an eel the length of her body, and I saw a stingray dart away from the reef. The coral and fish were delightful. What was not so delightful was the way both Arab men and Arab women dressed—or didn't dress as the case tended to be. There was little hidden. It was as if the liberty gained had to be stretched beyond its propriety. Freedom not stewarded well is as troubling as freedom denied. I don't think we'll return to that beach.

We left the beach to visit a house church of expatriates. In the varied body of Christ there are multiple expressions, and this house church is influenced by Bethel (Redding, CA). While I don't agree with everything that comes out of Bethel (and neither does the leader of this house fellowship), I can say that the people were loving, friendly, welcoming, kind, gracious, generous, and enthusiastic worshippers. The pastor had prepared well, was gregarious, had some excellent truths, illustrated his sermons well, was transparent, was an excellent communicator, and oozed love and joy.

And what was most striking to me about the pastor was this last point: joy. He has lived in Narnia for over twenty years, and he radiates hope, faith, love, joy, and blessing. Jesus beams out of him. I marvel and magnify the Lord for this vibrant representative of Christ in this barren land, and that after all these years of toil and service he still shines with the joy of Jesus and beams out the blessing of the Bridegroom. So, while this particular house church is probably not to be our spiritual home, I do want to shine like the people and pastor: full of love, hope, and joy, kind, diverse, welcoming, gracious, and passionate for Jesus. What a testimony it will be to Muslims if, like this precious pastor, we live here for years radiating the great joy of the Lord.

I pray a blessing on him and have a holy jealousy to shine for the Savior even as he does.

The church planting lesson is that it is important to find ways, places, and people that give rest and spiritual renewal. There are usually several good options and the Lord can lead us to the right one. It is also true that there is no perfect option (if this group is too charismatic, the one we will likely join is probably not charismatic enough for our preference), and when we join a body of believers, we do so also for what we can give, not just for what we can receive or for what makes us comfortable. Sabbaths are not intended to be selfish, and the Lord has the capacity to help us find rest even as we give it, to be blessed even as we bless. Whatever that ratio and synchronism, it is important to find it for long-term joy in service.

DAY 12

PURSUING JESUS:

Let those who love Your salvation say continually, "Let God be magnified" (Psalm 70:4). Jesus, let me pursue You by continually magnifying Your name. Let me be aware that Satan can enter "one of the twelve" and cause betrayal (Luke 22:3). Rather than making room for the enemy, let me prepare a large furnished room for Jesus, doing my part for Your visitation (v. 12). Perhaps a Jesus Celebration Center in the city! Thank you that You are so generous. Your poured-out blood and Your poured-out Spirit, both extravagant, both without measure (v. 20). Let me remember that betrayal hurts me in the end more than it hurts You (v. 22) and that You are among us like one who serves (v. 27). Oh, Jesus, how little I act like You do! Truly let me pray and long: not my will but *Yours* (v. 42). Pursuing You means fleeing myself. From now on, Jesus, You are seated at the right hand of the power of God (v. 69). May that not only be true cosmically, but also in my daily life and obedience. I have no need of further testimony of Your divine rights when I hear them declared from Your own mouth (v. 71).

My mouth must always proclaim Christ (Acts 8:5). I pursue You in part by proclaiming You and I proclaim You by insisting (both for myself and others) on the necessity of post-conversion Spirit reception in multiple, ongoing fillings (vv. 4–12). I need the Spirit's help to identify, convict of, and forgive the impure intentions of my heart (v. 22), which are many and repeated. Wherever I find myself (v. 40), my assignment is unchanged: I must keep preaching Christ. The patience to appeal in love is based on the authority to give orders (Philemon 1:8–9). Because God has all authority over me, He can appeal to me in love. When we do have authority over others, it is for their edification, and our modus operandi should be love appeals more than orders, service more than demands. Is God confident of my obedience (v. 21)? To pursue Him with sincere integrity I must be quick to do what He says, prompts, appeals, or orders.

Pursuing Church Planting:

I took a prayer drive to a religious town yesterday. Technically, we (a younger missionary colleague went with me) drove to a city perched on the edge of a mountain range, but our route ran through the protected city. I wanted to see if it was possible to drive into the city past the central mosque. There was a checkpoint to navigate, but the bored looking soldiers attending it did not stop us or ask questions. We were able to drive through and right into the center of town. We took a couple wrong turns but otherwise navigated our way right to the mosque. It was a little surreal. We did not get out of the car, but it did feel strange to be so close to the spiritual and emotional center of Islam.

I have been examining my motives since returning. On the positive side, I did truly want to pray, and I did want to see if it could be done and how close we could get. I did want to push against the spirit of fear and intimidation, and I did it with a brother in Christ so that we could pray together and be of mutual encouragement. On the negative or carnal side, I did it knowing it is forbidden to non-Muslims (it would be silly to be kicked out of the country for this). I did it in a friend's car, not my own, and I did it, if I am honest, to be able to tell others I did it. There is still that little (or perhaps big?) part of me that wants to be thought brave. Pride is still a sickness I struggle with on a daily basis. And I note that I struggle to rationalize my actions by focusing on the good motivations while suppressing the arrogant ones. There is a thin line between courage and folly, and I wonder if I crossed to the dark side yesterday.

Lord, forgive the twisted intentions of my heart (Acts 8:22). In church planting wrong motivations so easily creep in: To be known, to be respected, to be thought brave, to be praised, to be elevated, to gain position. How easily correct but secondary motivations become primary: To be a good steward, to earn and keep the trust of supporters, to be a blessing to the people of God, to be an example to those who are tired or afraid, even to be fruitful. How difficult it is to keep the primary motivation central: to be faithfully obedient for the glory of God.

Constantly we must marshal our energy to strive for the purest motivation. We must rigorously examine ourselves to seek out false or mixed motivation. We must carefully listen to the Holy Spirit for His convicting correction. This is a battle for humility and a battle against pride; or better said, it is a war with many battles. We must constantly revisit it, and all the more if the Lord in His mercy would grant us any fruit.

Pursuing Jesus:

Jesus Himself (not a place) is my refuge (Psalm 71:1). Jesus is the rock of habitation to which I may continually come, my fortress, my hope and confidence, my sustainer (vv. 3, 5–6). Lord, let my mouth be filled with Your praise and glory *all day long* (v. 8). I will pursue You with glad praise, hope continually, and praise You more and more, telling of Your righteousness *all day long* declaring to this generation and *all to come* (vv. 14–15, 17–18). Thank you, Jesus, that You will revive me again; thus, I will praise, sing, and shout, and I will utter Your righteousness all day long (vv. 20, 22–24).

Jesus is under no man's or king's jurisdiction (Luke 23:7). Loud and incessant anti-Jesus voices begin to prevail. They must be combatted and conquered with praise and adoration, both private and public. The most beautiful act of God in time and history (giving Himself to save evil man) and man sneers (v. 35). Jesus makes the seeing blind as well as the blind to see (Acts 9:8). Vision comes from humble and desperate prayer (vv. 11–12). We are to be His chosen instruments to bear His name before Gentiles, kings, and the people of God with both the promise of suffering and the Spirit (vv. 16–17). There is no good time to proclaim; we must *immediately* begin to proclaim Christ (v. 20). When we see Jesus and He talks to us, we can speak boldly (v. 27). The fear of the Lord *and* the comfort of the Spirit, they go together.

God has spoken to us in His Son and makes His ministers a flame of fire anointed with the oil of gladness and a ministering spirit sent out to render service of salvation (Hebrews 1:2, 7, 9, 14); all this of angels, let it also be thus of men.

Pursuing Church Planting:

Yesterday included the more routine aspects of church planting.

Abiding: This is the starting place, spending time with Jesus. My routine is to get up at 5:45 a.m., prayer walk from 6 to 7, read my Bible and worship until 8, worship and journal until about 9, have a quick bite to eat, shower, and then spend two hours writing. At 11, language school begins three days a week and runs until 2 p.m. Then I answer email and begin meetings with either neighbors, friends, other missionaries, business contacts, or other appointments necessary for life.

Meetings: At a shared office space a few days ago, I met an interior designer, a Narnian woman, and had arranged for Jennifer to meet her. We had a lovely visit with her and expressed that we were pastors, supported by the church, here to help with intercultural education and leadership development. She was kind and open, and we are praying that it will be a friendship that can develop for Jennifer. We went to meet another Narnian businessman, but he was late coming to the office so Jennifer talked to his interns for a while. I met a Narnian and when I asked how he was doing, he replied, "I am crowded with grace!" We had a nice chat; I would like to meet him again.

Errands: From there we had to cash U.S. dollars to pay our language school bill, find a solution to our internet problem, purchase a few household things, pay for our language school, get the car washed (I inadvertently parked under a pigeon roost), and get lunch. After many stops and starts, and meeting many lovely Muslims, both Narnians and Sudanese, we returned home around 4. We need to remind ourselves that in the course of errands, God can lead us to divine appointments, and we need not be so hurried that we don't evangelize in our routine. Evangelism should not be relegated to a few focused hours of the week (though that is helpful) but should be woven into the fabric of our daily lives. I did not do this very well yesterday. I want to be more intentional about gospel witness and Scripture distribution.

Organizational and office work: On returning home we had our afternoon chai, worked on the internet for an hour, and then paid bills and answered emails, doing some calendar planning and organization. This took us past supper to 8.

Reading: We went to bed early and laid there reading. I am reading a book which is an illuminating history of Narnian Arabia. I want to be informed about the people and powers that made this nation what it is and be aware of the people and powers that now shape this nation into what it shall be. The better we understand context, the more shrewdly we can contextualize the gospel.

Nothing we did yesterday was spectacular. We met with several Narnians. We furthered relationships. We paid bills and became organized. We took a few more steps to get structural things in place so we can have more focused time on evangelism and being with Narnians. But the reality still is, these practical steps out and about are rife with witnessing opportunities.

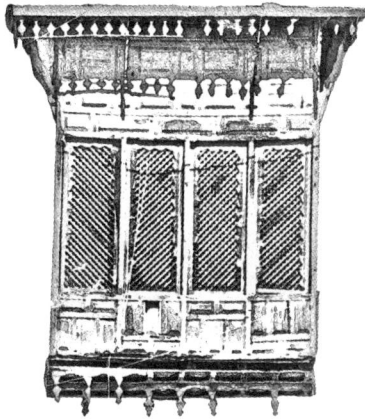

CONFLICT RESOLUTION

1. Intervention is both empowering and disempowering.

Interventions both empower and disempower. There are times we do need to intervene, but we should do so as a last resort knowing there will be both blessing and pain to the leader we circumnavigate or remove from the loop. We do need to provide recourse to our people, but we must do so carefully as it has ramifications. Interventions are usually better done not by removing a leader from the conversations, but by bringing the next level leader into the conversations and having him lead the way forward with all parties talking directly to each other.

2. All levels of leadership need to stay on the same page.

When multiple leaders are involved in a conflict resolution scenario, it is imperative that the leaders stay on the same page. Conflicts become more and more confusing when our brokenness plays off each other. At the leadership level there is a fine line between being the "safe" leader to talk to and undermining what you need to accomplish together as a leadership team. At all costs, the leadership team needs to stay united in message, tone, feel, spirit, and decisions.

3. We need to create a climate where creative, apostolic leaders can thrive.

Many leaders who cause conflict are excellent missionaries and strategists. We must strive to give them liberty within certain boundaries to be creative, being sure to stay principle-based in how we lead. Sometimes the rub is not in fact but in feeling; even then we are liable. If my creative followers don't feel free to be creative leaders, that is on me. We should be doubly careful that principles are not becoming rules, and that we are not wittingly or unwittingly putting our most creative, apostolic leaders in boxes where they cannot thrive, initiate, or innovate.

4. Not everyone is teachable, not everyone will buy in.

While you can be apostolic and teachable, you can also be apostolic and hardheaded, non-teachable. Not denying leaders make mistakes, at the end of the day we must still follow and submit biblically. Some apostolic leaders, though, repeatedly think they know better and often correct their leaders. Many times, they are right about the leader being wrong, which makes the situation trickier. We can't force someone to be teachable; it is a choice only they can make.

Some leaders have a strong desire to reframe principles in their own lingo and style. Reframing is not bad, but it can veer into unhelpful if it's done just to be different. Team members on a team can feel increasingly isolated from the wider family if their particular leader wants to shape everything to his/her comfortability.

5. Competencies should not trump character.

Some leaders have off-the-charts mission skill in language, evangelism, discipleship, church planting, media savvy, intelligence, charisma, etc., but they also have some essential character challenges that all those skills cover over. At the end of the day, if there is emotional un-health within the leader or their spouse, it cannot be compensated for with all the skill and competencies in the world. When you are internally unhappy, you often find someone else to blame.

Character must precede competencies in evaluating ourselves and potential leaders. But I don't think we start with character. I think we start with calling. God calls us when we are still a mess, and He works on our character. When our character is being refined, we can be trusted to employ our competencies, which likewise grow. The progression leads us to church planting. In other words, the flow is:

- First: God calls us.
- Second: We need to be persons of character, whole.
- Third: We need to have competencies, skills for the work.
- Last: We plant churches.

I don't think many of us will plant churches without legitimate calling, godly character, and requisite competencies; all are needed and they build on each other.

6. Be careful to honor all sides.

The personalities in any given conflict can be very convincing. In one scenario as a peacemaker, I found that when I listened to one, I felt he was right. When I listened to the other, I felt he was right. I was sometimes rash in drawing conclusions in my head and then making decisions or pronouncements, even if that was agreeing with the person venting to me. I should have brought the disagreeing parties into the same room and had a conversation with all present. I made the mistake of agreeing with the one I was listening to. I should have held my peace and deferred judgment until I had heard all perspectives and had time to pray about it.

This process of patience will often mean you disappoint both parties involved in a conflict, which is what happens anyway when you try to please both. This process will also mean you need to absorb criticism and swallow injustice. Some things you know you can't say as they were expressed to you in confidence. This can make your decisions seem arbitrary. To truly honor all sides can mean that you take some heat from multiple directions. It is the weight of leadership.

This lesson is also true when leaders you lead are not in conflict. I have found that often the recent conversation can be the most convincing. Impulsive decisions cause great collateral damage, and I am learning that even with good people who are not at odds with anyone, I need to wait to hear other perspectives before making a decision.

7. You need to meet with your leaders (husband and wife) regularly (spending time and money to do so) in order to get buy-in, shared DNA, and common culture.

Group DNA is formed over multiple, frequent meetings, and if a leadership couple misses that formative process, it is very hard for them to buy in. Without buy-in (DNA, trust, understanding) small problems become big problems and big problems become impossible. We need to make the effort to meet often as leaders and to work and rework on our common values and vision.

8. Trust among leaders in times of conflict is absolutely indispensable.

Conflict can make your insecurities intensify. In one scenario, a team leader upset with me was talking to my leader about a situation I had been managing (or mismanaging). I had no idea what was being said and had no ability to defend myself. There was one supreme confidence I could hold on to—I trusted that my leader would not throw me under the bus. I could trust my leader to hear the legitimate grievances and filter out the illegitimate ones. I could trust my leader had my best interest at heart (as well as the best interest of the TL, the team, the organization, the BAM, and most importantly the work of church planting). Because I could trust my leader, I could live with the angst of not knowing, of feeling exposed and vulnerable. If I did not trust my leader, I don't think I would have made it through the situation.

9. Sometimes time is your only way forward.

Some things get so messy and so complicated and so hurtful that there is no way out of them in the now. Sometimes the only thing you can do is wait, and let time be a balm. Perspective, healing, forgiveness, and reconciliation sometimes require a waiting period. Because we are all broken and bring our brokenness to the table, sometimes our interactions with others cannot be well until we have healing and resolution within. I have had to trust Jesus that He will heal the things in me that are sick and that He will heal the sickness in others. Sometimes we can't really work things out with others until the Healer works the sickness out of us.

Time tends to lend perspective that the heat of battle and disagreement denies. Time also justifies, and that justification is usually granted to both sides of the conflict. It's hardly ever true that one person was all in the wrong. Time helps us to be humbler as it can gently point out where we were wrong.

10. It's okay to let people go.

At the end of the day you need people on your team who are bought in. If they are not bought in, release them with grace. Let them find a fit that is better for them. I can't lead everybody well. Other leaders will lead some people better than I can. If it is better for the person and/or the team that remains behind for that person to move on, find a way to do it graciously. Sometimes good people just fit better in a different context with a different leader. I need to be okay with that, and I need to bless it.

11. Go the extra mile.

If someone is going to leave (the team, area, region, organization), let it be done with generosity on your part. Assume the best. Be generous practically and financially. If they do decide to leave and we desired them to stay, let them not leave because we were stingy or cruel. Let us do all that we can in kind, gracious ways. At the end of the day, others will do what they feel best; let us treat them well whatever they decide.

12. Too many changes too quickly (even if they are right) are destabilizing for followers.

In one scenario where I was coaching a leader, we both failed to realize that others don't adjust quickly to new ideas. In our minds we were just tweaking and improving, or sometimes thinking out loud, throwing ideas against the wall to see what would stick. This is not a stable way of leading. Creative thinkers can frame and convincingly present a half-baked idea, then move on from it while their colleagues are still grappling with the idea, wanting to buy in, spending great emotional energy to buy in, only to have the idea discarded and the next exciting idea be forcefully presented. This is exhausting to goodhearted and stable, loyal team members. In the mind of followers, every tweak or change requires emotional adjustment. Our followers are goodhearted and want to buy in, but at some point, too many changes too quickly overload their emotional circuits and they resist, not because they are bad people, but because they are overwhelmed. Our tacking back and forth can unsettle and de-stabilize those we lead. You can lose your team if you make too many changes too quickly.

13. Trust the Lord to defend you.

In complex situations of conflict, you must brace yourself to take short-term hits. Not everything can be said or revealed in the moment. Decisions have to be made for the good of all, which means that someone will be hurt or frustrated and they will likely take it out on you. For conflict to be managed and de-escalated, you will have to absorb some unfair criticism without defending yourself, as will others. Besides, when you do attempt to defend yourself, it's usually out of vanity, which makes things worse.

14. We must default to thinking the best.

When feelings are hurt, disappointments high, relationships strained, and roles and futures in question, it's all too easy to assign the worst possible meaning to any action, words, decision, or behavior. When emotions are raw and wounds are open, we tend to think the worst about the others' motives and character. We tend to vilify the other and build a case against them in our head—and often with our tongues. We must be super intentional about granting the other the benefit of the doubt and assigning the best possible meaning (tone/intention/heart/spirit) to their email, comment, or decision. So easily we lose the basic Golden Rule—treating (and interpreting) others how we would want to be treated (and interpreted).

15. Nobody wins when you gossip or talk out of turn.

The biggest mistakes we can make in conflict are with our mouths. We can err in many ways—saying too much or too little. In one scenario the leader reporting to me was frustrated and the team members reporting to him were frustrated. It became clear to me that the best scenario for all was for this leader to move to a different role. When his followers came to me with their grievances, I said too much. I said something to the effect, "Just be patient. In a little while he will not be in that role." In doing so, I betrayed the leader with whom I was processing. I should have said less; I should not have said that the leader would transition on. I was too agreeable and sympathetic with those who were struggling under their current leader.

The second mouth mistake I made was with the leaders themselves. They were hurting and not physically healthy, and I was not completely candid with them about my concerns. In my judgment I felt they were not in a place to hear criticisms directly from me. Even when they pointedly asked, "Is there anything else that you are concerned about?" I said "no" as I thought they would not react well to it and I wanted to wait for a better time (a face-to-face meeting) where we could talk about the thorny issues. As a result, they felt lied to and lost trust in me. To further complicate it, I talked with others about my concerns, but not with them directly, and eventually those concerns came around to them, as they always do. I messed up, lied, sinned against these friends; I hurt them deeply in multiple ways.

I cannot remember the source, but one leader talks about the "uncomfortable eight minutes" of confrontation that, though difficult, can spare everyone involved much pain down the road. I failed in this. I did not address my concerns head on with the persons in question and instead talked too much to others about the issue. In the end, everyone lost, and much pain was inflicted. To this day I carry regret for my wrong actions and poor leadership in this scenario.

16. Don't give people free rent in your head.

Omar Beiler is the first person I heard say that we should not allow people free rent in our thinking. We can find situations of relational conflict so painful that it becomes difficult to shut it from our thoughts. We think of it when we sleep and when we rise. We mull over it all day long. We agonize over it and spend so much emotional energy on it that we're not at our best for others and for other decisions and interactions. We must learn to shut the issue in its own room, lock the door, and not open that door unless it's the time determined to deal with it. This takes repeated discipline as multiple triggers (emails, questions, phone calls) reopen the door. We have to learn to answer the point in question and shut the door again. It is all too easy to linger in the room or even in the doorway. Over and again we must shut that door and move to other people and issues that need emotional and spiritual investment.

17. When we fight among ourselves, we don't fight for souls.

One of the greatest tragedies in extended tension or conflict is the energy spent in conversation, communication, intervention, justification, grieving, manipulating, framing, discussing, adjusting, accusing, repenting, and reconciling by all involved. All this is primary energy diverted from evangelism. When we fight among ourselves, it saps considerable energy and focus from fighting for the lost. We become consumed with being proved right or proving the other wrong. When we fight among ourselves, everyone loses, especially the lost.

The devil is very adept at entering situations of conflict between colleagues to make things even messier and more twisted. In most conflicts, both sides make mistakes. There are many variables and personalities at play. The accuser, the devil, takes advantage of our weaknesses and makes things worse. We should not blame all problems on the devil, as problems tend to start in our collective brokenness, but I think the devil takes advantage of our weakness to cause greater damage. We must be very aware that when conflict arises due to our fallen human nature, the devil smells it like a shark smells blood. The devil speeds towards missionary conflict and pours fuel on the fire. In the heat of conflict may we recognize that we daily need the Spirit's help to pour water on the fire, for we are not ignorant of the devil's devices.

SUMMARY

Conflict is inevitable. Our goal (planting the church where it does not exist) requires apostolic figures—hardheaded men and women who are visionary and determined. Having hard heads does not mean we also have hard hearts. May the Lord who teaches us both to fight and to make peace grow our conflict resolution skills. May the Lord teach us to lead others through their conflicts. May the Lord help us concentrate our firepower on the lost. May the Lord in mercy forgive us our many sins against one another and against Him.

DAY 14

PURSUING JESUS:

L ord, refresh me that I may "come down like rain" and refresh others, that the whole earth may be filled with Your glory (Psalm 72:6, 19). Help me embrace the reality that suffering comes before glory (Luke 24:26). Speak to me and let my heart burn; let me recognize You in the breaking of bread; open my mind to understand the Scripture; and fulfil Your promise to clothe me with power from on high that I may worship You with joy and continual praise (vv. 32, 35, 45, 49, 52–53).

Thank you, Jesus, that You are Lord of all, all peoples, everywhere (Acts 10:36). Father, raise up Jesus in Narnia and make Him visible (v. 40). Let me obey Your order to preach and solemnly testify that Jesus is the judge of the living and the dead (v. 42), that Arab Muslims might believe in Him to receive forgiveness of sins (v. 43). Father, pour out Your Spirit on me that I may speak in tongues and glorify God (v. 45). I want to be a full gospel disciple, experiencing everything You intend, obeying everything You command, glorifying You in all things, great and small.

Lord, I realize that drift is possible as is neglect (Hebrews 2:1–3). Keep me true and help me turn my eyes from the rebellion of man to focus on Jesus (vv. 8–9). Let me remember that sons are brought to glory through suffering (v. 10) and that when we suffer for and with You, we join a brotherhood You are not ashamed of (v. 11). Thank you, Jesus, that in our frailty You are a merciful and faithful high priest, a propitiation maker, able, willing, and active in coming to the aid of us who are tempted (vv. 17–18).

Pursuing Church Planting:

Yesterday was a grind-it-out day, the norm of church planting. Woke up, exercised, abided in Jesus, wrote, Arabic lesson, e-mail correspondence, newsletter, spoke with potential Narnian business partners, read a book about Narnian culture, and went to bed. Jennifer and I are striving to "work the plan," to stay focused on the five critical things in this entry phase:

1. Abiding in Jesus
2. Arabic fluency in Narnian dialect
3. Prayer
4. Partnership development
5. Professional identity

Along the way we are of course meeting Narnians, sharing our faith, trying to pass out Scripture, inviting to Bible study, and looking for persons of peace. We know that to do church planting and evangelism well over the long term we must pursue and solidify the above five things.

I remain convinced that openhearted transparency about being a pastor sent and funded by the church is the best identity for me. In that light, the Government Investment Authority and the Narnian company that issued me the multi-year exploratory visa asked me for a summary of our business concepts. This is what I provided:

Dear Mohamed,

Greetings! My name is Richard Brogden and we spoke briefly by phone this week. I am an American seeking to open a business here in Narnia that I own, possibly with other expatriate stockholders depending on what is allowed. You asked me to send a short summary of the business idea.

I actually have three business ideas, which depending on your advice may be combined into one business or perhaps registered independently as three businesses. Part of the equation is how many residential visas each business allows for expat stockholders and employees (as I would like a way for my core staff to join me in country), but we can address that in due time as the first consideration is gaining Investment Authority approval.

Before I summarize the business ideas, let me give a small introduction. I have been living in the Arab world for the last 27 years [Mauritania (1992), North Sudan (1996–2011), Egypt (2012–2018)]. I am a minister with the Assemblies of God church and the church has been my investor for the businesses we started. I am not asking to register the church; I am just explaining they are my donor base and the investors who have provided the capital for our businesses. This is a tremendous blessing—the church wants to invest in Narnia in a way that adds value to Narnian citizens.

The previous businesses have all been in the training/consulting/education sector and are both professional and non-sectarian (i.e. they serve all people regardless of religion, tribe, or race). We started an international school, an adult education center with ten franchises across Sudan, a ladies community center, a development service, and a language and cultural center.

That said, here are three services we are interested in developing in Narnia:

1) Intercultural Training

2) Leadership Coaching

3) Shared Workspace

Please let me know if any or all of these ideas fall under the allowance you provide for foreign-owned companies to be registered in Narnia. We are open to your advice and suggestions. We are open to starting one business or three separate businesses.

Many blessings,

RICHARD BROGDEN

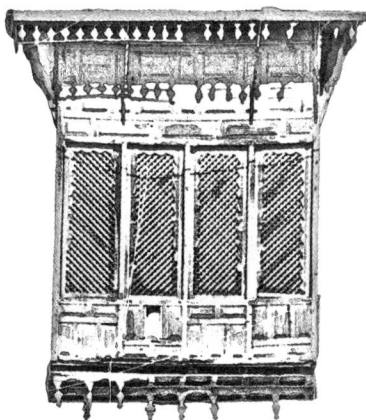

SPIRITUAL WARFARE AND OUR THOUGHT LIFE

Recently a worker here in the Arabian Peninsula had to be sent home for conduct unbecoming to a minister of the gospel. Whenever sinful choices lead to tragic consequences and difficult decisions, we should pause and examine our own hearts and hedges—as "there, but for the grace of God, go I."

The details of this particular case were shocking and made me wonder again how those who love Jesus and who have given their life for Him can so betray Him, their loved ones, and themselves. The wonder is not based in judgment, but in sobriety. I am sobered that the enemy of our souls is so adept at deceiving our minds, so canny in tempting us towards what we know will destroy us and those around us.

One primary way the enemy attacks us is in our thought life. Serving among unreached peoples in locations where Satan has his throne and where he has ruled for centuries puts us in a position that threatens him and his holdings. He then lashes out, and through his cunning those lashes work to twist truth in our minds. I have been appalled at what my mind has conceived and entertained while serving in pioneer contexts. I have thought despicable and blasphemous things with reoccurring frequency. But what a relief and necessity it is to recognize that these are not my thoughts; rather, these are the vile and twisted suggestions of the enemy.

As far as defeating the devil's attacks on our minds, it is critical that we bring these thoughts into the light, that we recognize they are not our thoughts but his invasive suggestions, that others are being similarly attacked (we are not unique or alone), and that the word of God, the blood of Jesus, and the Holy Spirit can wash our minds of the filth and folly from hell which the enemy deviously tries to make us believe is ours.

I'm not saying these attacks on the mind are unique to pioneer contexts. The devil is remarkably consistent and uncreative, primarily because his tactics are so effective against those unaware or unprepared. I'm just saying these lies of the enemy, the lies that attack the very foundations of Christlike, biblical thought, if you live for any amount of time in the places where the devil has dominated, are exacerbated and vehement.

Transparently then, I want to share some common ways the enemy tries to attack me in my mind. What liberty, joy, and hope I found when Jesus assured me that these are not my thoughts, that these thoughts do not define me, that these thoughts are NOT who I am, and that these are but wicked darts of the enemy that have no rightful place in me. My hope is that as you read how the devil has lied to me, you will recognize how subtly and stubbornly he tries to deceive you. My hope is that in realizing that he lies to all of us in similar patterns, we will have solidarity in resisting his lies and resting in our true identity in Christ.

THE LIES AGAINST SEXUAL PURITY

Infidelity, perversity, homosexuality, confused identity, child abuse, rape, promiscuity, self-gratification. Have you thought about these things? Have you had nasty dreams about them? These are not your thoughts; these are not you. These are from the pit of hell and have no part of you. When these thoughts come, pray in the Spirit, plead the blood of Jesus, read Scripture, sing out your worship, lift your voice in praise, and remind yourself: "These are not my thoughts. I will give no place to them or their suggestions." You are not sinful because the devil threw a dart at your mind or because he questioned your God-given identity. You are normal and under attack. Quote Jude and remind the devil that the Lord will rebuke and defeat him. Tell someone you trust about the errant thoughts, for in doing so you bring the lie out into the light and break most of its power. Don't freak out. Relax in the realization that the enemy is trying to insert his lies into your psyche and that he tries this same trick on all of us. Relax in the confidence that Jesus and His word define who you are; the Devil and his wiles do not.

THE LIES AGAINST CHRIST'S IDENTITY

Is Jesus really God? Can God really be both man and God? Is the Bible really trustworthy? Is the cross really necessary? Is there not some other way (or ways) of salvation? These along with any other doubts about the essential nature of Christ seemingly come out of nowhere and circle us, seeking any opening in our armor. In his cunning the devil attacks our weakness, and in his hubris attacks our strength. Don't be surprised when the enemy launches a doubt against the very core of your faith, against a truth you have taught with passion a thousand times, against the very heart of the gospel and our Lord Jesus Christ. When these lies come flying at you, recognize their origin and keep your shield up. Don't argue with them—they are lethal, not logical. Simply stand on the promises of God, quote or read the Bible out loud, and let the washing of the water of the Word purge all the nonsense from your head.

THE LIES AGAINST RELATIONAL UNITY

Jealousy, competition, striving for acceptance, critical spirits, suspicion, judgmentalism, the "in-club," marriage tension, team dysfunction, division in the local church or missionary community, loneliness, exceptionalism (no one understands, no one has it as bad as I do, no one is as aware/informed as I am). The enemy loves to divide because the unity of the body of Christ threatens him. The devil loves to make mountains from molehills and to brew tempests in teapots. We fight him by refusing to allow small cuts to fester, by refusing to take offense, by being the pain swallower, by keeping short accounts, by being peacemakers, by living out the Golden Rule, by following Matthew 18 principles for conflict resolution, and by praying the mercy prayer for those who hurt us. When hurt is spreading, we absorb it rather than pass it on. We forgive rather than attack. We extend grace rather than demand it. The devil has no answer for those who live the crucified life, for those who end the conflict by accepting the nails into their own hands and the whip on their own back with love for the other. We don't bury our heads in the sand, but we do bury our hurts in the cross, and in so doing we diffuse the lies against relational unity.

THE LIES AGAINST LEADERSHIP AND AUTHORITY

Disobedience, partial obedience, refusal to submit, gossip, frustration, rebellion, pride. As pride was the original sin of the devil, even so it is still his favorite poison today. So easily he tempts us toward the Absalom spirit: "If I was in charge, I would do this…and this… and this." It starts as a critical attitude in our hearts. It then sprouts into indirectly undermining our leaders or authority through faint praise, gilded criticism, coalition building, seeking out other wounded followers to commiserate, and becoming the "safe" one to complain to, secretly feeling better about ourselves as people grumble about our mutual leader. The devil lies to us by telling us we are treated unfairly, that we know better than our leaders, and that our peers would be better served if we were in charge. The enemy is adept at making bad seem good, at convincing us that ends justify means, and at making our rebellious attitudes and behaviors feel justified. But there is no justification for dishonoring authority, not even when our authorities are less than honorable. The truth is, we must always trust that God rules in the kingdoms of men, always trust the sovereign Lord to defend us, and always believe that when all is said and done, the safest path is the submitted path.

THE LIES AGAINST EMOTIONAL STABILITY

Fear, selfishness, suicide, murder, violence, rage, deception, depression, schizophrenia, delusion, theft, irrationality, folly. In my experience the devil uses fear as often as he uses pride. Pride tends to damage others, while fear tends to destroy ourselves along with those around us. Fear can make us irrational. It clouds our thinking. And if we succumb to it, we consider (and enact) things we would never do if in our right mind. If the devil cannot destroy our spirit and body, he attacks our mind and emotions. If subtle lies don't work, he attempts outlandish ones. When we are hungry, angry, lonely, tired, and sick (HALTS), we are more vulnerable to crazy thoughts. When we are emotionally depleted, we have less resistance to the ridiculous, and it somehow becomes more believable. We tend to recover from physical and spiritual depletion more rapidly than emotional exhaustion, and when we are emotionally empty, somehow the most horrific ideas seem strangely appealing. The devil suggests that some wild act will bring relief and rest, when in reality it will only bring hell. Spiritual warfare thus includes such simple things as eight hours of sleep and occasional naps, daily exercise and healthy eating, industry and a healthy work ethic alongside holidays and Sabbaths, date nights and family games, accountability groups, and counsel and counseling as needed (with no shame). It means friends you can laugh with and don't need to try to spiritually impress. It means your feet on earth while your head is in heaven and "recharge" time, whatever that means to you.

CONCLUSION

A primary theater of spiritual warfare is in our heads and thoughts. The primary weapon of the enemy is deceit. He starts with attractive little lies and half-truths, and works his way up to blatant, ridiculous, perverted nonsense. Winning the battle for truth in the mind is critical to winning the war. If we lose enough of the little skirmishes, we can believe and do any wicked thing. If we daily combat lies with light and truth, we will stand firm, by grace, unspoiled till "that day."

PURSUING JESUS:

So easily am I distracted from pursuing You, Lord. So quickly my mind and heart turn to other, lesser things—some benign, some evil. The constant presence of Jesus is my only hope. Lord, I repent of my wicked, prone-to-wander heart. Thank you that Your presence explains difficult things (Psalm 73:17). Thank you that Your presence clarifies, frees, and counsels when bitterness tries to blind and stupefy (v. 24). I am the fool that desires wicked things. Let it be true that besides You I desire nothing on earth because You are the strength of my heart and my portion forever (v. 26). May the nearness of God be my good and my refuge, that I may tell of all Your wonderful works (v. 28).

Apart from You, Jesus, I can do nothing, for You are life (John 1:3–4). Thank you that I need no rights but to be a child of God with the promise of being filled with the Holy Spirit (vv. 12, 33). Thank you for grace upon grace in Jesus, for grace perfectly blended with truth (vv. 16–17). Lord, teach me to confess who I am not, to be ever conscious that I am not worthy, and to ever *only* minister that Jesus be manifest (vv. 20, 27, 31). Jesus, let me have faith that radical monotheists will fall and worship You, even as did the radical monotheists of Your day. John the Baptist declared, "This is the Son of God" (v. 34). And Nathanael echoed, "You are the Son of God" (v. 49). There was something so compelling about Your presence that You won them over to Your deity and Your worth. Do it again, Lord Jesus, in Narnia, from the sovereign and the princes down to the simple, special needs youth on the street.

Lord, help me today to speak words by which Muslims may be saved (Acts 11:14). Let me begin to speak and the Spirit descend (v. 15).

Let me not stand in God's way (v. 17). Let whatever consequences (scattering, persecution) that result from gospel allegiance lead to preaching Jesus and gospel advance (vv. 19–20). Let me be content and joyful in being a Barnabas, a good man, full of the Holy Spirit (v. 24), who finds a Paul and steps back so that Paul can bring considerable numbers to You (v. 25).

Lord Jesus, let me be faithful to Him who has appointed me (Heb. 3:2). Let me ever remember that the builder of all things is God (v. 4). Let me ever strive to be faithful as a Son, holding fast to confidence in You (v. 6). Let me ever work at keeping my heart soft and to take care not to have an unbelieving heart (3:8, 12, 15). Let me never be hardened by the deceitfulness of sin, holding fast to our assurance to the end (vv. 13, 14).

Pursuing Church Planting:

In the twists and turns of figuring out long-term credible presence (and professional identity), there are various options. Yesterday, I spoke with a firm that can offer a residence permit, which is necessary to rent an apartment in my name, buy a car in my name, open a bank account in my name, etc. We can function on a multi-year visa, but it is more complicated and does not allow for certain legal and necessary actions. What this firm can offer is a status in which I am paid by my church in the U.S. but that payment is channeled through the firm for a monthly management fee. They can also handle payroll and billing, etc (also for a fee). We are continuing to research our options and to pray about the best long-term status.

I had a conversation with Mohammad, the Sudanese Muslim doorkeeper of our building. He shared frankly about racism in Narnia and how it affects him and all expatriates, primarily those who are not white. I pray that God uses this ugly sin to disenfranchise Muslims about Islam and that accordingly, the body of Christ here would be inclusive and welcoming without prejudice. May the Lord help us establish indigenous churches that are missionary minded, reaching across their own tribal and cultural lines. There can be a danger to the homogeneous principle if it becomes prejudiced and inward.

On a Skype call with one of our team leaders from a neighboring country, I was reminded that many Muslims live in bondage to fear. The leader reported that a survey showed the main felt need in her city was deliverance from spirits and demons. We talked about the need to have a spiritual identity and that the gospel (which included guilt/innocence, shame/honor, and fear/power) has arbitrary insertion points. In other words, it may be the fear/power dynamic that frees a Muslim woman from evil power that then opens the door to the forensic truths of justification by grace. Perhaps Muslim women need to be freed from demons before they can be freed from sin. All aspects of the gospel must be preached and lived, but the starting point may vary. What is clear is that we need a robust spiritual identity that gives us access and opportunity into the cultures we serve. Perhaps this team leader can gain access to her community by being known as the Jesus follower through whom there is power to cast out devils. This is an exciting and sobering possibility. And it calls to mind the warning: "Jesus I know and Paul I know, but who are you?"

In Narnia, I am drawn to the E. Stanley Jones model of public lectures, speeches, and teaching on who Jesus is and how He relates to society. Winsome, respectful, articulate, but uncompromising. I think there is in the new Narnia space in the public sector for such a presentation. I want my identity to be as a Jesus-Bible devotee, a pastor who loves Narnia and Narnians and lifts my voice to talk about Jesus as He is described in the Gospels.

PURSUING JESUS:

Thank you, Jesus, that You have established *all* the boundaries and You have made the seasons of life of ministry (Psalm 74:17). I can relax and trust You. Thank you for Your kind and cultural heart. You made 120 to 180 gallons of wine for a societal event using vessels dedicated to ritual washing (John 2:6)! You blessed a young couple and assured their honor before others, and this is called a manifestation of Your glory (v. 11)! Then immediately, You went to the temple, made a scourge of cords, and, consumed with zeal, attacked what was culturally unholy (vv. 13–17). This too was glorious! And You did this on resurrection authority (vv. 18–19), which proves you are divine. Jesus, You stand as Lord over culture—You both created and correct them, You set the limits and boundaries, You rejoice in what is good, and You cast out what is vile. Teach me to follow in Your steps.

When God tells me who I am (v. 25), I don't need (or rely on) the affirmation of others. When I don't know what God has asked of me, I am unstable, seeking praise, affirmation, and confirmation where I should not.

Prison is good for prayer, both your own prayer and that of the church (Acts 12:5). We can sleep between intimidating soldiers with the confidence that bigger soldiers watch over us. Peace in adversity is linked to seeing the unseen, the forces that are for us, God for us and Christ within us, the hope of glory. If we don't give glory to God for deliverance, fruit, and ministry success, we will be eaten by worms, *but* the word of the Lord will continue to grow (vv. 23–24). Jesus, help me remember that You don't need me; it's a privilege to be used by You. Help me remember that arrogance leads to painful death. Help me remember it is always about You and the Word going forward. I am expendable, wonderfully so. Let me remember and rejoice that it is all about You.

Let me fear, lest the Word not be united with faith in my heart (Heb. 4:1). Reintroduce me to godly fear, and forgive me for long-held flippancy, deadness to Your awesome presence. Thank you that You are outside time and Your works were finished from the foundation of the earth (v. 3). Let not my disobedience preclude entering the rest/presence/sanctuary of God (v. 6). Let me labor to enter into rest (v. 11)! Thank you that the word of God can judge the thoughts and intentions of my heart and that all things are laid bare to Your *sympathetic* eyes (v. 13). Jesus, today let me draw near, receive mercy, and find grace to help me in my time of need (v. 16).

PURSUING CHURCH PLANTING:

We are enjoying language school again, and every day I attempt to make our language nurturer laugh and to hear some gospel truth. I have been singing songs to her in Arabic to illustrate words. When we learned the word for knee, I sang in Arabic: "He is Lord... Every knee shall bow, every tongue confess...." When we learned the verb for touch, I told her the story of the woman with the issue of blood reaching out in faith to touch Jesus. When we learned the word for lips, I sang a chorus in Arabic to her: "Thy lovingkindness is better than life... My lips shall praise Thee!" It has benefited us to have Sudanese Arabic. It makes our lessons are very conversational as we learn Narnian words, but it's not in a vacuum. The point I'm making is that in the creative tension between learning language and evangelism, it's not an either/or. The language learning process can be a wonderful time to share faith, Bible stories, and truth from Scripture. The guard of the building, Mohammad, wants to visit tonight to learn some English, and I will suggest to him that we do so from the Bible. There is a nice edition of the Bible that contains English and Arabic side by side.

Yesterday we had lunch with a delightful brother. He has been in Narnia nearly thirty years, speaks Arabic well, and has an influential position here in town. He is full of the joy of the Lord. I marvel that he so sparkles after being in this context for so long. After spending just a few hours with him, I noted some practical disciplines of his which I believe have engendered longevity:

1. He talks to Jesus all day long. He constantly says: "Glory to God!" "Thank you, Jesus!" "Praise the Lord!" "We love You, Lord!" He constantly lifts little prayers to the heavens. He is careful to always give God glory and direct attention to the Lord. He lives and breathes prayer. He seems to commune with Jesus constantly.

2. He radiates joy, kindness, and acceptance. It is evident that he spends time in the Word. He quotes scripture freely. He chooses joy, and it's not manufactured, but a choice. He has chosen to be kind, loving, gracious, and welcoming. He shares his possessions and his information freely. He is openhanded and openhearted. He thinks about others and encourages constantly.

3. He combines courage with prudence. He listens to the Spirit and adjusts to the times. He is careful without being over cautious. He takes necessary precautions and necessary risks. He has smuggled Bibles, has led locals to the Lord, and has endured the ups and downs of resistance.

4. He is disciplined, hardworking, and culturally engaged. (He knows Arabic poetry, understands the Arab mind keenly, and is appropriately respectful.) He has figured out how to get the most from a busy day. He brings others into his routines and makes them natural.

I am thankful for this brother and see Jesus in him. I too want to praise and thank Jesus all day long. I too want to constantly give Jesus the glory and others time and attention. I too want to shine and smile with the joy of the Lord. I too want to be irrepressible in witness. Thank you, Jesus, for this example of 29 years and still shining for Jesus, brighter and brighter until that glorious day.

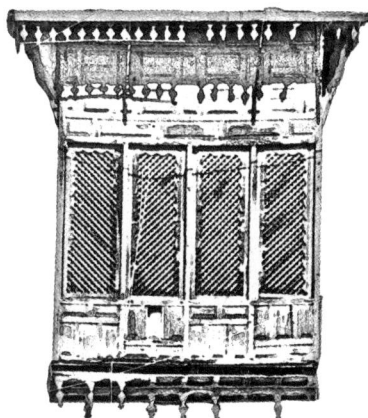

HEAVEN'S HIGHEST HONOR

Three unconnected Christians died on the same marvelous day and entered their heavenly home together. Sister Pam, Farmer Jaeger, and Businessman Bob met at the gates of glory and introduced themselves to one another before quietly walking through.

Lined with giant oak trees, the path gently rose up a pleasant hill. The rise of the hill became the immediate horizon, obscuring the pilgrims' onward view. All was quiet and calm, and the three friends walked on gladly. Cresting the hill, they saw an immense valley and in the center was a radiant city. Broad avenues from four directions converged on the city, their path being but one of the four. The avenues were slightly sunk into the valley floor, with natural grass terraces cascading down towards them. Along the broad path of these three new arrivals was a magnificent crowd, multiple thousands deep, stretching all the way to the city steps. There were millions of beings along their road, angelic and the redeemed.

As Sister Pam, Farmer Jaeger, and Businessman Bob crested the hill, the throng of millions erupted into a thunderous roar. They cheered. They clapped. They whistled. They lifted their hands to pump their fists. They high-fived the pilgrims and each other. They cried. They smiled. They jubilated. The three pilgrims were stunned and stopped in their tracks. The crowd roared even louder as intimate friends and family detached themselves from the cacophony and ran up to gather the pilgrims in fierce hugs. Their loved ones grabbed their hands and propelled them onward—the noise and acclaim somehow increasing as they walked.

The path brought them to a series of elegant marble steps that led upward towards the joy of their being, for Jesus stood radiantly at the top of the stairs. He just stood there smiling. The crowd fell into a comfortable silence. The families and loved ones of the pilgrims released their hands and let them climb the steps alone. The pilgrims climbed steadily, eyes transfixed on Jesus. Their legs climbed slowly, but their hearts and spirits raced forward, embraced and enveloped in love and satisfied joy even before their bodies arrived. They reached the top step and stopped. And Jesus smiled and simply said, "Hello, beloved. Welcome home."

Jesus first turned His attention to Sister Pam, and in an instant all the weariness of a difficult life vanished. He said to her, "Pam, I'm so proud of you. You endured rejection, loneliness, and pain with great grace. You fed the hungry, welcomed the abandoned, loved the least and the lost, served the church, gave to the poor, and you did it all with joy. You kept My word and you represented My heart. You reached out to the unreached in your city and state. You translated My heart for all peoples to your local congregation. You led your leaders and your followers to have a single eye on My glory amongst the nations. Pam, I am so proud of you." Pam smiled and looked down, her eyes filling with contented tears.

Jesus then looked at Farmer Jaeger with a twinkle in His eye. "I have a special love for farmers, and you have been a good one." Farmer Jaeger beamed, and his weather-beaten face glowed. "Farmers understand My laws of sowing and reaping. Farmers honor Me with hard work. Farmers understand seasons and anticipate harvest. Farmers are humble, loyal, dignified, faithful, and steady. Man, Jaeger, I love farmers and I love you. You not only raised crops; you also raised godly seed. You harvested godly children who represented Me all over My earth. You prayed on your tractor, you gave in your pew, you supported your pastor, you served the body of Christ, and you gave of your best so that I would be glorified in every tribe, tongue, and nation. Jaeger, I am so proud of you." Jaeger and Jesus held a long knowing look. No more needed to be said. The farmer just looked and nodded at His King, and both were happy.

Last, Jesus addressed Businessman Bob. "Bob, you are the real deal. There is nothing false about you, and I love that. You always obeyed Me, and I love that, too. I asked you to go to Harvard, and you did it. I asked you to live in the business world with integrity, and you did it. I asked you to give generously to missions, and you did it. I asked you to carry My heart for the unreached, and you did it. I asked you to lead the missions committee at your church, and you did it. Whatever I asked, you did, and Bob, obedience is My love language. You have loved Me and the nations well." Bob just beamed.

Jesus then extended His arms out wide, as if to gather all three pilgrims in His embrace at once, smiled again, and said to them all, "Well done, My good and faithful servants. Enter into the joy of the Lord."

And the crowd roared, and the three pilgrims raced into the arms of Jesus. Family and friends raced to join the group hug. Tears of joy streamed, hearts burst, and the happy throng turned to enter the celestial city. For heaven had just conferred its highest medal of honor, and the new saints wore it well as they sauntered home.

PURSUING CHURCH PLANTING:

Yesterday consisted of a prayer walk, Arabic study, office correspondence, and communication back and forth with the business that can issue me an *iqaama*. I then had two evening appointments. As I emailed back and forth with the Narnian business partner, I became discouraged as I discovered piece by piece more costs for the annual residence and work visa. There is a fee to the government because I am not a Narnian. There is a fee for each dependent. There is a 5 percent value added tax (VAT). I have to buy full medical insurance (even though I currently have my own insurance). Etcetera, etcetera. The costs kept coming and piled up as I researched, making the prospect daunting. The total cost came to $33,000 or so for the year, just in administrative costs, taxes, and fees. And this is before renting office space or any other operational costs for doing business here.

I was getting discouraged as I waded through yet another spreadsheet that gave a clearer picture of how expensive it is to settle here under this option that allows an *iqaama*. As I was sinking into discouragement, an email opened on my screen: "We have decided to give you a grant of $25,000 to help register the business in Narnia!" I could not believe the timing. This was from a foundation that I forgot about, and in the very moment I was struggling with how to manage the costs, the Lord sent a wonderful encouragement. In that moment I had done nothing—He did it all. I must remember that in church planting the responsibility is on Jesus. "I will build My church," He said. He will do it all.

I had two appointments set up for last night: one with Thomas after he collected his daughter (he is divorced and shares custody) and the other with Mohammad, the guard. Mohammad wants to improve his English, so I hope to study the Gospels with him using a Bible that has Arabic and English side by side. Thomas was to call me around 8 p.m. and I told Mohammad that he could come to the apartment around 10. Thomas never called and Mohammad did not come, so around 10:30, I began to wind down for the night and headed to bed to read. I thought about calling them, or in Mohammad's case walking downstairs to see if he could come, but I was too tired and I didn't.

A complementary truth to God doing all the work of church planting is the necessity of our sweat equity. What I should have done was fight though my fatigue and walk downstairs to see if I could find Mohammad and invite him up. What I should have done is called Thomas to see if we could meet somehow. It is unacceptable to do nothing; *and* I must *actively* expect God to do it all. I play my little part as He does the primary work. I can't wait for the fish to jump into the boat; I have to cast my net *again*, even if I have been fishing all night. Yes, indeed, in church planting God will do it all when we practically obey and keep casting out the gospel net even when we're tired.

DAY 18

PURSUING JESUS:

God is to be feared. Who can stand in His presence once He is angry (Psalm 76:7)? Even the wrath of man shall praise You (v. 10). Lord, let my zeal be for Your house and channeled towards Your purposes, not a destructive wildfire. Let me make vows and give gifts to You who are to be feared (v. 11). Lord, You have no tolerance for false worship. You bluntly told the Samaritan woman that her religion was wrong and that she worshiped what she did not know (John 4:22). In the same breath You debunked second temple Judaism, saying that neither mountain (Gerizim or Jerusalem) defined true worship, for true worshipers were anywhere in spirit and truth (v. 23). Lord, I want to be moved (in both love and hate) by what You love and hate. Only You have the wisdom to hate lovingly. Help me, Lord, burn for You in focused heat that brings life not death.

Thank you that others have labored and done the hard work (v. 38). Let me ever be thankful in missions for those who have prayed, given, and gone ahead of us. I pray that those Muslims I share Jesus with would hear for themselves, know, and believe that Jesus is indeed the Savior of the world (v. 42). When we face opposition to this truth, may we respond by spending time speaking boldly with reliance on the Lord who acts and testifies to His truth with miraculous signs and wonders (Acts 14:2–3). If they stoned Paul, let me not be dismayed by smaller pebbles, for indeed it is by *many* tribulations we must enter the kingdom of God (vv. 19, 22). Lord, on that day when *You* break through, let me be able to report all that God has done through us with joy and humility (v. 27).

Relationship and covenant are conditional. It is possible to abuse grace and so insult God that salvation is impossible, and you become cursed and burned up (Heb. 6:4–6, 8). Let me retain a healthy reverence for Almighty God. Let me also trust that faith and patience will allow me to inherit the promises just as Abraham patiently waited to obtain his promises (vv. 12, 15). In the interim, be my refuge and let me take hold of You and take hold of hope. Thank you that in the storm, my anchor can hold within the veil (v. 19). I can actually hold on to the presence of Jesus while I wait for His promises to come true.

PURSUING CHURCH PLANTING:

Yesterday we had a lovely time with brothers and sisters in a little home church. The message was on John 7 and how Jesus fulfilled the expectations of the feast by promising springs of water. Let us drink deeply of Jesus. It is the only way to survive. In the afternoon I spoke to a group of new missionaries (online) about longevity in missions. The average length of service for those intending to plant churches among Muslims is shockingly down to about four years. The obvious challenge is that not much church planting happens in four years (outside God's divine intervention). If we are going to make disciples, it does not happen overnight and there is no spiritual microwave. We must abide (remain) for a long time in context in order to be fruitful. And in order to remain for a long time, we must drink deeply of Jesus. Longevity is not the goal, obedience is; and drinking from Jesus helps us be obedient over time (where fruitfulness is derived).

We spent the evening with Thomas, and I was able to clearly share the gospel with him using the Exodus Passover story bridged to John declaring Jesus is the Lamb of God. I was able to tell Thomas that only those under the blood of Jesus are saved from the wrath of God. He still has not read the Bible I gave him, but interestingly he has asked other Narnian friends if they wanted to read the Bible. They laughed at him and said no, but I was encouraged that at least he asked. If he ever comes to faith, I think he will be an evangelist. I affirmed to him that I would love to sit with his friends and him to talk about Jesus and the Bible. We will now pray and see what God does. I do want to strive for open proclamation of Jesus from the Bible to groups of Narnian Muslims. Lord, have Your way. You alone can open these doors.

In house church yesterday, I had a great sense of the peace of the Lord in the season we are now in—unknown again (largely), without much responsibility or position. It is a sweet spot to be in and I felt His encouragement to enjoy it. In my flesh and insecure pride, I want to be known and recognized. This is shortsighted folly. May Jesus help me enjoy the quiet seasons, preparing for whatever He wants me to do in the future, being faithful in the little things now.

DAY 19

PURSUING JESUS:

G rief (pain, discouragement, disappointment, etc.) lies to us (Psalm 77:10). God's way is holy, for He is both the earth shaker and the One who leads His people like a flock (vv. 13, 18, 20). Thank you, Lord, that Your awesome terror and Your tender care do not cancel each other out for zero effect, but that You are multi-directionally magnificent. Thank you, Father, that You never stop working (John 5:17). Un-resting, un-hastening, Father and Son are ever at work. It is amazing that Jesus reminds us the Son can do nothing of Himself (vv. 19, 30), and yet He has life in Himself, for He is the *Son of Man* (vv. 26–27)! How much more can I do nothing; if the Son of Man who has life in Himself depends on the Father, so much more must I. Further, God the Son did not seek His own will, but the will of the Father (v. 30). How much more must I pursue the will of the Father. When we seek glory from men and not the glory from the one and only God, we are acting in unbelief (v. 44). God will not bless me when I seek my own glory. God will not share His glory with a presumptuous fool like me.

Lord, Jesus Christ, Son of God, Son of Man, have mercy on me. All my motives are mixed, and many of them are completely vain. My soul thirsts for glory, praise, and recognition from men. I repent of this vanity. Lord, purge me, cleanse me, and sift out of me all that lusts for self-glory. Teach me to long for, work for Your glory alone. Forgive, Lord, my presumption and childish attempts to draw attention to myself.

Thank you, Jesus, that You are the One who makes choices among us (Acts 15:7). I don't need to strive for status or place among the brethren. You determine what, where, and when for the good and joy of all. Let me trust You and revel in the assignment You give me. Thank you, Lord, that You concern Yourself with taking from among the Gentiles a people for Your name (v. 14). Let that be my concern, my total concern as I leave all other lesser concerns to You. Let me walk in unity with brothers in the faith under the Lordship of the Holy Spirit so we can say with the apostles: "It seemed good to the Holy Spirit, and to us" (v. 28). Thank you that there are *always* others preaching and teaching Christ (v. 25). Let me not compete, compare, or criticize; rather, let me bless and affirm in the generous spirit of Jesus.

Thank you, Jesus, that You are a better hope because You have the power of an indestructible life; thus, You have the power to save forever (Heb. 7:16, 19, 25). You can forever save since You always live to make intercession. Oh, what wonder! Jesus, God, Son of Man spends His time praying! He doesn't need to spend time on rituals or religion. Jesus with all the fullness of the Godhead prays! Holy, innocent, undefiled, and exalted above the heavens, He spends His time praying (v. 28).

Jesus, God of very God, does nothing without the Father and what He primarily does is pray. I, frail and fallen, try to do so much without the Father and spend very little time in prayer. Lord, I am indeed a fool. Have patience with me, I pray. Teach me to depend completely on the Father. Teach me to spend much time in prayer.

PURSUING CHURCH PLANTING:

We hosted a young couple who are praying about coming to Narnia and figuring out what that will look like. We enjoy being a blessing to God's team in country, a team from all nationalities, and hope we can help create unity and trust between missionaries. Mohammad, the building guard, came by for a visit as he wants to improve his English. We read the first portion of Mark, and I helped him understand the meaning with a Bible that has English and Arabic side by side. After working through the

DAY 17

PURSUING JESUS:

God puts one down and exalts another (Psalm 75:7). Lord, forgive my anxiety about where I fit in, what my role should be, and whether or not I am respected by others. Teach me to relax and trust You and to enjoy seasons of anonymity for the lack of pressure they afford. Thank you, Lord, that You rule in the kingdoms of men, setting over and removing whom You choose.

Let what is born in me be of the Spirit (John 3:6). Let flesh life die in the womb before it draws breath. Spirit, will You blow where You wish, do what You want (v. 8)? I don't have to understand or be central or even be a part at all of what You do. Help me, Lord, receive the heavenly things because I believe *You*, so that the light will manifest that my works have been wrought in God (vv. 12, 18, 20). Let me ever remember that I am *not* the Christ, or even *a* Christ. Let me live for Your increase and my demise, setting my seal (lovely imagery!) to this: that God is *true* (vv. 30, 33)! Thank you, Father, that You do not give the Spirit by measure (v. 34), but in torrents and tidal waves; thus, it is altogether just that if I don't obey Jesus (when all authority and power is available) for the wrath of God to abide on me (v. 36).

Let me remember that God is opposed to all deceit and fraud (Acts 13:10). Let me remember that ungodly jealousy leads me to say and do foolish things (v. 45). Let me continually be filled with joy *and* the Holy Spirit (v. 52) so that there is no room for silly flesh. God, forbid me from taking honor to myself in ministry but only to receive ministry with the calling of God (Heb. 5:4). Forbid be (disable me) from glorifying myself (v. 5). Teach me obedience through suffering (v. 8). Don't let me become hard of hearing, rather train my senses to discern good and evil, first within and then without (vv. 11, 14).

passage, I stepped out to get him some coffee and told him to write down ten vocabulary words he needed to study. I was delighted to come back and see on his list "Son of God" and "Messiah" alongside "belt," "sandals," and "send." This was not a Bible study per say, but it was a Bible reading time, and he read the Arabic enthusiastically. When we began talking about racism in all its forms (including the prejudice of the rich against the poor), I showed him James 2 and he read that text eagerly. Principally, I don't want to spend a lot of time teaching English, but if I can teach English from the Scripture, that is a good investment.

Later in the evening, the director of the GPA Arabic learning program came by and we had a long talk. He loves Americans and is a religious pluralist. I hesitated to say anything as he (Michael) is connected to other missionaries here who have invested in him and I am unaware of their approach. I listened for a while but felt convicted that I needed to be more concerned about biblical truth and the character of Jesus than anything else, so I sought a way to gently show him that I did not think the Bible agreed with him. I said something like:

> *Michael, thank you for those thoughts, but the reality is, the Bible does not agree with them. It is indeed easier to say that many ways lead to heaven, but in the Bible, Jesus says He alone is "the way, truth, and life, and no one comes to the Father but by Him." So, we can be friends and love one another yet disagree. According to the Bible, it is not like this room where any door can exit. According to the Bible, the idea is more like all mankind has fallen down a deep well and we cannot escape or lift ourselves out of it. There is only one way out for all of us—if Jesus rescues us.*

It was a gentle conversation, but I did want to be clear that according to the Bible, all have sinned and Jesus is the only name under heaven by which men can be saved.

A very interesting item from yesterday was a telephone conversation with an MBB from Syria (who has a marvelous testimony of Jesus healing and saving him) who is in conversations with Narnian officials regarding the official functioning of an international church here in the city. The idea is that the government will provide land and build a church according to the specifications of the Christian community, that public worship for Christians will be allowed, and that clergy visas will be given for international church pastors. It is part of the liberalization program the country is undertaking.

We have been thinking, praying, and asking about this, and God is so far ahead of us. There are dangers, of course—being monitored, yielding up the prophetic voice in order to curry favor, compromise of various kinds along the way. There are also opportunities, and to have a public church where the people of God can come worship Jesus, pray, and hear Bible teaching will be a huge encouragement to the believers in Narnia. There are evidently 1.5 million expatriate Christian workers in Narnia and over 1,000 house fellowships. The number of Narnian believers in house churches is unknown.

This MBB brother from Syria believes this church registration will happen and has offered to help me get a visa as a pastor as well as visas for my staff (team members). This is an exciting possibility and potentially an answer to prayer. We will see what God will do. The plan would be to publicly encourage Christians and privately train and equip them to make disciples of Narnians and all unreached peoples around them, gathering them primarily in house churches.

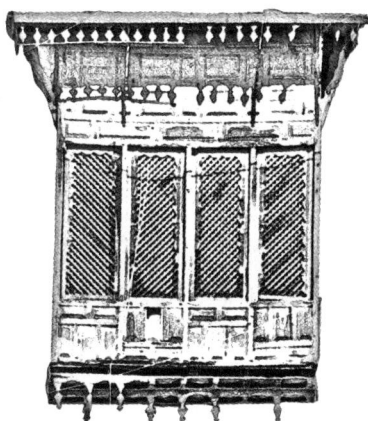

FEELING STUCK IN INTERACTION WITH A LEADER?

1. Have you followed Matthew 18?

2. Have you started to vilify the leader in your spirit (i.e., build a case against him/her)?

- Do you remember that the leader loves Jesus and does what he does because he thinks it is best for the lost?

- Are you praying blessing or judgment on the leader?

3. Have you followed the Golden Rule?

- Treat the leader as you would want to be treated.

- If you were in his/her shoes, how would you want to be treated?

4. Is the leader asking you to cross any moral lines (conscience/conviction)?

- Is this a matter of opinion or morality?
- Have you changed whatever you could without crossing a line of moral conviction?

5. Does anything he/she asks stop you from making disciples or training missionaries?

- Have you remembered the best job in the world is not leading or training but making disciples and planting churches?
- Is what is happening a gift in painful disguise as it opens more time for you to focus on the best job in the world?

6. Are you bowing on the inside?

- Make the leader look good to others.
- The job of an orderly in the military is to make his superior look good to his followers. Have you done that?

7. Have you identified the truth in the criticisms?

- There is almost always a measure of truth.
- Have you come to terms with your own weaknesses in leadership? Do you know what they are? Have you articulated those to your leader?
- Is there an appropriate means of intervention at the next level of leadership? Or has that been tried and not helpful?

8. Have you repented wherever and to whoever you could?

- Do you recognize that at some level you are reaping what you have sown (painful as that admission is)?

9. Are you emotionally tired and in a place where you can't see clearly?

- Do you need a mini sabbatical of three months or so?
- Do you need to get away for a while and clear your head and spirit?

10. Is God asking you to wait and not react? Is He asking you to endure?

- Do you trust Him to vindicate you?
- Are you willing to let time, circumstance, and the Judge of all the earth sort this out and be your honor, lifter of your head, and your defense?
- Is this your cross, your death to self, your live dead, your crucifixion? If so, are you dying well or are you spitting and muttering from your cross?

This last one is hard. It is so ingrained in us to submit to authority and to die to self (and we have asked so many others to do so) that we have difficulty knowing if we are just struggling with dying to self or if there is some spiritual manipulation (that we do to ourselves or is being done to us).

Time sometimes is our only balm. Time and space away from the situation. We can come to a place where we cannot think clearly. We have to give up the desire to understand or be understood, to figure it out. How we are being treated and reacted to sometimes will not make sense. We see no way out of it. There is no good way to defend ourselves, and it seems there are no good options. At least none other than waiting, trusting Jesus, and staying silent. That is where we have to park for a while: waiting, trusting, and staying silent. If you are like me, some days I say too much and trust too little. Jesus, help and mercy us!

PURSUING JESUS:

Psalm 78:70–71 records that God chose David His servant and took him from the sheepfolds, from the care of the ewes with suckling lambs to shepherd His people and Israel His inheritance. It is ever encouraging that God sees all and has the power to choose and place as He sees fit. I don't have to strive, compete, manipulate, preen, boast, posture, or position myself (all of which I am prone to do). All I have to do is to be faithful and trust the Lord. He can pluck anyone from obscurity and put them anywhere. He can also return to obscurity in His great wisdom. In my own life I am ashamed to confess there are multiple levels of arrogance. Lord Jesus, please keep refining me, correcting me, forgiving me, helping me to live humbly—something that is absolutely foreign to my flesh.

John 6 raises some critical questions for me as I struggle with pride: Why *do* I seek Jesus? What *am* I working for? Do I believe (vv. 26–27, 29)? For the work of God is to believe in Jesus and to do all things for Him. Ashamed, I confess that much of what I do is for me—to be known and respected. And even when I want to do things for Jesus, it is usually not purely so. There is a perverted mix of motive in my heart—some glory to Jesus if a little bit will go to me. Jesus, I repent of this. To whom shall I go with my messed-up motives and ambitious heart (v. 68)? Only *You* have the words of eternal life, and only *You* can purify my motives. Have mercy, Lord. I am an arrogant, self-seeking servant, a glory hunter/gatherer. I am ashamed.

The Holy Spirit forbid Paul to speak in certain places (Acts 16:6). The Spirit of Jesus did not allow Paul to go to certain places at certain times (v. 7). The Lord then called to the place and persons of His choosing, and Paul preached Christ then and there (v. 10). Jesus, thank you for

Your loving "no." Let me accept it gladly and wait patiently for Your empowered "yes." Then in those moments let praying, preaching, and singing cause spiritual earthquakes (vv. 25–26).

God takes His people from handholding when we are young in Him to putting His laws in our minds and hearts (Heb. 8:9–10). We grow into being internally led, not externally guided. Lord, help me mature in this regard. May I be sensitive enough to You that You can prompt me with the still small voice and You don't have to resort to the rod. Discipline gives the Father no pleasure, even if it's an act of love, when the child should know better, when the child should respond to the gentle prod. Lord, I should know better; yet You often have to prod me. Forgive me, Father. Let me bring You the joy of quick obedience, of being so attentive to Your leading that I don't need handholding, for Your will is written on my mind and heart.

Pursuing Church Planting

We learned a little bit of what not to do yesterday. We learned what is not found in certain shops. We learned again that shops are shut during the prayer times. We learned that the British Consulate hosts the Anglican service, not the British Consul, and missed half the service. We learned that a thank you text to the "lunch group" which meets on Fridays that mentions the components of the meeting (with names) is not appreciated by some. I had sent a WhatsApp message after the service thanking the ones who preached, led worship, and led the service and that broached someone's comfort level as far as security.

There is a vast difference of opinion on how careful to be about who we are and what we do. By conviction, I tend to be on the far end of openness, but others (who are good people) see it a different way. In this regard I do feel I erred as I should have been more considerate of their concerns and used the code they prefer: Thank you for the good main course and thank you for the dessert. In one sense I think it's unnecessary, but I suppose this is what Paul means in honoring one another. It also seems to me that Narnia is changing, that caution can as easily blend into fear as courage into folly. I do need to attempt to be bold according to my convictions without offending brothers and sisters (and/or jeopardizing them) as much as possible. It won't always be possible; but let me not necessarily offend or break trust. I am praying for wisdom and humility so that I can follow my convictions (and perhaps be a source of encouragement, a model of a different way to approach the challenge) without unnecessarily making others uncomfortable or uneasy. It won't always be possible, but if it does happen, let it not be because I was arrogant, cavalier, or foolish.

DAY 21

PURSUING JESUS:

Psalm 78 reveals how the human heart (including mine) wants God to bless us and judge others. He often surprises us by blessing others and judging us! God is both more merciful and holier than we imagine. Only God perfectly blends and applies both mercy and judgment. Lord, teach me to want for others what I ask for myself.

Jesus had the patience to wait for His time, not rushing to be known (John 7:6). In the interim His life matched His rhetoric and teaching as godly teaching is verified (or annulled) according to the active obedience of the teacher to the will of God (v. 17). If I do not obey Jesus, I cannot with conviction or authority ask others to obey Him. Jesus, You warn that those who speak from themselves seek their own glory (v. 18), and I stand guilty of that more often than not. Lord, teach me to restrain my mouth and teach me to not speak until my heart is ready to seek Your glory. There are snatches of pure desire in my heart for Your glory, but they are riddled and overcome by the motive for self to be glorified. Lord Jesus, help me. I can only stay true by seeking You and Your glory. Thank you that if my heart truly desires to glorify Your name, that no one can lay a hand on me here in Narnia until my time has come (v. 30). Thank you that if I truly desire Your glory, if I believe in You, if I act and speak in a way that gives You glory, that out of my innermost being will flow rivers of living water (v. 38).

When my heart is right, I can rightly upset the world and my spirit can be provoked to gospel witness without being in the flesh (Acts 17:6, 16). Let me be faithful to preach Jesus and the resurrection to focus on the deity of Jesus (v. 18). When my heart is right, I can lovingly and powerfully confront wrong thinking about Jesus (v. 29), clearly stating that God has overlooked their times of ignorance in the past but *now* declares to all people everywhere that they should repent (v. 30). This text (along with Romans 1) is an answer to those who ask about days gone by, when there were areas of the world where the gospel did not extend. We may have some consolation that in the past God overlooked some ignorance, but *now* commands men everywhere to repent.

Thank you, Jesus, that the best things are yet to come both in ministry here on fallen earth and forever in exalted heaven (Heb. 9:11). Thank you that Your blood is so much better (v. 14). Thank you for Your simple law that without the shedding of blood there is no forgiveness of sins (v. 22). Thank you that You appear in the presence of God for us (v. 24); we have an advocate with direct access! Thank you that You have been manifested to put away sin by the sacrifice of Yourself and that You will appear a second time for salvation, for all those who eagerly await you (vv. 26, 28). Jesus, today I am thankful for the gospel message and that it applies to me personally and that You have saved me from the wrath of God unto His eternal joy by Your great love. I ever want the simple gospel to be profound to me, so that I can powerfully extend it to others.

Pursuing Church Planting:

Yesterday was a delightful morning of exercise, abiding, writing, and admin work. For dinner we met with a missionary kid who is away from the Lord. He manages the Cheesecake Factory here in the city and is very kind and gracious. We talked of general pleasantries, and then I inquired about his faith. He said he believes in a higher power and prays, but he cannot say one religion is right or wrong. Church is "not my jam," he said. I pray for him what I pray for all our missionary kids—I claim the promise of the Psalms: "This one was born in Zion!" Lord, I ask for this man's repentance and his salvation. Bring him back into the family of God, shatter his pluralism, and let him encounter Jesus as Lord of heaven and earth as the King who demands worship.

From dinner my teammate Andrew and I went out to do some evangelism. We decided together that we will be intentional about wide gospel sowing once a week. I am a little bit more direct and bolder than Andrew so hopefully I can be an encouragement to him to take more risks for the gospel. He is wise and steady so hopefully he can teach me prudence and wisdom. Having the partner to pray with, debrief with, and hold accountable to diligence in evangelism is helpful.

We had three good conversations about the gospel. The first with Adam, a Thai man born and bred in Narnia; that conversation was all in Arabic. Then we met Kareem, a young man who has travelled the world and has excellent English. He allowed us to explain what the gospel is over an extended time and agreed to give me his phone number so I could send him some scripture verses. As we disengaged from him, he gently warned us that not all Narnians are as openminded as he is regarding Christians sharing their faith openly on the streets. It did not seem like a threat or a rebuke, but more like a kind caution. The third conversation was outside a coffee shop with Matthew. He had been in the States and found Americans friendly. To all these men I introduced myself as a pastor and Matthew immediately asked me how Jesus could be God. We had an extended conversation in English and I had him read the beginning of John 1 in Arabic. He agreed to receive an Arabic Bible from me as a gift and we exchanged phone numbers.

In the first conversation Adam was bemused and then gently disengaged. In the second conversation Kareem listened politely but didn't seem animated in response. In the third conversation Matthew sincerely wanted to understand what we believed about Jesus but could not wrap his head around Trinity and incarnation. This is no surprise, and we were reminded again that we must be articulate and clear but that only the Spirit can illumine. At the end of the day the cross (the God-man dying to redeem and rising from the dead) is a stumbling block.

I do want to be excellent (as much as depends on me) in explaining the gospel from Scripture and through story and example. I do want to be passionate and ooze love when I share about Jesus. I want to celebrate who Jesus is and to have my enthusiasm match any erudition. Knowing full well that salvation is a work of the Spirit and no man can come unless the Father draws him, whatever is my part I want to do with excellence: language, culture, tone and tenor, apologetics, attitude, wisdom, and authenticity. I would never want a surgeon, dentist, or pilot to carelessly or unprofessionally approach their task when I am in their care. Lord, let me be a diligent, well-prepared, highly skilled, attentive, and dedicated witness. You then do all You do.

"God calls upon us, until the world is utterly destroyed with fire, to go on saving men with all our might and main. Every year that passes is meant to be a year of salvation. We rightly call each year the year of our Lord. Let us make it so by more earnest efforts for the bringing of sinners to the Cross of Christ." – Charles Spurgeon

DAY 22

PURSUING JESUS:

Revive, Jesus, and I will call upon your name Psalm 80:18. Lord, I need You to initiate revival and renewal. I cannot awaken myself; I need Your help, Your instigating mercy. Life me, Lord, that I may seek and pursue You. I can't pursue You without Your animating help. I can't seek You in my own strength.

No one seized Jesus because His time had not yet come (John 8:20). This assurance and confidence, however, is based on some understandings. When we lift up Jesus, knowledge follows, and we have insight into how to act (v. 28). We should do nothing of our own initiative; we should speak only what the Father teaches (v. 28). We must always do what pleases the Father (v. 29). We must not launch out on our own initiative (v. 42). We must honor the Father (v. 49). We must not glorify ourselves (v. 54). We must know Him and keep His word (v. 55). Immunity (until the ordained time) is not a blanket guarantee regardless of our folly or disobedience. When we walk in the above covenantal understanding, nothing can harm us (until the hour comes).

It is on the above basis that Paul was told, "Do not be afraid, but go on speaking and do not be silent, for I am with you, and no man will attack you to harm you, for I have many people in this city" (Acts 18:9–10 NASB). Jesus, help me settle into the city and teach the Word including public and powerful refutation that demonstrates from the Scripture that Jesus is the Christ (vv. 11, 28).

At the same time, teach me how to wait (Heb. 10:13). Jesus with glorified power is my example. He is at the right hand of the Father waiting for the right time. Lord, teach me this blend of covenantal obedience, fearless proclamation, and waiting. In the interim let me draw near with a sincere heart in full assurance of faith (v. 22). Let me hold fast the confession of my hope without wavering, for He who promised is faithful (v. 23). Let me consider how to stir up others (and be stirred up) to love and good deeds, and let me not forsake assembling together, encouraging others (vv. 24–25).

PURSUING CHURCH PLANTING:

Yesterday was an Arabic study day. We had the chance to explain to our Muslim teacher that we fast because we are hungry for Jesus to return. He is the Bridegroom that we long for, and hunger in our physical bodies reminds us that nothing will be fully well until Jesus comes in glory and power. She knows an influential man who works in the field of intercultural training and she has offered to introduce us. I am thankful for dialogue and interfaith meetings, but I never want to give up conversionary goals or invitations. Our approach to dialogue should by all means be gracious and courteous, but we are evangelists and must ever call for repentance as we do not stray from gospel truth.

After Arabic I did a little writing, took a little nap, and then had a Zoom call with a generous foundation. From 8 to 10 p.m., we make ourselves available on Zoom for any team leader that wants to chat or pray. Last night all was calm, so I wrote about security, identity, and community (see page 147).

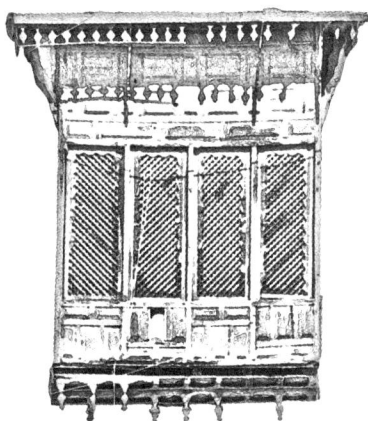

10 GUIDING HEART QUESTIONS WHEN IN CONFLICT, DISCOURAGED, OR HURT IN MINISTRY

1. **What will glorify God?**

   - What action/reaction brings Jesus the most glory?

2. **What is the crucified path, the Calvary way?**

   - Is my heart submitted to my leadership?
   - Am I bowing on the inside?

3. **What is best for the other?**

   - Am I unselfishly choosing what is best for Christ and His kingdom?
   - Am I sacrificially acting for the good of the one with whom I am in conflict?

4. **Have I prayed about it?**

   - Have I taken time to listen to the Holy Spirit?

5. **Will it matter in ten years?**

   - If not, does it matter enough now to take me away from giving energy to the lost?

6. **Is it mission critical?**

   - Does the disagreement adversely affect life and ministry, or is it just style, preference, and personal approach?
   - Does the other have a valid (if different) point that I need to humbly accept?

7. **Is it my responsibility and/or obedience to ask for clarity, disagree, or even object?**

   Or is this inappropriate for me to speak to, and should I leave it to others to address?

8. **Is this something to leave in the hands of Father God and/or father time?**

9. **Am I being reactionary, emotional, defensive, self-righteous, vindictive, too sensitive, wimpy, self-justifying, or immature?**

   - Have I admitted my mistakes and asked for forgiveness?
   - Do I acknowledge to myself that I could be wrong?

- Have I conceded the good points of the other?
- Have I put myself in the other's shoes and fairly listened to and understood their perspective?
- Am I just being argumentative? Does my pride want its own way?

10. **Am I doing the right thing the wrong way?**

- Have I followed the Golden Rule?
- Am I in the flesh at any level?
- Have I gossiped, talked too much, or tried to build a case with others?
- Is there any rebellion in my spirit?
- Have I remembered that I have blind spots? Is my heart lowly?

Pursuing Jesus:

"God takes His stand in His own congregation; He judges in the midst of the rulers" (Psalm 82:1). "Arise, O God, judge the earth! For it is You who possess all nations" (v. 8). John records that "if anyone confessed [Jesus] to be Christ, he was to be put out of the synagogue" (John 9:22). Jesus said, "For judgment I have come into this world" (v. 39). God has very clear dividing lines. His judgments remove what is vile so what is pure can grow, or His judgments remove us from what is vile so that we can grow. We can't stay in sin; we can't remain in religious contexts that deny the deity of Jesus. What is evil must be purged out of us, and we must be purged out of what is evil. If we say that "we see," our sin remains (v. 41). Jesus, help me to realize how blind I am and how much I need You.

Even for Paul, judgment (splitting away) was sometimes necessary. In Acts 19:9, he "took away the disciples" from the synagogue and fellowship with the Jews, and for two years taught daily in a public lecture hall (v. 10). The result was that all who lived in Asia heard the Word. Sometimes you need to come out to go on, for at the end of the day all false religion must be dethroned (v. 27).

Hebrews 11:2 reminds us that we gain God's approval by faith. Moses chose to endure ill treatment with the people of God, rather than enjoy the passing pleasures of sin (v. 25). He considered the reproach of Christ greater riches than the treasures of Egypt, for he was looking forward to his greater reward (v. 26). There can be an allure of power, especially here in Narnia, thinking that relationship with authorities or the rich is helpful for Kingdom advance. It can be confining, limiting, the exchange of your personal freedom (or ease) with the cost of the repression of others. We must be careful to align with the people of

God, not the powers of earth, even if that costs us. This, too, is faith. And all of us will gain approval through our faith (v. 39).

Pursuing Church Planting:

Yesterday I met with a team leader from another organization. There is currently no regular meeting of TLs for strategic coordination of church planting work in the area. There is a partnership that meets twice each year for all (team leaders and team members), which is a little general and informative, and there are networks of collaboration and media follow-up, all of which is wonderful. We would like to volunteer to help with follow-up as is needed and would be very interested in a monthly meeting of church planting team leaders. I will defer to the veterans who have gone before us as they know the history and context better (these partnerships tend to ebb and flow). I do have the conviction that the different organizations need to seek ways to partner together and that this is best done through team leaders meeting regularly for prayer, relationship, strategy, and cooperation.

I also met with an expatriate who leads a house fellowship and is very connected to the other house movements. This is positive, as Narnia is one of the few countries remaining that does not allow expatriates to worship publicly. This is also dangerous if it means that the authorities will shut down all the private house churches on the grounds that there is a public place they can meet (and be monitored easily). We are praying for the both/and of a public venue and ongoing house fellowships. With over 1.5 million expat workers in the country, one (or even a few) locations will not suffice.

There is even the subtler danger that public allowance will undermine desperation for Jesus and evangelistic zeal. The goal must ever be on the gospel going forward to all the nations, every unreached people, not the comfort and ease of the found. Jesus left the 99 and sought out the one uncomfortably lost. Recognition and ease can be a curse, not a blessing. Jesus, help and lead us.

Team meeting was a joy. Just four of us worshiping Jesus and praying over our lost Muslim friends. It is difficult to have follow-up meetings with Narnians. It takes persistence and the wooing of the Spirit. Oftentimes, encouraging initial conversations have no follow through. This is where media ministries that have pre-identified the hungry are both helpful and efficient.

¢¢¢¢¢¢¢¢¢¢¢¢¢

DAY 24

PURSUING JESUS:

God will not remain silent when His treasured ones are conspired against (Psalm 83:3). God will terrify those who try to "possess the pastures of God" *that* they (the oppressors) may seek His name and know that He alone is Most High over all the earth (vv. 12, 15–16, 18). Jesus is so beautifully redemptive. We think only to our own deliverance from oppressors. Jesus does deliver us, but in that deliverance, He has the deliverance of the oppressors in mind. Lord, grant me this same heart of compassion for all men, no matter how violently they act.

Jesus is the door (John 10:7). Thank you that we are saved and go in and out through You to find pasture, life abundantly (vv. 9–10). Thank you that You are the Good Shepherd that lays down Your life for us sheep; that You know us; and that You will bring in other sheep so there is one flock and one Shepherd giving us all eternal life (vv. 11, 14–16, 28). Jesus, You are so wonderful. Thank you, thank you for life eternal. I understand that life on this earth will require humility, tears, and trials (Acts 20:19). Let me faithfully teach publicly and from house to house, willingly bound by the Spirit (vv. 20, 22). Not needing to know anything other than being known by the Shepherd,

I can face the opposition that awaits in every city. My life is not dear (v. 24) in the sense that it's not important in contrast to eternal life with You. What matters is faithful proclamation of the gospel right to the end. So, Jesus, let me not shrink back from declaring the whole gospel, even admonishing with tears (vv. 27, 31).

In order to be a faithful preacher of the gospel to the end of life on earth and on to the beginning of life eternal, let me obey what You have asked in Hebrews 12: Lay aside every encumbrance; fix my eyes on Jesus, my faith Perfecter; consider Jesus and the hostility You faced; resist, strive against sin even to the death; not regard the Lord's discipline lightly; discipline and train myself to peaceful righteousness; strengthen what is weak and make straight paths; pursue peace with all men; see to it that no bitterness arises and no immorality; never refuse God's voice; show gratitude to Jesus with reverence and awe; for God, You are a consuming fire (vv. 1–5, 11–12, 14–16, 25, 28–29). Let me never lose my awe. Open my eyes in new and fresh ways to Your terror, awe, majesty, and the wonder, that the God of fire became flesh and brought me near.

Pursuing Church Planting:

Yesterday we had the opportunity to visit an Asian pastor and his wife who have been in Narnia for 22 years. They came as nominal Christians and got wonderfully saved here. They have been pastoring a house church for about the last 15 years. Both are employed full-time in the medical sector. They are sweet and kind. He had an experience in which he says he died and went to heaven and an angel told him he had to come back. He feels he doesn't have long on this earth and so wants to make every day count. He is 51. They live in the same apartment where the house church is located and have soundproofed the walls by adding carbon sound-absorbing materials in between the cement walls and the drywall they installed on the interior. They say things are under much less pressure now than in the 1990s and early 2000s.

I am grateful for men and women like this. They have a heart for the Lord. Some are very cautious about witness to Narnian Muslims saying that we can't say anything about the gospel, that we should just live exemplary lives. I do not deny that things in Narnia have been difficult (as house churches were often raided and people kicked out, and Asians have no embassy protection or leverage), but I also think the season is changing and we must open our mouths in witness. Jennifer and I need to learn that obedience in this context in this season. If we are faithful, I hope the Lord can use us to encourage these expatriate workers to have more boldness themselves. They are bold in their own way and faithful. May the Lord help us all be vibrant, courageous proclaimers.

DAY 25

PURSUING JESUS:

Jesus, let me ever be praising You (Psalm 84:4); thus, going from strength to strength, for a day in your courts at the threshold of Your presence is better than a thousand days outside, and I would rather be at the edge of the things of God than in the center of the world with all its power (vv. 7, 10). How much better to be in the center of the things of God. Thank you, Lord, that You are a sun and shield, giving both grace and glory (v. 11). You are my defense and my offense, and I am blessed when I simply trust in You (v. 12).

Help me, Jesus, to walk in the day, the light with nothing duplicitous about me (John 11:9). Help me to believe You at every level. Your acts are so that I may believe (v. 15); everyone who believes will never die (v. 26). If I believe, I will see the glory of God, and if I believe, it will result in others believing (vv. 40, 42, 45). This is such great responsibility and opportunity. Let not harvest in Narnia be limited because I did not believe!

Help me, Jesus, to be led of the Spirit in the balance between boldness and discretion. Paul was warned "through the Spirit" not to set foot in Jerusalem (Acts 21:4). The Spirit said that he would be bound (v. 11). Paul declared he was ready to be bound and die, and the implication was that the will of the Lord will be done (vv. 13–14). There is discussion on whether Paul disobeyed the Lord or if the Spirit was just warning and preparing Paul for the consequences. I lean towards the latter (while not wanting in my own experience to despise the former). As much as I can discern what the Holy Spirit is saying to me about Narnia, I think my course is in the same direction as Paul's (consequences are the will of the Lord). I must go forward in wise and obedient boldness, and if prison or death is the result, I am ready. Or if there are less dramatic difficulties, I am ready. I think the Spirit warns and prepares us for the cost of being obedient. He also redirects and cautions us. Jesus, I need ongoing help to discern what You are whispering to my spirit. If I press on to bonds and death outside Your will or timing, it will not bring You glory. If I press on according to Your good will, whatever happens will glorify You and contribute to the church being planted and established in Narnia. For those goals I will gladly be bound, restricted, suffer, and die. Jesus, let this not be arrogance or boasting. Jesus, let it be pure. Refine all that is not holy in my heart.

Hebrews 13 gives practical advice on how to be equipped for every good thing glorifying God. Whether dramatic or daily, if I obey these commands of Scripture, Jesus will be glorified: Love the brethren; show hospitality; remember prisoners; stay pure in marriage; stay free from greed being content with having Jesus; remember those who lead/teach me; not worried about men as Jesus is ever the same; not get carried away by various and strange teachings; keep going to Jesus outside the camp sharing in His reproach; seek the city to come; continually offer up a sacrifice of praise; do good and share; obey my leaders and rejoice in them; and pray for my leaders. It's wonderful how daily, normal, and practical living for Jesus is, and anything more dramatic is only powerful if it's the result of the daily, obedient, simple, faithful living. Jesus, help me be simple and obedient. You take care of the rest.

Pursuing Church Planting:

Yesterday we spent the morning fellowshipping in a house church of mostly Western expatriates and the afternoon in another with a more multicultural mix. The first one is sedate and conservative in theology (Baptist/Reformed/Evangelical), and the second is more charismatic (Pentecostal/Bethel). I spoke on John 15 in the second one, and in my sermon I tried to gently oppose dominionism and prophecy that portends to speak for God. The message overall seemed well received; however, the enthusiastic "amens" dried up a bit when I talked about suffering. We love the multi-cultural, enthusiastic, and loving feel of the second group. The first group is probably where we will spend time more regularly, though they are less animated than we would like. May Jesus help us bless and be blessed by both flavors of His church. We don't have everything right either.

At the first meeting we talked about the possibility of renting the villa adjacent to the house church as a safe house for MBBs in transition, a prayer room for discreet meetings, a guest house for missionaries passing through, overflow space for the kids, and house church on Fridays. The idea would be that a missionary couple could live there as hosts. I have inquired with Voice of the Martyrs (VOM) as to whether they would be interested in funding this and with Assemblies of God World Missions. It is expensive as it is a 4-bedroom villa in an upper-class part of town, but the location and privacy make it a little more conducive for a safe house. Jennifer and I are willing to set it up and are thinking about our Egyptian colleagues who will move here in August 2020. It could bless them with free rent, and they speak both Arabic and English and have the ability to host and understand both cultures.

How beautiful is the body of Christ! It is a blessing to be connected to groups like VOM who have the capacity to help those under pressure. They are very generous. How critical it is to have good relationships and understanding with these entities as it can open the door for ministry. We don't rely on money, and money can be detrimental (undermining dignity and creating dependency, which we must always be vigilant against), but it is a neutral (if powerful) tool that can be used for great good if stewarded wisely.

In between gatherings I had numerous exchanges with a Narnian Muslim named Matthew. On the one hand he seems to be a serious inquirer, but on the other he also sends me a lot of Islamic videos and teachings refuting the deity of Jesus. After numerous exchanges (I also sent him some teaching videos), he seemed to shift and back away from that exchange of information to a more personal interaction. I am learning that some things can be done digitally, but that informational exchange needs to have relational support. We will back the train up a little and work on some more face-to-face interaction.

Another case was the taxi driver who wants to learn English. I told him by text I would be happy to teach him from the Bible as I am a pastor and church leader. He said thanks but then stopped communicating. On the one hand, I want to quickly establish what I am about so as to not waste time; on the other hand, things in writing are more serious. I read in a cultural book about Narnians that they are so private they distrust those who disclose too much information about themselves too quickly. Perhaps the better way with this taxi driver would have been to meet him first and then disclose that I am a pastor and church leader that I was happy to teach from the Bible. Putting it in text may have scared him away. I want to be open about this identity but I'm learning good and not-so-good ways to do it.

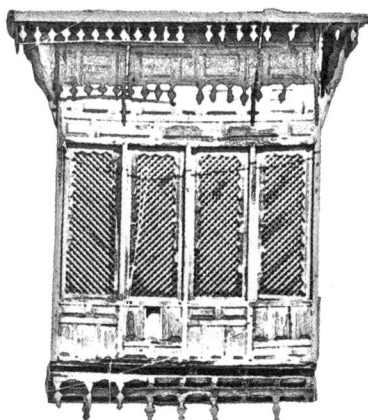

LESSONS FROM THE MONGOL ARMY[4]

Igleaned the following lessons from the Mongol army that have church planting applications.

1. The Mongol military consisted entirely of cavalry—armed riders without a marching infantry.

2. The Mongol army traveled without a commissary or cumbersome supply train other than its large reserve of horses.

3. The poorest Mongol soldier ate mostly protein, thereby giving him strong teeth and bones.

4. The Mongol army spread out over a vast area (it did not congregate in columns).

5. The Mongol army organized around the number 10.

    • No leader led more than 10 men.

    • Each leader of 10 was a member of a cohort of 10 with its own leader.

    • The system was repeated up to ten units of 1,000 (totaling 10,000).

    • Each unit of 10,000 functioned like a miniature version of the whole army: The commander of 10,000 moved at the center of his unit of 1,000; the other nine units around him to the left, right, front, and back (even as his unit of 10,000 did the same for the total army).

    • In other words, everything was scalable. Rather than a hierarchy of military units, Genghis Khan organized his men into a set of concentric circles.

6. Each unit of 1,000 travelled with its own medical unit.

7. At camp, all tents were lined up in specific ways, and the interior of the tent was arranged in the same way, so any soldier of any unit felt a degree of familiarity and when in trouble knew exactly where to look for what he needed.

8. At the most basic level, after supper, warriors slipped out into the night and slept in groups of 3–5 men in hidden places in the area. At daylight they reassembled in orderly units. It became impossible to ever surprise them or attack at night.

9. Because orders were given orally, officers composed their orders in rhyme with fixed melodies and poetic styles, which could then be improvised according to the meaning of the message. For a soldier, hearing the message (new order) was like learning a new verse to a song he already knew.

10. The soldiers sang as they rode. They sang their laws of obedience and rules of conduct. By memorizing their laws and constantly practicing the format of their message-songs, every man was ready at any moment to learn a new message.

11. Genghis Khan had generals who were with him for 40 years. He also understood each general's strengths and weaknesses. One of his commanders would fight fast and furiously, taking unusual chances and inspiring resolute courage among his men in battle; while another commander moved slowly and methodically but could sustain broader and longer assignments.

12. The Mongol army tried to win the battle before the first arrow was shot by defeating the enemy through breaking his spirit by fear and intimidation and by creating confusion. They wreaked havoc in the countryside and then disappeared, only to reappear suddenly and attack again just when everything felt safe.

13. They exploited any weakness of internal social turmoil or rift. Their first effort was to divide the ones they were attacking through masterful propaganda campaigns. They presented themselves as a liberating force that would empower the oppressed and marginalized.

14. Genghis Khan concentrated on capturing scholars of all sorts in efforts to apply their knowledge to his aims.

15. They *did not* conquer through superior weapons. The Mongol success arose from their cohesion and discipline of working in small groups connected to their steadfast loyalty to their leader.

16. Genghis did not ask his men to die for him. He waged war with this strategic purpose in mind: preserve Mongol life. His whole tactical approach was to save his soldiers' lives; he would never willingly sacrifice a single soldier. At the same time, every Mongol soldier was to live as a warrior under the assumption that he was immortal and that no one could harm, defeat, or kill him.

17. The Mongols did not find honor in fighting; they found honor in winning. They had a single goal in every campaign—total victory. There was no bravado or moral victories; they did smart things, even if it took longer.

18. For the Mongol warrior, there was no such thing as individual honor in battle if the battle was lost.

19. Their ingenuity was to turn the enemies' greatest asset into a liability. If the enemy had huge numbers, the Mongols found a way to make that work against them (mobility, food, attacking the surrounding civilians and driving them to the army or city so that the local defenses, supplies, or resources, human and physical, were exhausted).

20. On the system of ten, each Mongol warrior had to capture ten of the enemy and then turn them into manual labor for the army. If one slave died, the warrior had to replace them so that each base soldier had a crew of ten captured enemies he put to work. The Mongols were always vastly outnumbered, but they figured out how to put the indigenous population to work for Mongol army goals.

21. More than capturing equipment and new weapons, Genghis was intent on acquiring the engineering intelligence needed to create them. They eagerly recruited engineers or sought them out in vanquished foes and elevated their status so that after every battle the technology was improved and upgraded for the next fight.

22. The Mongol army constantly pretended to retreat. It lured an overconfident enemy to ground where the Mongols had an advantage; the enemy spread out and then the Mongols counter attacked. They lured the enemies from safe cities by pretending to be defeated.

23. The Mongols learned how to fight on the move. They learned to shoot arrows while riding away from the enemy. Both directions represented fighting. A fleeing conquest was just as effective as an attacking one, and in this way they saved Mongol lives while taking others.

24. They carried valuables with them to war, so if overcome or surprised, they dropped their treasures on the ground to distract their enemies. The enemy began to pillage or squabble among themselves and forgot to pursue. The Mongols escaped, doubled back, regrouped, and attacked again.

25. They lit extra fires at night to make it appear that they were more numerous than they actually were. They tied branches to the tails of their horses to create more dust so that from faraway the army appeared much larger than it actually was.

PURSUING JESUS:

Jesus, You have covered all my sin and turned away Your burning anger and withdrawn all Your fury (Psalm 85:2–3). The wrath of God is real, yet so is Your reviving power and in that I rejoice (v. 6). Lord, covered and revived I long to hear what You will say, for I will fear You (vv. 8–9). Glory will dwell in our land, lovingkindness and truth married, righteousness and truth kissing (v. 10). Only in You, Jesus, do these wonders meet, and only in You can they meet in me. Grant it, Lord.

Jesus, I pray that my whole house will be filled with the fragrance of my extravagant worship of You (John 12:3). What a wonder that we can be intimate with the great King who comes to us in such lowly fashion (v. 15). Thank you that understanding follows glorification (v. 16). When I give You glory, I begin to understand, and when we give You glory, the world will go after You, including Greeks (Gentiles) who want to see Jesus (vv. 19–21). It's interesting that we can't really see Jesus unless, like a grain of wheat, we fall into the ground and die (v. 24). For the purpose of Jesus being exalted, we have come to this hour, we have come to the reality of dying, dying to self and dying to the world that the *Father* might be glorified (vv. 27–28). Jesus, we join You in that great prayer: Father, glorify Your name. The way we work towards that goal is by lifting up Jesus who will draw all men (v. 32). So then let me not seek nor love the approval of men, rather let me seek and love only Your applause (v. 43). Let me not speak on my own initiative but only speak as the Father has told me (vv. 49–50).

In this wonderful assignment of being a witness of Jesus to all men including the Gentiles (Acts 22:21), let me not forget that I am first appointed to know His will, to see the Righteous One, and to hear an utterance from Your mouth (v. 14). Help me, Jesus, that as familiar as I am with the concept of abiding, not to lose its praxis: the delight of being with You, knowing You well, cherishing intimacy with You, hearing Your voice, and then from Your presence representing You faithfully in every evangelistic and discipleship endeavor among the unreached.

Let me not forget that joy follows trials and testing of faith and endurance (James 1:2–4). Let me experience that joy comes in the midst of trial and that trial leads to being complete and crowned with life (v. 12). Along that road, thank you, Jesus, that You give wisdom generously and without reproach if I will but humbly ask for it. And I do ask for it—help me with the humble part. Let me not allow any place for destabilizing doubt or lust that leads to sin and death (vv. 8, 15). Thank you that all good things come down from the Father of lights in whom there is no variation (v. 17). You are always good, and because You are good, You can help me be good and quick to listen, slow to speak, and slow to become angry (v. 19). Let me ever remember that while wrath is part of Your nature, the wrath of man does not accomplish the righteousness of God (v. 21). Rather than carnal wrath, wrap me in humility so that I can receive the word of God, no matter the source, no matter the pain, bridling my tongue, being kind and holy (vv. 26–27). 'Tis a lot to ask in one day, Jesus, but it is Your word, and I ask You to sand, chisel, smooth, or strike as You see best. Thank you. I trust Your kindness.

PURSUING CHURCH PLANTING:

In this context, evenings are in high demand for meetings and ministry, so date nights are becoming date mornings. Jennifer and I had a date brunch yesterday and had a nice chat about where we are and what Jesus is teaching us. We are finding that our Sabbath may very well be parts of two days: Friday afternoon and Saturday mornings. It is important that we keep the principle even when the application varies.

In the afternoon we were invited to attend the ministers meeting for the Asian churches that meet in town. They have a collaborative union with all the pastors of house churches which organizes collective prayers, outreaches, and praise or teaching events. They are very sweet and there were about 20 in attendance. It is wonderful to see how God has His people everywhere. One pastor mused about going public soon (all the churches are underground), and we had a good conversation of implication and consequence. To be public and legal is not worth it if the price is ease or agreeing not to evangelize. All the pastors see both the benefit of a recognized church and the dangers. We are all praying for God to lead us to find the win-win. How can this be done in such a way that the gospel advances, not retreats? We need the Lord's wisdom. It is encouraging to see how many underground churches are scattered across this land.

DAY 27

PURSUING JESUS:

All nations will come and worship Jesus (Psalm 86:9). In this light, unite my heart to fear Your name (v. 11). Ministry and missions are so dissatisfying outside a vibrant walk with You, Jesus. It is so easy to slide into prayer and Bible study as the mechanics of producing content, but that is a soul-stifling journey and process. I feel the dry encroachment of putting in spiritual time outside personal renewal of the Spirit. Jesus, I do long for the nations to come and worship You, but I also know that I am wretched if I don't personally walk with You in intimate worship. Unite my heart, Lord, to fear Your name. Bring me back to the simplicity of just having Jesus. Let me live out what I teach and know. I sense the slide towards knowledge without intimacy, a form of godliness but no power within. Arrest this slide,

Lord Jesus. Awaken me to whatever it is in me that contributes towards it. Protect me from whatever forces of evil drag me towards it. Overcome my internal flesh and all outward devilry and draw me to Yourself. I cannot survive without the reality and simplicity of *You*. You and I must precede the world and me.

Thank you, Jesus, that You love us to the end (John 13:1). Let me have the same enduring love, knowing that the Father controls all (v. 3). Let me serve even as I struggle with the wonder of having You serve us (v. 8). I get that wonder all confused, sometimes abusing it and sometimes resenting it. Help me understand it, Jesus, by washing others' feet (v. 14), so that You may be glorified and glorified immediately (v. 32). Be glorified today in a dozen little private ways, thoughts, actions, and obediences. Let tomorrow's grand glories take care of themselves. Remind me, Jesus, that You are known when we love one another, and You are glorified when the nations see how Your children love. Jesus, I know that I *must* glorify You, and that when I do, I am most satisfied. Yet I fail with such regularity. I default to glorifying myself and find it so dissatisfying. Jesus, have mercy on me, for I stubbornly evade what would enrich my soul.

Jesus, let me also solemnly witness in the halls of power in such a way that does not lust for glory or recognition (Acts 23:11). I realize there is still so much in me that wants to be known as an influencer. I carry within foolish fantasies of being greatly used by You, which are just thinly disguised ambitions of being greatly known and respected. I repent of this indecency, rebellion, and perversion. At my heart I twist giving You glory as a means to give myself glory. Lord Jesus, have mercy on me; my heart is vile, and I cannot cleanse it. I can only confess to You and plead for both Your forgiveness and Your cleansing power. I can only cling to Your character, the promise that mercy triumphs over judgment (James 2:13). Let my works support the profession of my faith (v. 22). Today, let me deny my own constant striving for glory and labor for Yours instead. I cannot do this in my own strength. I need Your divine help to overcome my earthly folly.

PURSUING CHURCH PLANTING:

Yesterday, we took time for a cultural tour of the Old City with a Muslim friend. At lunch he spoke openly of his admiration for American society. We were able to point out the link to the Protestant work ethic which has its roots in biblical character which is founded on Christ. This led to inviting him to study the Bible with us (my colleague Andrew and I). He agreed, and we are scheduled to begin next Monday. I had more ongoing texts with Mahdi and am trying to turn them to more relational testimony that references biblical stories of Jesus. We have agreed to meet this Friday (also with Andrew), so we are praying over that meeting. Mahdi seems to go back and forth between interested and hostile. It is wonderful to have a brother to process all these things with, both for prayer and insight. Andrew is more introverted than I am and more naturally cautious with a calm wisdom.

In the evening we spoke at the 16th anniversary of one of the Asian Christian fellowships. It was a sweet time of celebration, and Jennifer and I were moved at the strong lyrics to their simple songs which detailed the cross, suffering, and preaching even at the cost of blood. We thank the Lord for their presence here in Narnia all these years and we pray that God encourages them and equips them to bolder sharing of the gospel with Narnians (and other Muslims). There is understandable fear about losing their jobs if they are open witnesses.

PURSUING JESUS:

The Lord loves some people and things more (Psalm 87:2). Our human sense of justice is initially offended at this notion, until we realize that we love our family more than anyone else (at least we should) and that love multiplies, not divides. It grows and ever expands because God is love and God is infinite. Therefore, God has a special affinity for those that were born in Zion (vv. 4–6). The Most High will establish them, and then we shall say, "All my springs of joy are in You" (vv. 5, 7). This psalm is the basis of my prayers for missionary kids. They were born in Zion, and the Lord loves them "more." He will establish and keep them, and for those who have wandered away, He will bring them back and joy will spring up in their parents and their "uncles and aunts."

Jesus, let not my heart be troubled (John 14:1). Let me believe in You. Let me lift my soul to the promise that You are coming again to receive me to Yourself (v. 3). Grow my belief in You and the greatness and mystery of the Godhead. Grow the glory that Father, Son, and Spirit receive (v. 13), so that all I do ever lifts Jesus up, exalted by seraph and angels. Thank you that You (marvelously!) grant what we ask; but let me realize that this is based on me doing whatever You tell me (vv. 14–15). If I ask You anything, You will do it—if I do anything and everything You ask of me! There is a reciprocal understanding. Thank you that when I completely obey, the Father loves, the Godhead comes and abides with me (v. 23). Oh, glory! Thank you, Jesus! This is the foundation for not letting my heart be troubled, not fearing, and being at peace (v. 27). And if Father, Son, and Spirit dwell within me, then it can be blessedly true that the ruler of this world has nothing in me (v. 30) because You have all of me and there is nothing left for anyone else.

Jesus, if I am fully Yours, I can be a holy beast, a sanctified terror "stirring up all" (Acts 24:5), but in the Spirit not in the flesh. I love how Paul, full of Jesus, was cheerful, fearless, articulate, and spunky (v. 10). Help me, like him, when under duress to admit and testify to what I believe (v. 14), to be confident in the central gospel: "There will certainly be a resurrection from the dead" (v. 15), even as I affirm my love for nation (my own and my adopted) (v. 17). Give me the holy courage to demand integrity and justice and the insight to control the argument and the messaging even as Paul brought the focus back to the one statement on resurrection (vv. 20–21). Let me never dilute biblical truth or teaching when under pressure, but focus on faith in Jesus, righteousness, judgment, and self-control (vv. 24–25). Let me also not be naïve about challenges whether they be based in fear, greed, or other (vv. 25–26).

Along the way, in public testimony or private discourse let me remember that teachers will face a stricter judgment and that my tongue is a fire that can be lit by hell, a restless evil full of deadly poison (James 3:1, 7–8). Let me ever be mindful that wisdom is gentle and that when I am jealous, selfish, and ambitious, I open the door to every evil thing (vv. 13–14). Lord, grant that rather than a fiery tongue broadcasting the evil thoughts of my heart, I would have wisdom that is godly, pure, peaceable, gentle, reasonable, full of mercy, unwavering, and without hypocrisy (v. 17). Jesus, grow *You* in my heart, so that out of the abundance of *You* in my heart, my mouth may speak.

Pursuing Church Planting:

Yesterday, our leadership team had our monthly Zoom call which reminded me of two essential components of church planting: accountability and intimacy.

The principle of accountability is greater than the personalities, styles, or competencies of the leader involved. My leader right now used to be my follower. He is a good man that came to the field as an experienced minister and joined our team in Cairo. When my prior leader resigned, my follower became my leader. This has not been without some challenges, but this man is humble, wise, mature, godly, gracious, and empowering. He is a good and kind leader. But even if he was not, it would not matter. It is healthy for me to bow; it is good for me to be under authority. Spiritual authority is a covering. Missionaries need to learn to bow from the heart as unto the Lord, trusting that God does indeed rule, not just in the kingdoms of men, but also in mission agencies and churches. It has not always been easy for me (or for him), but it has always been good for me to submit to authority. I was created to submit, even as I was created to lead and created to be collegiate. All are true, and I am only whole if I function in all aspects: leading, following, and brothering.

The principle of intimacy was encouraged on the Zoom call by a guest presenter who is a beloved friend and pastor. He exhorted us that, while spending time with Jesus in our abiding is good, we must be sure to press in for the simplicity of Jesus—not just disciplined time, not just ministry inspiration, not just empowerment for the task—but first and most essentially, just the pleasures of God, the joy of who He is. I notice it is a reoccurring danger of mine to abide for others, to receive something to pass on. This is not wrong, but neither is it primary. I first must be intimate with Jesus for who He is and for the personal joys and pleasures of God. Jesus, help me not to lose sight of You when I am spending time with You.

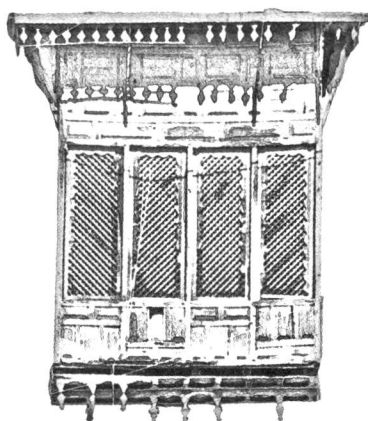

IDENTITY, SECURITY, AND COMMUNITY

SYNOPSIS

God is light and in Him there is no darkness at all (1 John 1:5). It is impossible for God to lie (Heb. 6:18). Jesus is truth (John 14:6). God incarnated as Word (John 1:1). Jesus was anointed to preach and proclaim (Luke 4:18–19). We have been sent in the same manner that Jesus was sent (John 20:21). Faith comes by hearing and hearing by the word of God. (Rom. 10:17). There is nothing false or deceptive about God, and as His children there should be nothing false or deceptive about us. The Bible is clear over and again that God is a revealer of Himself, not a disguiser, and in these last days He has revealed Himself to man through Jesus (Heb. 1:2). At its pragmatic core the missionary task is both verbal (preaching/teaching) and relational (make disciples). We are to preach to all peoples (Matt. 24:14) and all the creation (Mark 16:15), to preach the word in season and out (2 Tim. 4:2), and to make disciples (Matt. 28:19) that make disciples (2 Tim. 2:2).

No Bible-based missionaries quibble over our role being centered on teaching, preaching, and making disciples that make disciples in integrity. All Bible-based missionaries agree that we must identify with Christ and boldly open our mouths to point to Jesus. How, when, and where that is done, and through what identity, is where discussion (and sometimes heated debate) take place.

The missionary community, especially in countries where missionary or church-related visas are unlikely and missionary activity is not always welcome, has a broad range of praxis as regards their identity. Some are very cautious, never use the word "missionary" (not even around their children), while some are more open. The prevailing wisdom leans toward a careful use of nomenclature, social media, and identity. Without criticizing that position (I do affirm all should be led by the Spirit, their conscience, and their context), I would like to make a case that a more open identity is a viable option and for some may be preferable.

BACKGROUND

I have worked in the Muslim world for 27 years in places considered challenging: Mauritania, northern Sudan, Egypt, and now Narnia. I have not been in Narnia long, so while I have started to implement the below principles here as well, I do not yet have length of experience in Narnia. When I started in missions, I was much more careful and cautious about my spiritual identity but quickly realized the problematic nature of a veiled identity (for me, my calling, my personality, and my own emotional health), so I migrated to an openly declared church/pastor (and sometimes even missionary) identity. What follows are a list of convictions and realizations that have played a part in forming my position.

CONVICTIONS AND REALIZATIONS

1. Biblically, we are proclaimers not concealers.

Ezekiel 3 and 33 make it clear that the prophetic and missionary people of God have the duty to warn others of approaching death and destruction. Our primary assignment is open our mouths and tell the good news (Isa.61:1), but logically good news only makes sense in the context of bad news. We must warn the nations that all men are under the wrath of God and must repent and seek mercy (Jonah 1:2). Even if the message is difficult or causes us trouble, we must speak it, for it is a fire shut up in our bones (Jer. 20:9). Whoever our biblical examples are, Old or New Testament, they all opened their mouths and pointed to the Savior. John the Baptist quoted Isaiah to identify as a voice in the wilderness (John 1:23). Layman Stephen would not stop speaking (Acts 6:13). Paul declared woe upon himself if he did not preach (1 Cor. 9:16). The end does not come until more are slain because they proclaim the word of God as faithful testifiers (Rev. 6:9).

In order for me to be faithful to my commission as a watchman, town crier, voice in the wilderness, messenger, and preacher of the gospel, I have to open my mouth and talk about Jesus constantly and consistently. My whole orientation must be towards revealing not hiding. My posture, passion, and focus must pulsate with the desire to disseminate news, to announce, to speak, to spread what I know of Jesus to everyone I can, everywhere. I need an external identity that propels me to this inward conviction, that holds me accountable to my assignment, and that orients me to proclaiming Christ constantly. I need to develop habits and disciplines that spread news, not restrains it.

It is absolutely critical—non-negotiable in my view—that missionaries have a public identity that clearly and early reveals that we are Jesus-and-Bible, light-of-the-world people (Matt. 5:14–16). There are many ways to do this. To me the easiest one is to state that I am a pastor, a spiritual leader of Christians, an elder in the church, a minister who has studied and prepared to help all people follow Jesus. I'm not saying it is the only way to get there; I'm saying it is the easiest and clearest in my case. These past (almost) three decades have debunked the myth that this church-related identity is problematic (in an unresolvable way) to Muslim ears and hearts. In fact, it seems to have helped and protected incredibly.

To be direct, I am not saying that every missionary should (or can) call themselves a pastor. I am saying two things: First, every missionary should have a clear and open Jesus and Bible identity, and second, identifying as a pastor is an incredibly easy, understood, and accepted way to get there. For the many who cannot call themselves a pastor, there are still ways to identify with the church as an elder, a member, or representative, as someone gladly connected to the visible body of Christ. My experience of identifying as a church representative in northern Sudan, Libya, Egypt, Oman, and Narnia and of being understood and even welcomed in these places has shown me it is possible and can be positive.

2. Truth brokers must live truthfully.

John 18:20 reminds us that Jesus spoke openly to the world, even when it brought danger and opposition. Paul told the Corinthians that he had spoken freely to them with a wide-open heart (2 Cor. 6:11). He told the Ephesians that he kept back nothing helpful and taught publicly (Acts 20:20). He told the Thessalonians that he cared so deeply with them that he shared not only the gospel, but his very life (1 Thess. 2:8). Both Christological and Pauline models are transparent. Indeed, the texts above refer to teaching (which necessitates a more public spiritual identity) while not excluding basic honesty and a life that holds no secrets.

Representing the truth, we must speak truth and we must live it. There should be nothing deceptive about me, especially as I live in contexts well-versed in deception. I cannot be a faithful minister of gospel truth if there is deception or duplicity in my life. I understand fully that we don't have to speak *all* the truth *all* the time, that there is a need for situational discretion, but there is a fine line between withholding truth and misleading. I would rather err on the side of living free and far from all deception and bear the consequences.

3. The problem and solution are not really in the words, but in the behavior.

John 8:43–47 reveals that Jesus used words of truth that were misunderstood because His hearers did not want to understand. The problem was not in the words that Jesus used, but in the hearts of the hearers. Jesus did not soften His language or dilute the forcefulness of His message (even when inflammatory) to please His hearers. The implication of the John 8 text is that intentionally misleading language is a tool of the devil, and not the nature of Christ. By contrast, Jesus grants understanding of truth, even to difficult concepts (1 John 5:20). Paul did not incessantly coin new terms; rather, he explained and clarified what was meant by common expressions (Rom. 9:6). He retained the title "Israel" but explained what it meant to be the "Israel of God." When terms were inflammatory, shameful, or misunderstood (like cross), Paul did not back away from the term; rather, he explained the theology behind the term (1 Cor. 1:23–30).

An intriguing lesson in clarification can be learned from Muslims in how they handled the public reaction to the 9-11 bombings. What is most intriguing is what they did not do; they did not abandon any of their terms: Islam, Muslim, or jihad. They just carefully and repeatedly defined what it meant and what it did not mean. "No, Islam does not mean this; it means this." "No, Muslim does not mean this; it means this." "No, jihad does not mean this; it means this." "No, extremists will not be allowed to define for us what Islam, Muslim, or jihad means." The Muslim community retained all the terms that extremists had sullied and won the war of definition.

If we keep changing our terms because history, nominalism, or even the behavior of some of our own have sullied them, we set ourselves up for the problem of having to change those terms again at some point. The problem is not in the terms, it's in the people or the praxis of those who use the terms. The behavior that our words explain (for good or bad) is the real issue.

The knee-jerk reaction of missionaries to the understood and very real objection that Muslims have to words like missionary, church, Christian, pastor, evangelism, and so on has been to change our terms. The problem with this approach is that biblically and morally we cannot change the behavior that those terms define, and the objection is not really towards the term, but the behavior (activity). Evangelism is offensive to the Muslim, the humanist, and others, but if we change the name, we must still evangelize; and so, whatever we call that behavior (sowing, sharing, shining), the name will ultimately become offensive, too. The huge danger then is that in avoiding inflammatory titles and names we actually change the praxis along with the name. Bluntly, because evangelism (word and function) is offensive, what usually happens is we abandon both the word and activity. Which is sin.

Rather than changing our titles and words, I think a better option is to keep them and to work hard at defining them. The definition should correct misunderstandings (which abound) without removing the conflict the term demands (which is unavoidably biblical). Let us take a lesson from our Muslim friends: "No, missionary does not mean a cultural exploiter or a predator of children. It means that God has sent us to tell all people the good news about how to have sins forgiven and eternal life assured." "No, Christian does not mean crusader, invader, philanderer, drunkard, or life-taker. A Christian does what Christ did: we love you so much that we will lay down our lives so that you can go to heaven." "No, evangelism does not mean we want to force you to be American. God by intention created all the languages and cultures of the world, and therefore, He rejoices in yours. Evangelism actually means 'good news' and we want to talk with you about the good news of how our sins are forgiven because we love you so much and we want to see you in heaven."

If we change our terms now, we will have to change them again in 10 years. They are intrinsically offensive (in part), and we have to navigate that tension. They are misunderstood (in part), and we must explain what we mean and don't mean by them. The words are simply titles and summaries of our behavior, and as gospel behavior will always be a stumbling block, it doesn't really help to change the titles. A better way is to make sure our behavior is biblical and Christlike, deal with the tension, and explain what we mean and don't mean by the titles.

When we backpedal, stutter, or equivocate when asked if we are a missionary (Christian, pastor, evangelist), we look guilty, confused, or ashamed. We must have a way to boldly say, "Yes! But not in this way, but in *this* way. Isn't that grand?" Muslims have taught us this. They are not ashamed of their titles and names; they simply dismiss the misconceptions and concentrate on the positives (to them) of what those titles mean. I believe we should do the same.

4. Transparency is appreciated.

Paul found a way to be transparent even in challenging circumstances. Before Felix, Paul spoke directly about faith in Jesus, righteousness, self-control, and judgment (Acts 24:24–25). These were not easy topics to unpack before a corrupt ruler, and in fact, Felix became frightened. The point is that Paul stayed true to his assignment. Earlier, Paul had recognized the crowd and called out his Pharisee credentials to gain some public support in a hostile context (Acts 23:6). In both situations he had a choice to make—he could have equivocated and tried to cloak either his theology or his identity, but instead he chose to find a way to use his identity to his advantage and to broadcast his theology. And the implication is that (for some) it was appreciated. Even when others disagreed with him, they seemed at least thankful that they didn't have to guess at who he was or what he really passionately believed in.

Whenever I am open with my Muslim friends about being a pastor or missionary and that churches support me to do what I do in their country, I have almost always been thanked for my honesty. My friends may not always agree, but they have always been appreciative and have often given me counsel. Some years ago, I invited a Sudanese friend who is an influential leader to the prayer breakfast in Washington D.C. He is the leader of a very devout, well-known Muslim family and has been very kind to us through the years. I openly shared with him how much I loved the Sudanese people, that I was a missionary with the Assemblies of God church, and that I felt God called me to be in his country so that I could share the gospel with Muslims. I mentioned we believe that believing in Jesus as God and Savior is the only way to have sins forgiven and to gain eternal life. He thanked me for my honesty, acknowledged that what I felt led to do in Sudan was difficult, and then gave me advice on how to go about my calling respectfully. We remain friends to this day and I hide nothing from him.

5. Disagreements are not deal breakers when there is respect and love.

King Agrippa was no angel, yet he tipped his cap to Paul in Acts 26:28–32. Paul found a way to respectfully articulate the gospel in a potentially hostile setting. Festus thought him crazy while Agrippa was intellectually intrigued even if unrepentant and unconvinced. These officials conferred, and though they didn't agree with Paul, his forthright explanation of the gospel revealed to them that he was not worthy of death. The text even indicates they would have helped him if they could. The point from this narrative is simple: the Holy Spirit can help us communicate the gospel clearly, lovingly, and respectfully to authorities (and others) who strongly disagree with us.

In our interaction with Muslims, I have found it's more important (for evangelism) to talk about our dissimilarities than our similarities. This is directly tied to my theology and my understanding of the lostness of all peoples outside biblical faith. I do not spend much time agreeing with Muslims; I concentrate on where we disagree, namely on Christology. I do this in Arabic. I do this with wit and grace. I listen, use stories, affirm where I can, and object where I need to. What I have found is that when my Muslim friend sees and feels that I love them, they have no problem with me disagreeing with them theologically, even when the disagreement is profound. In this regard, culture and language skill matter. I do not advocate a young missionary getting off the plane and in cultural ignorance with no language capacity lambasting local people or their thinking publicly. I am a fierce proponent of learning language and culture and sitting at the feet of our host community to learn their wisdom and culture. I'm not saying we wait until we are fluent to evangelize. I believe in a both/and approach and have seen how language learning gives constant evangelism opportunities. I am saying when we love, respect, listen, are humble, and use wit and wisdom, we can strongly disagree about critical eternal issues.

6. Credible services to communities we live among empower church/ missionary identity.

Both Jesus and Paul had credible identities in the context of their day. Jesus took up the legitimate role and identity of a rabbi, which was not only accepted but respected. He added value both through teaching and through miracles (healings, deliverances, provisions), and so the common people heard Him gladly (Mark 12:37). Jesus was able to say difficult, new, and provocative truth *because* He operated from an identity that was understood, contributed, and won popular support. Paul, too, was a scholar. He started out in the synagogues for scholarly and/or religious debate or seasonally worked in the marketplace in a viable trade or used public educational halls as the center for his teaching and preaching (Acts 17:2; 18:3; 19:19). At other times he started in the *agora* (Roman marketplace) as in Acts 17:17. The point is that both Jesus and Paul had identities that were both understood and respected in context, which propelled them into verbal witness about spiritual matters—as should we.

When we add tangible value to society through legitimate business, employing locals, paying taxes, providing services, physically improving our natural surroundings, and integrating into culture, it empowers a church-based identity. Globally, men and women appreciate work done professionally and value added to their community. In advocating for a public identity that is church based, missionary in name and function, I insist that this orientation is placed on the foundation of real service at the highest quality that serves the broad community. In Sudan, for example, I had a church visa and an identity as a pastor. I started a Bible school and an open church. In that church I preached without reserve on missions and evangelism. I talked about unreached people groups and we organized mission trips, all completely out in the open. We also started an adult education center that at its peak had 1,200 students each day, a ladies community center, an international school, and a local development agency. We had 150 employees, we made money, and we were model citizens. Our upfront identity as church and missionary people was buttressed by undeniable and appreciated service in and to the community.

I saw no need to downplay my pastor/church identity in order to not jeopardize my business. I saw that it actually worked the other way around. Doing business and service well allowed me to be even bolder and clearer about being church-sent and church-aligned. I used the fact that my donors were churches to further witness. I used the fact that I was supported by churches openly and positively to express love. If I was asked if I was paid to tell people about Jesus, rather than backfooting it in nervous denial, I "frontfooted" it enthusiastically: "Yes! Absolutely! Isn't God amazing? He loves you so much that He not only sent me here so we can talk about Jesus right now, but He also blessed all these people in America to pray and to give sacrificially so that we can talk right here, right now about heaven and how sins can be forgiven! My beloved friend, not only does God love you, not only do I love you, but there are dozens of churches and thousands of Christians in America who love you. They have made it possible for us to meet and to talk about Jesus. Isn't that marvelous?"

It is my experience that church connections (identity) is an advantage, not a disadvantage. It clarifies right away that we are not CIA, military, or embassy, and it does so with a category (institution) that every person in the world has some (almost always positive) familiarity with. Thanks to those that went before us (including Catholics, thank God for them), the church is known as the institution that brought education and health to most of our countries. At worst the church is a neutral but known entity. For me, open church connections have allowed my friends and associates to immediately place me in a non-threatening category in their mind, and often it's a positive starting place. At least they know that I am not a spy.

My identity as a pastor, church-sent and body-of-Christ-connected, is not incompatible with being a businessman. An official international church pastor identity (or chaplain) is certainly possible, but it is also possible to be a businessman who is a pastor, a pastor who is a businessman. Here in Narnia I am both—without tension. I explain I am a pastor, sent by the church, connected to body of Christ locally (expatriate Christians) and globally, who loves this country and her people and who serves them (without prejudice or bias) through a credible business that does intercultural training and coaching.

7. Security forces are smart and know everything we do (and probably say).

I don't think it is a matter of keeping secrets from the men and women trained in surveillance and tasked with the responsibility of protecting their citizens. Obviously, we are not a threat when it comes to committing acts of violence, but we all understand civic unrest and in the mind of officials anything causing agitation must be monitored. It is my conviction that security police know exactly who I am, that I am church-based and church-sent, a missionary. I have no desire (nor capacity) to hide that from them. I further believe that if I'm doing my job, that if I'm seeking to make disciples by preaching repentance and faith in Jesus, the God who became man to die on the cross for the sins of the world, if I'm doing that, then security police better know I am a missionary. If they don't know, then I'm not being faithful.

The point is not to hide from the authorities who we are. It's more about respect and not embarrassing them; it's about not causing public unrest. The vast majority of the time we can have a very public church/pastor/missionary identity without causing civil strife (if we are respectful, relational, culturally astute, professionally serving, linguistically capable, and Spirit-led). Not all the time, but most of the time, at least for a season. Security either knows you're a missionary, knows who you're meeting, and knows your activities, *or* you're not a very good missionary. That sounds harsh and I don't mean it to be condemning, but it is connected to my conviction that we are sent to proclaim and announce, and if we proclaim and announce, it is impossible to not be known who we are and what we do by those whose job it is to know. We don't hide what we do; we just work to do it respectfully.

In some Muslim contexts it is possible to have pastor or missionary as the reason for your visa, and the above point has less grey to navigate. In other places to get a visa as a church-related worker is more difficult, and in these cases I would argue you can be church connected without that word/concept being stamped in your passport. In Narnia, for example, I have been explaining to business friends that I own a business that does intercultural training, that I am a pastor sent by the church, that the church has funded the business, and that we are training Christians how to live and work in Narnia and the Middle East loving Muslims and living out their faith respectfully. My visa does not say "church," but my explanation does.

In 2011, we voluntarily left Sudan to work in Egypt. In 2012, there was a general purge of all missionaries in Sudan. Every single missionary agency was affected. Those that were open, those that were super cautious. Those that would not meet with other missionaries, those that hosted the partnership events. Those that led Muslims to Jesus, those that had barely arrived in country. Security knew everyone, they knew everything, and they kicked everyone out. Let us give security police their due—they know. Let's not spend energy on trying to hide things from them. Let's focus on being respectful and not embarrassing them, not causing a public ruckus it can be avoided at all (and sometimes it can't).

8. If we are not careful, digital security leads to self-censorship in verbal witness.

Related to the last point, I find it humorous that we ask people to "*pr@y to G.d for us.*" I find it humorous because I believe security is smart and has the capacity to read all our communication if they want to. I find it humorous because a second grader can crack the "code." I find it concerning because it makes us look sneaky. I find it troubling because I have observed that caution in our language and communication with one another *often* bleeds over to caution or code in evangelism. If we orient ourselves to be vague, we usually slip slowly to vagaries in witness (not addressing the real issues, looking for agreement, losing the shocking inflexibility of our message of repentance).

I often ask missionaries if they know anyone kicked out because of a newsletter, an email, or open text. It is rare that any missionary actually knows someone personally. Missionaries have been drilled in caution regarding their communication from a fear-based possibility, not a normal eventuality. I know examples of missionaries called in for questioning and shown their correspondence, but as I dig into those case studies, it was never the email, newsletter, or text that was problematic—it was the activity that communication detailed, and security wanted the worker to know that they knew. They would have been kicked out regardless. This point I admit can be interpreted two ways (i.e. the newsletter provided the fodder for security to kick the missionary out). In my experience, it is never the communication but the activity. And we must continue the activity, even if it jeopardizes the longevity. We cannot not be missionary *and* be faithful, and we can't allow our communication caution to seep into our evangelistic and discipleship praxis. We are to be bold and courageous. It's part of the job description. Yes, there is a fine line between courage and folly. Agreed. The other side of the coin is that there is a fine line between wisdom and fear. Today, I think most missionaries err on the wisdom/fear balance than err on the courage/folly continuum.

One final consideration on vagaries in our communication to supporters back home. I am concerned about the injury to potency in prayer and mobilization. Informed prayers tend to be more powerful prayers. Information about specific places is often used by God to call new missionaries to those places. If we are too general, I think the result is less effective prayer and mobilization. Of all censorships, self-censorship can be the most damaging and shameful of all. The devil need not intimidate us if we have silenced ourselves.

9. The goal is not longevity; the goal is the glory of God and an indigenous church.

If we judge Jesus or Paul by the criteria we usually establish for what is wise and what is foolish (usually linked to longevity or not upsetting anyone), neither of them pass the test. Jesus made it only three years and made enough powerful enemies to assure His death. It appears Paul never made it more than three years in any of his missionary assignments, and in all of them he stirred up opposition. The Pauline model is clearly to evangelize, disciple local believers, identify and train elders, and move on, and he did so in astonishing rapidity. Jesus is unique in that His primary mission was to redeem all men by dying on the cross. The point remains that Jesus' and Paul's success was determined by whether or not they glorified God through obedience to their assignment, not by their longevity. Jesus and Paul had short ministries (Paul never in one place long), but God received glory, for Jesus redeemed the world and Paul planted the church.

There is an interesting closed loop of logic that goes something like this:

- I am sent to be a witness and plant indigenous churches.
- In order to do so, I need to be in country long enough to make disciples.
- In order to make disciples, I must proclaim the gospel widely and boldly.
- If I proclaim the gospel widely and boldly, I will get kicked out of the country.
- If I get kicked out of the country, I can't make disciples.
- In order to not get kicked out of the country, I won't make disciples.

- Because if I make disciples, I won't be able to make disciples.
- So then, I won't do what I am sent to do, because if I am kicked out I won't be able to do it.

Silly, yes, but all too common. But the goal is not that we stay in a country for a certain amount of years so that our kids don't have to transition again—the goal is to plant indigenous churches. And yes, to do that will draw attention, and to do that will probably get us kicked out at some point. But that is not a problem *if* one of two things has happened: (1) if the indigenous church was birthed and able to grow without us and (2) if we were obedient and God was glorified, and in that obedience a gospel contribution was made that will one day lead to the church being planted and multiplied. Our actions of obedience may lead to us being kicked out *and* another step towards the indigenous church being planted at the same time. It is too simplistic to say that because we were kicked out our action was wrong, for if our obedience leads to dismissal, it gives God glory and He will use it somehow to build His church. On the other hand, if we are kicked out for foolish, stubborn, unteachable, proud disobedience, then we will do harm to the work of church planting and bring dishonor to God.

As an example, as I write, in a neighboring country two missionary men sit in jail, for they have been connected to an evangelism drop in which they saturated a remote area with gospel literature. The debate has already begun: Were they foolish? The easy answer is to say they were unwise and their actions jeopardized others. Would we feel the same way if we knew that a local person read that literature, got saved, and became a Paul-like minister used of the Lord to bring tens of thousands to faith? I don't know the answer, for only God knows their hearts (if they were obedient or willful) and what fruit has or will come. The point is, we can indeed fall off the horse on both sides. We can leave too soon because we were injudicious, and we can stay too long—never fruitful because we were too cautious or our identity too clouded. In either case, we must remember the goal is not longevity; the goal is God's glory exemplified in our obedience to Him (and longevity in the biblical examples is rather elusive).

One helpful qualifier to revisit at this point, I'm not saying that any identity leads directly to bold witness or fruit or vice versa. I could have a church/missionary identity and be lazy and a discredit to King and gospel. I have some friends with a non-church identity who are incredible and bold witnesses all the time.

10. Trouble is inevitable.

It has been granted to us on behalf of Jesus, not only to believe on His name, but also to suffer for His name (Phil. 1:29). Everyone who desires to live a godly life in Christ Jesus will face persecution (2 Tim. 3:12). Matthew 10:22 tells us we *will* be hated *by all* for Jesus' sake. We have come so far from this biblical reality. We have twisted trouble into an indicator that we have done something wrong. The shocking truth is that we are amiss, and woe to us if all men speak well of us (Luke 6:26). The sober truth is, if we are not being persecuted, facing trouble, being hated, we are doing something wrong. This does not mean we foolishly make trouble our aim; it is the simple reality that faithful gospel witness will bring trouble. Thus, we should not jump to conclusions that trouble means missionaries have erred. It may very well indicate faithful obedience.

No identity removes all the obstacles or all the problems. The Bible is clear that suffering comes before glory, that we will be hated, that we will be resented, that persecution is a certainty, and that it is by many tribulations we plant the church and enter the kingdom of God. Whoever our model—Jesus, Paul, the Apostles, the church fathers, missionaries through the ages—the cross is still a stumbling block and the enemy will always attack.

Trouble does not delegitimize an approach; if it did, then both Jesus and Paul were miserable failures in their mission. Neither does trouble endorse folly or bravado. We can't make a one-to-one correlation between trouble and a public church/missionary identity when trouble is promised to everyone who bears the name of Christ. If we do not get in trouble, we are either not fulfilling our mission or we are so ineffective that demonic powers are not threatened in the least and leave us be. Those that get in trouble in missions then (whether modestly or in martyrdom) should not automatically be considered either heroic or foolish. This is too simplistic when the biblical guarantee is that trouble will always find those who are faithful followers and proclaimers of the gospel.

In Morocco, one movement of churches has grown to 43. The leader of this movement has intentionally avoided incorporating believers who were discipled by missionaries to be super cautious. He very specifically only wanted to add new believers to the church, and he has woven a teaching on suffering into the discipleship process. His philosophy is that boldness breeds boldness. They just launched a media campaign that includes videos of Moroccan MBBs who live in Morocco and identify with the Moroccan church. One of the unexpected results is that after seeing people they know witness publicly, other MBBs in the churches are volunteering to participated in a video sharing the gospel. Boldness breeds boldness.

11. There are times and seasons.

In John 11, Jesus raised Lazarus from the dead, and then at the height of both His popularity and His danger, knowing the authorities wanted to kill Him, He withdrew to a safe place (John 11:54). He would still march with a face like a flint to the cross (Luke 9:51), but all in good time. Paul went over the Damascus wall in a basket (Acts 9:25) and then set his face to Jerusalem as well (Acts 21:13), where he would be bound and set on a course for his execution. Clearly in the Bible, there are times when we withdraw, reroute, stay silent, wait, or escape. We do not answer every person or every question the same way every time. There are times to be super direct; there are times to hold our tongue.

I have been telling almost every Narnian I meet here in the city that I am a pastor sent by the church, and that has led to amazing gospel opportunities. But I am not here on a pastor/church/missionary visa (yet). I have a legitimate business visa, and I explain that the church has funded the business and are my investors (or donors). I have also been able to explain what we do (intercultural training) and invariably have Jesus-centered conversations. *But* for the record, I did not say anything evangelistic at the airport. I just handed them my passport and wore my BAM shirt (with the name of my company on it).

My usual, consistent identity is as a pastor and church-connected Christian *and* I selectively use it. At other times I just buy gas, get my groceries, and act like a normal expatriate in country. When asked who I am and what I do, I weave my pastoral identity and church donors immediately into the explanation, almost every time. It is the identity that gives me the most internal harmony and the most external opportunities to witness. Further, this identity is something I have grown into and become more comfortable with as time has gone by and as I have learned more about myself and context. I started out very cautious, but over the years as confidence and opportunity have grown, I have become more and more open.

12. If we don't identify with the church, we don't model the body of Christ well.

God created all the nations (*ethne*) and languages (hence, cultures) of the world (Gen.10–11) *and* initiated His mission plan to bless them all through Abraham's seed (Gen. 12:1–3), which we know to be the Lord Jesus Christ directly from Galatians 3:16. We see the biblical metanarrative is ever inclusive of all peoples and that one day all peoples will gather around the throne (Rev. 5:9; 7:9). Our eternity will certainly be multi-cultural as should our collective present. The Antioch church was both multicultural and missionary from the beginning (Acts 13). I'm not saying there cannot be homogeneous churches (embedded in one culture using a heart language); I am saying that God considers the church to be one body intended to be inclusive and reaching out, and any healthy body must be self-connected (Eph. 4:16). No healthy church makes isolation (especially if the goal is self-preservation) a goal, for truly the lost (all men) will know we are Christians by our love for one another (John 13:35).

In full disclosure I am not a proponent of insider missiology when it is defined by encouraging Jesus followers to remain within Islam. My ecclesiology is that the church is "called out" of false religions. I believe Islam is a false religion. Islam must be defined by Muslims and Muslims deny the deity of Jesus; thus, it is impossible to be Muslim and follow Jesus in the biblical sense. This is what I mean by false religion—a religion antithetical to biblical religion. Therefore, I believe that followers of Jesus everywhere must be in fellowship with the wider body of Christ, with the church—this means the church historically (the church now at rest that has been faithful down through the ages) and the church militant (the church now on mission, actively obeying Jesus and loving Him all around the globe). We must be the church both organically (with all its beauty) and organizationally (with all its flaws). We can't have one without the other. If you have a house church, whose house? Who speaks? Who feeds? Who watches the kids? Who leads? Church is always both organic and organized.

The other reality is that to ignore the existing church in any context, whether expatriate (for example, in Narnia there are hundreds of house churches—Filipino, Indians, Africans, Pakistanis, Westerners, mixed, other, etc.) and a few indigenous Narnian house churches (MBB). To ignore either or both suggests an ecclesiology not expansive enough to recognize the incredible Kingdom potential that overcomes liabilities.

From this conviction comes the understanding that I, as part of the historic and global church, am to make disciples who will be part of the historic and global church. Indigenous? By all means. But not orphans. Brothers and sisters who are welcomed in to complete us. Giving correction and receiving it. Adding value and benefiting. If our job is to be church planters and if part of that responsibility is the union of God's global body, then there must be intentional identification with the church. We can't plant what we don't love, and if we are to be church planters, we must love the church, for what it can be (and will be). What I am saying is that having an upfront church identity helps this process tremendously—it opens doors, it clarifies, and it helps me set and hold the course. It lets the hounded and isolated believer know in those early, frail days of church planting that they are not alone, that a vast multitude loves and cherishes them. What I am saying is that I need to be a part of the church myself, for my own good, for the good of my family, not just for modeling, but also for experiencing.

THE STICKING POINT

Most missionaries would have no objection with most of what I have written above regarding this direct church association and identity, as long as it remains personal to me. Where it becomes challenging is when my personal identity becomes problematic for their identity due to association. In other words, no one really objects to what I do as long as it does not jeopardize them or does not jeopardize new believers. It's a fair question. Let me take the question in two parts: fellow missionaries and local believers.

Fellow Missionaries

If my identity is as a missionary/pastor/church man and other missionaries have chosen to go a different way with their identity, what are the implications for them if it is known that we spend time together (social gatherings, house church, training, etc.)? What are the implications on them if I am more direct in witness than they are, more open in communication than they are, more visually connected to the church than they are? How do we in good conscience interact with other missionaries who feel that our approach is dangerous for them?

1. We honor the consensus in context and the individual preference in private. In communication with them we adopt the language and security measures (VPN, secure email, secure communication apps, coded language) that they prefer. I may not agree with them and I may even think them wrong-headed, but if I want them to communicate or interact with me, I realize it must be on their terms. Partnership is worth this accommodation. There are missteps sometimes when we do not realize what others' comfort boundaries are (and I have made them), but we hope they are gracious enough to allow us to learn their "language." Simplistically, we engage them on their terms.

2. We are not offended if they chose to disassociate or avoid us. Before moving to Narnia, I discretely contacted the known leaders by email and explained who I was, provided links to our public profile, and said I would love to connect with them if they were willing. Some were willing, some declined. I respect their choice. Our posture is to freely invite others to friendship and partnership but understand if they decline. We understand if they think our position/identity jeopardizes them. We always want to be clear with our identity and profile to other missionaries and then let them dictate the terms of their engagement with us.

3. We offer the protection and benefits of our position (for all positions have some benefits and some liabilities). Our choice of identity can offer some sanctuary, and we want to be generous with extended covering. Essentially, a public church identity that the powers that be understand can be calming and empowering. If the authorities know exactly who we are (missionaries, pastors, church workers) and who we are not (CIA, spies, special forces, drug runners, money launderers, pimps, etc.), it often works in our favor and in the favor of all we associate with. Missionaries and church leaders are known entities and the challenges they bring are often the least of a government's worries.

Here in Narnia, I recently had a conversation with the pastor of a house church. We were meeting to get to know one another and I did not want to unduly jeopardize him or his underground church. I asked him to "Google" my name and get back to me. He did, watched some online sermons, and came back graciously beaming. He said, "Wow! With your online profile and the fact that they let you in the country and gave you a visa is a sign to us that you can offer us protection. Come and speak to our church and be free. We have no concerns, for you will bring protection with you wherever you go."

I know this is not always the case, but the point is that sometimes it is true, sometimes the best thing we can do for others is to have a clearly articulated and public church, pastor, or missionary identity that is known by the authorities.

4. We are very careful not to use their names, images, or any information in communication. This is simple professional courtesy and ethics. Pictures, references, data, info, etc., nothing should be passed on without their explicit permission and guidelines.

Local Believers

All the above holds true regarding being open on the front end, allowing local believers to determine the rules of engagement, being honest and upfront on who we are, allowing them to distance themselves from us or engage with us, honoring their comfort level in communication and verbiage, and especially not doing anything to jeopardize them through injudicious communication of their testimony, life, or circumstances. Any exploitation is heinous. In addition to these:

1. We want to model faith and courage. The research of Nik Ripken (author of *Insanity of God*) haunts me; it condemns us all. In a teaching time to our team in Cairo, he related how he discovered that the number one thing disciples of Jesus learned from missionaries was how to fear. We won't associate with one another; we are unwilling to baptize; we leave the country when things get rough; we ignore those being watched by security who are from our own teams; we care more about our own security than that of MBBs; and we protect our own visa more than we do those in danger.

In this regard, I always want to be willing to baptize (or be a part of the celebration when the MBB invites me as I do think it better for other MBBs to baptize whenever possible). I always want to be willing to meet them on their terms. I never want to hold my longevity or security as more important than their discipleship. If they want to meet me, I will bend over backwards to meet with them and pay any price. If they do not want to meet me, I will honor their lead. I want to demonstrate to them that they are more important than my visa or security.

We must demonstrate that we die daily and that we would die for them if need be.

2. Honor their boundaries, dignity, and comfort levels. As mentioned above, with pictures, newsletters, and all communications, I must interact from a posture of respect for their personhood and security. The above is more obvious than the subtle viewing of the disciple as a trophy or endorsement of my ministry. Even if I never brag to supporters about my relationship with a disciple but internally view that person as a number, target, or accomplishment, I have sinned against him. Certainly, we are sent to make disciples and we rejoice at souls saved and disciples made, but let's not depersonalize that wonder.

I must do no harm to their bodies, souls, or emotions if there is any possible way to avoid it. I must not be afraid of Christian discipleship and biblical teaching if the consequences of that obedience bring pain. If pain is to result, let it only be for the gospel and let it be shared. After all, compassion is to "suffer with." If something I teach, preach, or ask is cross worthy, it will apply to me as well as to them.

3. Give them full liberty to say anything they want about you to others, including security. On the one hand, we must model that we, when under duress, will not reveal anything about them that would cause them harm. We must determine, assure, and live out a refusal to be an informant, even to our own hurt. In most cases the extreme cost to us is expulsion, but even if it means prison, torture, or death (however unlikely), we must never be the ones to give up others' names or information. On the less dramatic side, we must be ready with good explanations for why that person visits our house, why their name is in our phone, why we gave them a Bible or some literature, or what our relationship is with them. Wisdom and respect lead us to have that agreement between us before it is required from authorities. As much as possible (when questioned about others), let us take all the responsibility on ourselves and protect the other in love to the highest degree possible.

Now on the other hand, because the likelihood is that they will face much more physical pain when questioned about us, we must give them the full liberty to say anything and everything they know about us. I always tell MBBs and CBBs that I partner with in ministry that they have my full blessing (and even request) to say anything and everything about me to security. I believe we need to set them free to do what their conscience allows and to assure them that we have no secrets about being Jesus, Bible, evangelism, church planting people.

CONCLUSION

God has revealed Himself in Jesus Christ and has commissioned us to preach Jesus, teach Jesus, and make disciples of Jesus. God revealed Himself in humble vulnerability, and it cost Him greatly. We are to do missions as Jesus and the Apostles did it, and their methods were vocal, transparent, public and private, and connected to the body of Christ. Jesus and the Apostles were revealers, proclaimers, announcers, and disseminators of information. They were people of truth, light, integrity, and honesty, even if it was to their own hurt. They were wise and bold, winsome and articulate, credible and acceptable in their roles, even as their message was inflammatory. They had understandable identities that were spiritual in nature and propelled them into verbal witness. They were also very different from one another with a wide range of method, scope, and gifting.

I'm an extrovert and I love a challenge. I love sharing the gospel. I'm Greek and enjoy a good passionate back-and-forth discussion. My wife is a peacemaker and an introvert. She does not employ the pastor/church identity as robustly or as often as I do, and I'm good with that. I can speak Arabic, I can joke around, and I'm comfortable with physical touch with Arabs. I love to affirm them and use proverbs, stories, and indirection. Being born in Africa and living 27 years in the Arab world have provided me some intercultural skills that a 22-year-old Yankee straight off the plane does not have. Further, I have an online profile almost impossible to hide, and due to my journey referenced above, have no desire to hide, both from conviction and efficacy. All these things factor into the equation. I am not trying to force everyone into this identity. I am merely making the case that it is a legitimate option for some.

We must, however, *all* be openly and immediately Jesus-Bible persons whose behavior is biblical, who never stop evangelizing, making disciples, and planting churches. A great way to do this is to openly have a pastor/church/missionary identity. It's not the only way, but it is a viable, powerful way to present ourselves. In my experience, this includes contexts that popular opinion consider "closed" or "hostile." The benefits can benefit other gospel workers and indigenous believers when we live and present ourselves wisely. I encourage missionaries to rethink their abandoning of historic terms. Let's retain them and explain them and broker them to advance gospel clarity. I encourage many new missionaries to prayerfully consider a very clear pastor and church-based identity, even in contexts where contemporary thinking has written that approach off. It may very well be the best way to go for many in these days, even as it was for many in the past.

PURSUING JESUS:

M any Psalms pull out from their nosedive of despair, fear, or complaint at the end, landing safely in the arms of a good and kind Sovereign. Psalm 88 is short on encouragement and long on the God of wrath, terror, and burning anger (vv. 7, 15, 16). At the end of the day, Jehovah is not a tame lion, and He cannot be domesticated. Sometimes we just need to be terrorized and awed, humbled at His majesty and sobered at His wrath. To never be afraid (not just reverent, but in despair) is to never really encounter Him. This is probably more necessary for those who have known Him longest than for those who are newly His.

I cannot bear fruit (make disciples and plant churches) unless I spend time with Jesus (John 15:4). Asking whatever we wish is not unconditional. I can only ask for anything if I abide always (v. 7), and only if I obey, am I Jesus' friend (v. 14), and only if we love one another are we granted whatever we ask (vv. 16–17; see also John 14:14–15). Yet, when we abide, the joy is of Jesus Himself (15:11), not in the answered prayer. We must be careful not to try too hard to have the world love us and ever remember that the world hates Jesus (vv. 19, 24). Joy is not in being loved by the world, but in being loved by Jesus, and if we love Him back, we will obey Him, and if we obey Him, the world will hate us. There is no excuse for sin (loving the world and living in such a way as the world will love us back) when the Holy Spirit has been sent to help us, sent by the Son from the Father (vv. 22, 26).

Paul exemplifies what our fate will be if we love Jesus. Leading members of the community will bring charges against us, many and serious charges, and all the people will appeal against us declaring we ought not to live (Acts 25:7, 24). We must be wary of the allure of being popular with the masses or the monarchs. As messengers, we have a message as unpopular as it is powerful to save. Ironically, the very truth that would deliver is despised. Jesus, help me guard my heart against the desire to be liked and respected. Let me take up the glorious cross of shame. Loving Jesus means being hated by the world. I testify that it is worth it; now help me live it.

James makes the same point when He bluntly says that friendship with the world is hostility toward God (4:4). It is, in fact, a proud act to want the world to love us, and God will oppose those efforts while gracing those who make no effort to earn the world's applause (v. 6). We must submit to God, resisting the devil's temptation (v. 7), the urge to be thought respectable by the host community and authorities. We must draw near to God (v. 8), which requires drawing away from the world, and in that withdrawal, we find that God has indeed drawn near to us, satisfying beyond measure, incomparably good. When God draws near, we realize what folly it is to desire the commendation and camaraderie of the world. In that sense it becomes simpler to humble ourselves in His presence (v. 10). Alongside drawing away from the world and drawing near to God, lifting Him up, we must also draw near to our brothers and sisters in Jesus, not speaking ill of them, not judging them, not arrogantly boasting about what we will do, and actively doing right (vv. 11–12, 16–17). In a hostile world, we need each other.

Pursuing Church Planting:

Yesterday was another language learning day in which we asked our tutor many questions about culture, generosity, and reformation. The country is changing so quickly, and there is a tension between the liberals (who embrace every new opportunity) and the moderates (who are pro-change but concerned that it is too fast and too broad and does not represent Narnia well). It's not clear what is best for gospel advance as liberalization certainly allows more freedom. But freedom politically, morally, and religiously does not automatically lead to revival and repentance; sometimes it works against it. Sometimes repression (which shows the true colors of a repressing ideology) is a better catalyst for turning to Jesus than moderate and liberal allowances. What we are sure of is that nothing can happen outside of the work of the Holy Spirit (whether the country continues to liberalize or whether there is a backlash from the moderates and conservatives and the pendulum swings back the other way as it has done over the last century).

We had a 2-hour Skype call with the team leaders in our cohort yesterday (from Morocco, Egypt, Bahrain, Oman, and the Indian Ocean) and nowhere do we have a church planted yet. We all are in desperate need of the Holy Spirit to break through.

John Owen (1616–1683) said it well about Christ, and it's also true of Christ's church. The birth of the church is indeed miraculous conception, a peculiar and special work of the Spirit: "The framing, forming, and miraculous conception of the body of Christ in the womb of the blessed Virgin was the peculiar and especial work of the Holy Ghost.... He was the wonderful operator in this glorious work." And regarding our role in church planting: "The Lord Christ had called his apostles to the great work of building his church, and the propagation of his gospel in the world. Of themselves they were plainly and openly defective in all qualifications and abilities that might contribute anything to it. But whatever is wanting in themselves...he promises to supply...by sending the Holy Spirit to them, on whose presence and assistance alone depended the whole success of their ministry in the world.... And this is the hinge whereon the whole weight of it turns and depends to this day. Take it away...and there will be an absolute end of the church of Christ in this world—no dispensation of the Spirit, no church."[5]

DAY 30

PURSUING JESUS:

Lord Jesus, You are awesome above all (Psalm 89:7). Let me keep my eyes on You and Your glory in all the earth, and thus, free from the deceptions of the enemy (v. 22). One of the deceptions is that we must be great, but the weight of great is crushing for any man. Only God is worthy and able to be great. There is freedom in being small, content in Jesus being awesome. Lord, forgive me (and keep me from) the folly of striving to be known and respected. That striving is a lust for what will kill me. Rather, let me rejoice in all You are, finding my joy in being small and simply doing what You created me to do.

Thank you, Jesus, that You can keep us from stumbling (John 16:1). Your Holy Spirit not only protects (defends) but also attacks (convicts the world, v. 8). Thank you that the Spirit of truth guides us into all truth (v. 13). What a wonder that God the Spirit does not speak of His own initiative but only glorifies Jesus (v. 14). If this is true of God the Spirit, how much more should it be true of me! Help me, Jesus, to simply talk of You and disclose You to others. In this there is a wonderful release from pressure. I don't have to be witty; I just have to glorify Jesus. Thank you further for Your honest warning that the pursuit of God's glory inevitably means earthly pain and anguish and for Your promise that on the other side of difficulty there is joy (v. 22). Thank you for the invitation to petition the Father with confidence, and for this, I pray: Take my will and make it Thine, forgive my sin and cover my shame, and make Jesus real to me. Lord, in these answers my heart will rejoice, and no one will be able to take my joy, for to have *You* is enough for me (vv. 22–23).

As life progresses, if I am to be in trouble, let it only be for the hope of the promise of the gospel (Acts 26:6). Let me never forget that

You have sent me to open eyes, turn Muslims from darkness to light and from the dominion of Satan to God, that they may receive forgiveness of sins and their inheritance among those who have been sanctified by faith in Jesus (v. 18). There is so much accommodation to false religion in our day. Let me stand clearly on Scripture with full fidelity to Your person, never in doubt that men and women need to be rescued from the dominion of Satan. Jesus, let me be obedient to this heavenly vision by continuing to demand repentance (of myself and others), by testifying to small and great, by proclaiming light, by uttering words of sober truth, and by doing all things openly, not in a corner (vv. 19–20, 22–23, 25–26). Let me openly and without embarrassment call for all men to become a Christian (v. 28).

In the obedience of this heavenly vision, Jesus, I need patience until the coming of the Lord, never losing sight of this goal and culmination of history. Let me be patient, for the produce of the soil takes time, and let me anticipate the early and latter rain (James 5:7). Let me live in the reality that endurance not only brings joy but *can be* joy even in the struggle as the outcome of the Lord's dealings are always mercy and compassion (v. 11). As I wait with endurance, teach me to pray, for the earnest prayers of righteous (believing, enduring, holy, lowly) men and women avail much (v. 16).

Pursuing Church Planting:

Yesterday was a grind-it-out day of abiding in Jesus, language study, writing and correspondence, travel across town, and team meeting. This is the norm of church planting. We must always be energized for the commonplace without allowing it to become routine busyness that does not engage the lost nor seek the glory of God. Routine must always be infused with a passion to seek the lost for the glory of Christ.

John Owen wrote, "Salvation is the end that God aims at in his choosing of us, in subordination to his own glory, which is and must be the ultimate end of all his purposes and decrees, or of all the free acts of his wisdom and love." We have been chosen and appointed to bear fruit, to see souls saved, to make disciples, and to plant churches. This is the goal of God *subordinated* to the goal of His own glory. Of first importance is that the glory of God and the saving of souls must be done in a way that glorifies God. Daily routine then has these two guiding questions as its riverbanks: (1) What am I doing in the daily routines of life that work towards souls being saved? (2) In my routines am I doing things in such a way that all things glorify God?

We can take great joy in days of grind-it-out endurance if they are contributing to souls being saved and Jesus being glorified. The church planter must ever be aware of the drift away from purposeful routine; it is all too easy to either be busy with things that don't lead to souls being saved or to be busy saving souls in a way that does not glorify God.

DAY 31

PURSUING JESUS:

Lord, *You* are my dwelling place in all generations (Psalm 90:1). Let me never forget that dwelling in You I am sheltered from the fury, anger, and wrath of God (vv. 7, 9, 11) and that the light of Your presence not only shelters, it also reveals secret sins (v. 8). I only safely dwell with You if I live in holiness by Your help. Teach me to number my days and confirm for us the work of our hands (vv. 12, 17).

The hour has come to glorify Jesus because Jesus has authority over all flesh and gives eternal life, which in essence is the intimate knowledge of God (John 17:1–3). Help me then, Lord, to focus in on glorifying Jesus and accomplishing His work on the earth (v. 4). Help me to manifest Your name that others can keep Your word (v. 6). Let me ever be mindful that all things are Yours and we should ever be one (vv. 10–11). Let the Scripture be fulfilled; in other words, let the will of God always be done that the joy of Jesus be made full (vv. 12–13). Let me remember that the joys of this world are ever at odds with the joys of Jesus, that we are not of this world; in fact, we will be hated (v. 14). In the midst of that hate, Jesus, keep me from the evil one (v. 15). Let him have no part of me; rather, sanctify me by Your word, Your truth (v. 17). Send me into the world that they may believe; send us in unity that the world see Your love and Your glory and that Your name be known (vv. 21, 23–24, 26).

Thank you, Lord Jesus, for the body of Christ globally and for care from friends (Acts 27:3). Do not let us be fooled into thinking that moderate winds (v. 13) are our friends; they mislead us into supposing we have obtained our purpose when truly they lead to violent winds (v. 16). Whatever the winds, thank you, Jesus, that You have guaranteed those who sail with us, so we need not fear (v. 24). I understand this does not mean immunity; it just means sovereignty. Let me believe God that it will turn out exactly as He has said (v. 25), again remembering that we sometimes must run aground. God is in control of shipwrecks. Let me model calm (v. 35) and trust, knowing that all will be brought to safety when the ship is going down (v. 44), which again is a status greater than physical pain or trial.

Thank you, Father, that You have chosen me, that I have been sanctified by the Spirit to obey the Son (1 Peter 1:2). Thank you that this sanctified obedience leads to grace and peace in the fullest measure. Thank you, Jesus, that it is the resurrection of Jesus (proof of His deity) that gives me living hope (v. 3) and that I am protected by the power of God through faith (v. 5). Let then my faith result in praise, glory, and honor at the revelation of Jesus—both now spiritually and on *that* day ultimately (v. 7). Thank you that grace is brought to us at the revelation of Jesus, that as Jesus is made known, grace is given to respond accordingly (v. 13). Let the center of my response be holiness as You are holy, as I have been redeemed by the precious blood of Christ (vv. 16, 19). Because of what You have done, help me fervently love my brothers and sisters in Jesus (v. 22), knowing that all of us are like grass and it is only the word of the Lord that will endure forever (v. 24).

Pursuing Church Planting:

Yesterday after language and writing, we had supper with a wonderful veteran missionary couple from another organization. We knew them twenty years ago in Sudan, and they are with an organization that tends to be quite secretive. Thankfully, they were super gracious to share their knowledge of this context and the different ministries going on. They walked the delicate balance of orienting a new missionary couple without betraying any other confidences—not an easy path to trod. I do think that transparency and voluntary sharing of ministry information is critically important for building unity, and I do understand that the betrayal of trust destroys unity rapidly, if not immediately. There is an ever-present tension then regarding not only the sharing of information, but also the different levels of openness that missionaries chose to adopt.

We talked about a Muslim friend who loves to be with Americans and is making the rounds. He has expressed interest in Bible study, but it's not clear if he just wants time with Americans or if he is hungry to study the Scriptures. Andrew and I are meeting with him Monday night to do the first Bible study, but as a small test of his sincerity, we decided to ask him to host a Bible study in his home to which he invites six friends. We want to see if he will mobilize others to study the Bible. It may be that he just wants English and American culture. The missiological principle is that we want to spend time with those who are serious and those who will spread what they discover right from the beginning, even before they get saved. We are looking for persons of peace who will host a Jesus-centered meeting in their home (not helpful to have the venue dependent on the missionary home) and will use their influence for the gospel. We are looking in collectivist societies for family or affinity groups (common interests or relationships) that could discover and decide to follow Jesus together. It sounds harsh, but as church planters we do need to spend the bulk of our time with those who can and will lead others to Jesus, and we need to do things with and in groups of locals as much as possible.

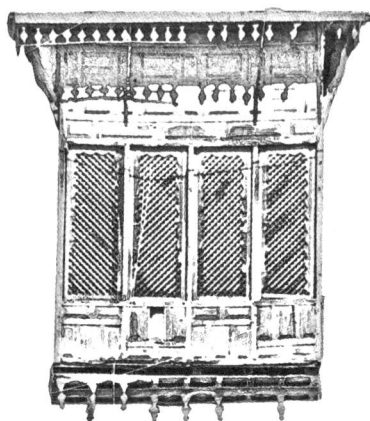

PRINCIPLES FOR SPEAKING HARD WORDS FROM A SOFT HEART

1. I have to keep a soft heart even if I must say strong words.

2. Standing with convictions doesn't mean we abandon compassion. Jeremiah's weeping is a good model.

3. Being prophetic is no license to become a critic.

4. Being liked is not part of the gospel.

5. You don't have to speak long or often if the message is potent.

6. Sometimes you need to wait. The one who casts pearls before swine is at fault, not the pigs. Timing matters as much as content. Persistence is needed, but the squeaky wheel sometimes gets the swift kick, not the grease.

7. I still have to earn the right to be heard.

8. If I am liable for the consequences of the decision (if I have to implement what I am proposing), it seasons and leavens my thoughts, ideas, and decisions.

9. Each step away from ground-level, hands-in-the-dirt practitioner involvement begins a decay of moral authority. We need to be judiciously considerate when asking others to do what we are not directly doing.

10. Truth without love kills. If your listener or follower doesn't deeply feel that you love them unconditionally, it is hard for them to hear correction or constructive criticism, no matter how true it is nor how badly they need to hear it.

PURSUING JESUS:

Jesus, help me to dwell in the shelter, abide in the shadow of the Almighty (Psalm 91:1). Lord, be my refuge, fortress, trust and deliverer, my cover, refuge, shield, and bulwark (vv. 2–4). Let me not be afraid of terror, arrows, pestilence, and destruction (v. 5–6) because You are my refuge, my dwelling place, my guard, and lifter of my head (v. 9). Thank you, Jesus, that You deliver those who love You that You are with me in trouble (vv. 14–15). Let me remember that life is not trouble free, yet I can be satisfied in You (v. 16).

Thank you, Jesus, that in all of my uncertainty You know all the things that are coming (John 18:4). Let me then drink the cup the Father has given (v. 11). Let me speak openly to the world, speak nothing in secret (v. 20). Let me remember that Your kingdom is not of this world (v. 36) and that You will bring us safely through the raging storms of this life to our heavenly home (Acts 28:1). I pray, Jesus, that You arrange "natives [who will show] extraordinary kindness" (v. 2), honor, and respect (v. 10), not for our personal ease, but for the lifting of the cross and the preaching of the gospel that we might have opportunity to pray, lay hands on and heal, and witness of You (v. 8). Thank you for brethren that give courage and national entities that allow our presence (vv. 15, 19); let me not speak ill of authorities You have ordained. Let any restrictions be borne with grace, for the hope of the people of God (v. 20). Let me remember that *You* will be spoken against everywhere (v. 22), even as You expect and empower us to everywhere solemnly testify and explain (to large numbers!) about the Kingdom as we try and persuade others about Jesus (v. 23). Some will be persuaded, others will not believe (vv. 24–27), so let me focus on those who will listen and preach to all the kingdom of God and the teaching of the Lord Jesus Christ with all openness, unhindered (vv. 28, 30–31).

Reconciled to the reality that there will be hostility and opposition (from inside and outside the family of faith), Jesus, help me put aside all malice, deceit, hypocrisy, envy, and slander and come to *You* with longing, knowing I will not be disappointed (1 Peter 2:1–2, 6). Thank you that I have been chosen to proclaim Your excellencies; thus, let me keep my behavior excellent by submitting to all authorities, silencing ignorant slander through holy living, honoring all people, loving the brotherhood, fearing God, and honoring the king (vv. 9, 12–13, 15, 17). Let me not forget that though we do all things with honor, we are still called to suffer and that if we walk in His steps, we will face scorn and loss (v. 21). Therefore, let there be no deceit in me, especially self-delusion (v. 22). When I am reviled (v. 23), let me keep trusting You and let me keep dying to sin (v. 24) as John Owen warned, "Be ye killing sin or sin be killing you."

PURSUING CHURCH PLANTING:

Friday morning was house church; the sermon was on John 9. A takeaway for me is that we should focus more on *how* circumstances can give glory to Jesus rather than on *why* they happened. After some Sabbath rest I went with Andrew to meet Matthew, and as it turned out, he brought a ringer with him, an expert in evangelizing Christians. The man (William) is Lebanese, witty, friendly, charismatic, and intelligent, and was armed with all the attacks against the deity of Jesus and the veracity of the Bible. We had a two-hour conversation where he asked the usual questions. He was a smiling assassin, and several times I pointed out that his point or his insulation was faulty, insulting, or even arrogant. If in gospel presentation there is both offense (evangelism) and defense (apologetics), this was certainly more of an apologetic session. I did the talking and Andrew did the praying. It was in a public café; nothing was hidden or muted. Others listened in with curiosity.

At the end of the day, though the good of these types of encounters is often limited, I rejoice that (1) the gospel was presented, (2) the conversation was in a public café where others listened in, (3) Andrew was encouraged and observed how to handle these situations and thorny questions (or at least saw one way, as I'm not saying it's the only way or best way; I did what I could and trust the Lord to do the work), and (4) all things were done respectfully and we ended cordially. As is ever the case with all men, no man can come unless the Spirit draws him (John 6:44). We now pray that the Spirit takes the things discussed and uses them to draw these two Muslim men to the Lord.

I also reflected on the types of apostolic questions we must ask ourselves in order to stay on point. I'm sure there are more than these, but these are the ones that came to mind (see page 186).

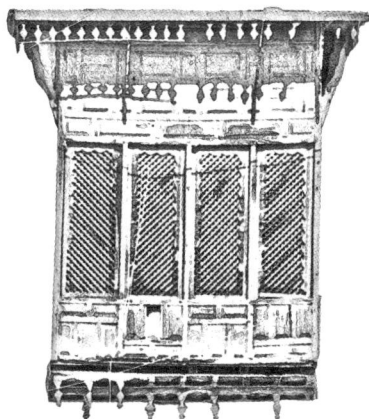

APOSTOLIC QUESTIONS

1. Is intimacy with Jesus the fount of all my ideas, inspiration, ministry, and efforts?

Before the ambition to make Christ known (Rom. 15:20), do I have the ambition to know Christ (Phil. 3)?

2. Where has the gospel not gone?

Have I done the research to know the state of the gospel in my context? What others have done and are doing? What strategically remains to be done that all peoples are evangelized?

3. What gives Jesus maximum glory among all peoples?

Cognizant that there are many good things to do and many important ministries that need attention, at this moment in God's redemption history for this context, what will give Him the most glory among those that have never heard? What is the best thing to be done right now?

4. Am I depending on the Holy Spirit?

Is the dream big enough that there is no possible way we can accomplish it without the dramatic and constant presence and power of the Holy Spirit?

5. Am I bathing my ideas in prayer?

Am I praying not just before the idea or ministry but during and after? Am I praying with my mind *and* my spirit (1 Cor. 14)? Am I sincerely asking for guidance, not just rubber stamp blessing?

6. What if it *does* work?

Rather than guarding against the dangers of ministry failing (being risk adverse) and being ashamed of failing, have we thought through the dangers of ministry success and put parameters in place to stay focused and not become proud, entitled, or comfortable?

7. Who can I partner with?

Who do I need to ask advice from, take counsel from? Where do I need to be careful to avoid duplication, complication, competition, confusion, and denominationalism?

8. What do I need to say "no" to in order to stay focused on the main mission (God's glory among all peoples)?

Am I guarding my heart against the temptation to "feel" fruitful by concentrating on those who are open to the neglect of those who have not heard? Am I intentional about leaving the 99 safe to find the one lost? Am I willing to do the hard work of sowing, not just the "fun" work of reaping?

9. Have I counted the cost?

Am I willing to suffer? To be misunderstood? To be criticized? To be slandered? Am I willing to put in the hard work and time required? Do I understand the labor that will be required, the toil over time? Am I committed to finishing, not just starting?

10. Am I dying daily?

Am I committed to living out the crucified life? Am I willing to do things God's way, in His time, in His Spirit? Am I under authority, covered by being submitted to my leaders?

11. Does this effort make disciples that make disciples?

Is multiplication in the DNA of the ministry (2 Tim. 2:2)?

12. Will this effort leave behind an indigenous church?

Am I making smart, difficult, long-term decisions that will leave a local, national, indigenous body of believers who are dignified and not dependent on me or outside entities?

PURSUING JESUS:

Jesus, only You can make me glad (Psalm 92:4) Do not let me look anywhere else for satisfaction. Thank you that You anoint with fresh oil as time and season require (v. 10). Let me focus on being planted in the house of the Lord, content and fulfilled in flourishing in the court of my God (v. 13). Thank you that You are my rock (v. 15), as steady and immovable as I am wobbly.

Jesus, I am so thankful that there is no earthly authority outside of what is given from above (John 19:11). I can rest in all those over me (nationally, denominationally) as they cannot hurt me outside of Your will. Thank you for the cross. What a moment it must have been when "knowing that all things were now accomplished," You gave up Your Spirit (vv. 28, 30). What deep satisfaction and joy must have flooded Your Spirit. Your physical dying was a sublime moment of rest, as with the Father's blessing You could say and feel that You had obeyed, You did what You had been assigned to do. Jesus, I strive for that similar rest—to be able to say (and feel!) that I have done my assignment, that I have done what You wanted me to do. Help me be faithful, to minister in such a way that Narnian Muslims here in the city, and around the world, would believe (v. 35), even if they are initially secret disciples (v. 38). Let them believe and then stand up for You when the time is right.

Along the way I ask for the imperishable quality of a gentle and quiet spirit, which is precious in the sight of God (1 Peter 3:4). Thank you for the reminder that this is how I hope in You, through an adorned and submitted spirit, a spirit that is not striving, harried, ambitious, defensive, or annoying. Jesus, here in Narnia, help me do what is right (in the right way) without being frightened by any fear (v. 6).

Let me remember that Jennifer is a fellow heir of the grace of life with me (v. 7), my spiritual equal, my human equal, my wisdom equal, and that as her spiritual head, I must dignify, cherish, and lay down my life for her (lest my prayers be hindered). In my relationships with other missionaries and ministers, help me to be harmonious, sympathetic, brotherly, kindhearted, and humble in spirit (v. 8). Help me to bless, not returning evil or insults with evil (v. 9), always remembering that the eyes of the Lord are toward those who do good and against those who do evil (v. 12).

PURSUING CHURCH PLANTING:

In a conversation with a veteran team leader (eight years in Narnia) and his wife yesterday, an interesting church planting question arose. We were expressing our desire to add value to the missionary partnership here in town through participation in a team leaders monthly meeting, hosting missionary kids twice each month in the afternoon or evening (so young parents can have a date night, do CP together, or take a nap), coordinating an activity once a month for the partnership (first month, men's event; second month, ladies event; third month, training/prayer; and repeat). The conversation was in the context of whether this was needed or wanted, and if so, would it justify the expense of us renting a bigger house so that we can host? We also talked about our public identity as a pastor being the way forward due to our history and online/public presence. The question we asked was whether our identity as pastors would make the missionary community reluctant to associate with us.

Traditionally, missionaries in Narnia have been quite cautious due to necessity. At one point, house fellowships were raided (until 2001 or so) and the religious police were very active, enforcing public conformity and Islamic hegemony. A gradual shift towards a more liberalized society has taken place over time, accelerated in the last two years (2017–2019) under the vision of the crown prince Mohammed Bin Salman. There is talk of a church presence (land, building, and clergy visas) being allowed in the near future. The answer from this wise couple was, "We don't know, maybe; there are too many other factors." What we all *can* see is that the country has changed and is changing, but what no one is yet sure of is what the implications will be. For sure there is more openness, but how the missionary community will adapt to that is yet to be discovered.

Jennifer and I talked about this, and our summary is as follows:

- Our primary calling is to see churches planted among Muslims.
- An international church role can easily become consuming; it can also be incredibly valuable and empowering.
- We feel strongly led to add value to partnership of those reaching Muslims directly.
- If it came down to a choice between being an international pastor or adding value to the missionary CP partnership, we would choose the CP partnership (if being full-blown pastors would make other missionaries unwilling to come to our house or to be involved in partnerships that we help coordinate).
- Whether that choice has to be made is still unclear; there may be a compatible way forward.
- It could be possible to have the private identity as a church-related pastor, even if that is not my main assignment or visa here in country.
- Members of our team could lead the charge as international church pastors, and we have a church visa, title, and behind-the-scenes or a less central role that gives us the church visa but primarily allows for other activities.

At the end of the day there are too many Narnian variables to clearly see the exact course of action, but we were able to clarify for ourselves that our main calling is to do church planting among Muslims. The ministry priority then would fall along this order: first, reaching Muslims ourselves; second, adding value to missionary partnership (helping them reach Muslims); and third, adding value to international community (helping them reach Muslims). We are resolved to work in the first two. How much we work in the third depends on the Lord's leading, our own energy and time capacity, the comfort of other missionaries, and the circumstances in Narnia. In the meantime, we bath this in prayer, trusting Jesus to choose for us.

♦♦♦♦♦♦♦♦♦♦♦♦♦

D A Y   3 4

PURSUING JESUS:

Jesus reigns, clothed with majesty and strength, and His throne established of old from everlasting (Psalm 93:1–2). Thank you, Jesus, that You on high are mighty, more than the breakers of the seas (v. 4) and that holiness befits Your house (v. 5). Lord, as a bearer of Your name, holiness also befits my house and heart. I know that pursuit of You must include a drive, longing, and dedication to holiness. Grow this desire in me and aid my feeble efforts. Jesus, make me holy, for I cannot make myself good.

Come, Lord Jesus, and stand in my midst granting Your peace (John 20:19, 21, 26). Let me rejoice at seeing You and understand what it means to be sent by You even as You were sent by the Father (vv. 20–21). Breathe on me, Jesus; I am in desperate need of the Holy Spirit (v. 22). Help me to reach, see, and put my believing hand in Yours (v. 27). Let me believe at every level, with every cell, that Jesus is the Son of God, and in that believing have *life* in *Your* name (v. 31).

Born in Saskatchewan, Canada, Margaret Clarkson grew up in Toronto. She spent seven years working as a teacher in the far north of Ontario. She desired to be a missionary on a foreign field but due to a physical disability, she was unable to go. One day she read John 20:21 (KJV), "Peace be unto you: as my Father hath sent me, even so I send you." In the north, she said, "I experienced loneliness of every kind—mental, cultural, and particularly, spiritual, for in all of those seven years I never found real Christian fellowship; churches were modern and born-again Christians almost nonexistent..."[6] She wrote a poem that reflected her experience and it was published as a hymn in 1954. "Some years later," she wrote, "I realized that the poem was really very one-sided; it told only of the sorrows and privations of the missionary call and none of its triumphs. I wrote another song [in 1963] in the same rhythm so that verses could be used interchangeably, setting forth the glory and the hope of the missionary calling."[7]

Here are the words to the two hymns, first the 1954 version followed by the 1963 version:

1 9 5 4

So send I you to labor unrewarded,
To serve unpaid, unloved, unsought, unknown,
To bear rebuke, to suffer scorn and scoffing
So send I you, to toil for Me alone.

So send I you to bind the bruised and broken,
Over wandering souls to work, to weep, to wake,
To bear the burdens of a world a-weary
So send I you, to suffer for My sake.

So send I you to loneliness and longing,
With heart a-hungering for the loved and known,
Forsaking home and kindred, friend and dear one
So send I you, to know My love alone.

So send I you to leave your life's ambition,
To die to dear desire, self-will resign,
To labor long, and love where men revile you
So send I you, to lose your life in Mine.

So send I you to hearts made hard by hatred,
To eyes made blind because they will not see,
To spend, though it be blood, to spend and spare not
So send I you, to taste of Calvary.

1 9 6 3

So send I you by grace made strong to triumph
Over hosts of hell, over darkness, death and sin,
My name to bear and in that name to conquer
So send I you, My victory to win.

So send I you to take to souls in bondage
The word of truth that sets the captive free
To break the bonds of sin, to loose death's fetters
So send I you, to bring the lost to Me.

So send I you, My strength to know in weakness,
My joy in grief, My perfect peace in pain,
To prove My power, My grace, My promised presence
So send I you, eternal fruit to gain.

So send I you to bear My cross with patience,
And then one day with joy to lay it down,
To hear My voice, "Well done, My faithful servant,
Come share My throne, My kingdom and My crown!"

Peter reminds us that we are to arm ourselves with the "purpose to
suffer" by no longer living for the lusts of men but longing for the
will of God, as we will give an account to Him who is *ready* to judge
the living and the dead, being that the end of all things is near (1
Peter 1:1–2, 5, 7). Jesus, help me then to have a sober spirit for the
"purpose of prayer." I wonder if one purpose of suffering is to help
us pray, as prayer is so much more effective than we realize. Because
the work of God goes forward in prayer, and because suffering aids

prayer, our good God ordains suffering! I should be thankful then for the difficult things that drive me to prayer, for they will indubitably work for gospel advance and the King's glory.

Along the way, especially if and when those difficult things pass to me through the hands of my brothers and sisters, *above all*, we must remain fervent in our love for one another as love covers a multitude of sins (v. 8). Jesus, help me/us to employ our gifts in serving one another as good stewards of the manifold grace of God (many different ways through many different people), speaking or serving by the strength God supplies, so that in *all things* God may be glorified through Jesus, to whom belongs glory and dominion forever (v. 11).

Peter exhorts us to keep rejoicing according to the degree of our suffering (v. 13 NASB). It seems that rejoicing in our difficulties here is practice or warm up for the great joy and celebration at His appearing, for in suffering "the Spirit of glory and of God" can rest upon us *if* we suffer for the will of God, entrusting our souls to our faithful creator (v. 14, 19).

Pursuing Church Planting:

After language I met for prayer with a brother, met with Thomas to see if he is interested in being our Narnian partner (for Step Global by helping put cars in the company name, co-branding, office rentals, official presence, etc.), and then met with MM regarding a possible collaboration on prayer room/guest house to serve prayer teams and the missionary community here in the city.

Four practical and essential components of church planting that are not necessarily dramatic but necessary all the same: language fluency, prayer and accountability, credible and enduring professional legal status in country, and partnership prayer and hospitality for the wider body. It does not make great newsletter material, but it is the daily substance on which evangelism and discipleship are built.

PURSUING JESUS:

Lord, You get a little frustrated at us when we are slow to understand (Psalm 94:8). Let me remember that You ever hear and see and that You will rebuke the powers that be in Your way and time (vv. 9–10). I don't have to worry or fret. You have it all well in hand; the Lord knows (v. 11). Thank you, Jesus, that Your omniscience also applies to my fallen heart and that I am blessed that You love me enough to chasten me (v. 12). Please don't stop, no matter how much I protest or flail under the rod of discipline. I know deep within it is mercy. Please keep "mercying" me; no matter how painful it is, it brings me life. If You would not have helped me through correction and if You do not continue to correct me, I will sink into sin, despair, and silent fruitlessness (v. 17). Thank you, Jesus, that Your lovingkindness will hold me up and I will not sink or drown in sin (v. 18). When my anxious thoughts multiply, Your consolations delight my soul (v. 19). You, Jesus, have been my stronghold and my refuge (v. 22).

Thank you, Jesus, that You manifest Yourself to us in practical ways (John 21:1). So many times we don't recognize it's You because You're doing simple things like cooking breakfast (vv. 4, 9, 12). Help me to know it's You in the common graces and joys as You continually manifest Yourself to me (vv. 12, 14). In those delightful manifestations, Jesus, give me something of Yourself to pass on as I shepherd and tend those You assign to me (vv. 15–17). Let any love I have for others flow from Your love for me and my loving You back. In the grand scheme of life and in the little common things (as You modeled), let me give You glory. In the little deaths to self and in the ultimate dying (whether at the hand of age or antagonists), let me give You alone glory (v. 19).

Daily, Jesus, let me wait for the Spirit (Acts 1:4) for all the practical and administrative components of my life, as well as the ministerial. I don't need to know times and seasons, but I do need to receive Spirit power to be Your witness to the uttermost parts of the earth (vv. 7–8). Thank you, Jesus, that You will come again, and to that end, help me to be of one mind with Your church, continually devoting ourselves to prayer and to being witnesses of Your resurrection (vv. 11, 14, 22). The ministry of apostleship is to point to Jesus as God, the Savior of the world, and the vibrancy of this message is sustained by prayer together and dependence on the Spirit.

The witness that represents You points to Your suffering and Your glory (1 Peter 5:1). But suffering always precedes glory; as it was for You so for us. Help me shepherd an example of suffering well (v. 3), not seeking glory but living out in my daily life that we must clothe ourselves with humility if we are to wear the crown of glory (vv. 4–5). Help me, Jesus, to humble myself, including by casting all my cares on You, by being sober and alert, by resisting the devil, by suffering (before glory), and by standing firm (vv. 7–10, 12).

Pursuing Church Planting:

Yesterday after our abiding morning, Jennifer went to the store to re-stock groceries and I did my daily writing. Then in the early afternoon we visited our language tutor and her family. She lives next to Old Town in a simple but clean home. I am always moved by the hospitality that the poor offer and how they sacrifice their minimal resources to provide a lavish feast for us. We had a nice, pleasant visit, and at the end I asked if I could pray for them. Rarely have Muslim friends refused a prayer like this. At the end our tutor's elder sister said of the prayer: "That was wonderful. We Muslims are supposed to do that as well, but we never do." It is important to pray for Muslims publicly and frequently, not for credit, but so that they sense the presence of God. When God answers prayers (after they sensed His presence when the missionary prayed for them), there is a witness that can overcome all the logical and illogical mental objections to the gospel. Prayer is effective evangelism, and we should never be shy to pray openly for and with our Muslim friends, for healing, for protection, for blessing, for truth.

From her roof our tutor pointed out a nearby building whose top two floors are vacant. She said that *jinn* (spirits) live there and everyone is afraid to live in those apartments. She also said there is a general fear of jinn in the area. This, too, can be a circumstance where prayer could demonstrate the power and presence of Jesus!

After three hours with our tutor, we went to Andrew and Kendra's house where we arranged to meet with Michael, a Sudanese Arab who is open to studying the Bible. He brought a young man named Abdullah along and we had an interesting discussion. I asked him to explain to us what he has heard and understood of the gospel from the Christian perspective (as he has met many Christians here in the country). We had a somewhat amusing dialogue where I played the role of the Muslim questioner and he played the role of the Christian explaining his faith. It was interesting to see what he understood well and what was still clouded by Islamic thought. We concluded the night by agreeing to a study next week in his home where we study the life of Jesus from one of the Gospels and discuss it together with some of his friends. He said that he and Abdullah will be there for sure, but he is unsure how many other friends he can bring. At least he is willing to try to collect others. From our side, we are trying to see (a) how sincere he really is, (b) if he could be a person of peace who brings others with him, (c) if the locus of the meeting can be in his home (not ours) which is a more natural bridge to a home church, and (d) if a corporate approach to conversion can be more sustainable for those who convert. While they are not Narnian Muslims (some are Sudanese Muslims, some Eritrean, etc.), they are still lost and precious to Jesus. It also gives us a chance to grow in our church planting approaches, to see what is possible and fruitful. We can then apply the principles to Narnians we encounter as well.

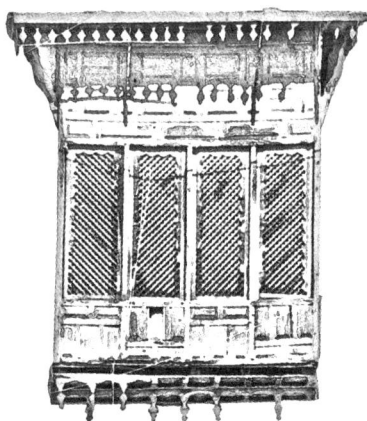

THE NOT-SO-GOOD METHOD OF CHURCH PLANTING

BY ROLAND MULLER [8]

Over the years I have tried to describe the church planting method that I and many others use but have failed to come up with a good description until now. I have called it the Not-So-Good method because it does not require an outstanding missionary, nor outstanding local leaders, nor wonderful converts. Rather, anyone, even the not-so-good missionaries can use this.

This method was developed because I was a not-so-good missionary. I struggled with the language, the culture, and personal issues in my life, such as timidity and uncertainty. But God kept pressing me that I should be involved in planting churches. So, as a not-so-good missionary, I looked around for a local person to work with. God in his infinite wisdom has never had a perfect local leader for me to work with so I have always ended up working with not-so-good people.

I have never had wonderful tools and materials to use either, so I have had to settle for some not-so-good tools. I now recommend the Discovery Lessons and the Discipleship Lessons by Abdallah Hawatmeh, available from my website, but you can use any other materials that God leads you to.

In this method, the not-so-good missionary asks the not-so-good local if he could teach him some lessons, and then the local will be available to teach others. I call him the teacher, but for goodness' sake don't tell him he is a teacher, because he may get a swelled head, especially if he is the not-so-good kind that God has always directs me to.

In this method, the missionary teaches the local teacher the lesson and then the local teacher teaches the lessons back to the missionary, to make sure that he knows them well and can teach others. If he really is a not-so-good teacher, get him to teach other missionaries as well. Then, start looking for people to teach. God usually led me to not-so-good people. Most of them had struggles and problems, sometimes outright issues, terrible issues, to deal with. But I am a not-so-good missionary, with a not-so-good teacher, so I accept not-so-good contacts.

In my book *The Messenger, the Message and the Community*, I share six steps to spiritually maturity. We usually start with Not Interested people which we hope will become Somewhat Interested people and eventually Seekers. I use stories, proverbs, incidental chats, and prayer to move them along. I like to call this Crummy Evangelism.

It's like catching squirrels. First you put out a few crumbs and stand a long ways away hoping the squirrel takes them while you watch. The next day you do it again, only a little closer, and bit by bit, day by day, you put out the crumbs until one day, hopefully, the squirrel eats right out of your hand. So we use Crummy Evangelism. We drop spiritual crumbs into our conversations and bit by bit move people along from being not interested to somewhat interested to being seekers. Then we ask them if they would like to have someone really explain what Christianity is all about; a local person. He can do it in a few hours. He is a teacher who can do a lot better job than we can because our language is poor and we are foreigners. After suggesting this several times, someone may eventually agree to meet the teacher. That is when I call in the not-so-good teacher who by this time should have also taken the discipleship lessons and had an opportunity to teach them back to us.

After connecting the new seeker with the teacher, I step out of the situation and pray for them while they meet. I do not attend. After all, I am only a church planter, not a pastor, and since I am a not-so-good missionary I don't even bother to attend the first meeting, nor the second, nor any of them. At the same time, I start gathering a few other not-so-good missionaries to help me. We meet with lots of people during the week and using Crummy Evangelism we urge them along until they show signs of being a seeker. Then we connect them to the teacher. It isn't long until the teacher is teaching some people the evangelism lessons, and some the discipleship lessons.

We continue to encourage the teacher, and pour our lives into him, but we don't bother to attend the new church. By this time the teacher will be very busy. He has led a number of people to the Lord, and we encourage him to start meeting with them regularly, to figure out which ones he should baptize, and to start breaking bread with them. Without knowing it, our not-so-good teacher has just graduated to not-so-good pastor.

When the teacher gets overloaded with people and ministry, we encourage him to choose one of the new believers and get him to help teach the lessons. This person doesn't have to be perfect; he can be not-so-good just like the rest of us. Once we have a second teacher, we start to send seekers to him. Soon we have two groups, then three and so on. Since we are not-so-good foreign church planters, we all end up leaving at some point, and the groups continue on their own, without missing us, since we never bothered to come to any of the meetings.

The amazing thing is this: God seems to enjoy transforming not-so-good teachers and not-so-good converts. Our only fear is that someday they may think they are really good teachers and stop training not-so-good people to teach the lessons. That would be terrible because good missionaries and good pastors always look for good leaders and good unbelievers to witness to, and these are very hard to find. So, if you cannot find good leaders, just settle for not-so-good people and get them doing Crummy Evangelism and using the Not-So-Good church planting method and see what happens.

PURSUING JESUS:

L et us sing, let us shout, let us thank (Psalm 95:1–2). Let us worship and bow down and kneel, for He is our God and we are the people of His pasture, the sheep of His hand (vv. 6–7). Oh, thank you, Jesus, that You tenderly care for us and lead us. Today, I want to sing, shout, thank, worship, bow down, and kneel in Your wonderful presence.

Thank you, Father, that Your Spirit still brings amazing things to life (Matt. 1:18). Help me not to be afraid of that which is conceived by the Holy Spirit (v. 20). Thank you, Jesus, that You save from sin by saving us from the wrath of God (v. 21). Let me never lose the wonder and the tremble joy of salvation. Let me never lose awe that God is with us (v. 23). In light of these wonders, let me awake, rise up, and do what God commands (v. 24), even if it does not seem right to others.

Lord, as I show my love to You through obedience, as I seek unity with brothers and sisters in Christ (Acts 2:1), would You send Your mighty Spirit from heaven (v. 2)? Let it fill the whole household of God so that all are filled with the Holy Spirit and begin to speak as the Holy Spirit gives them utterance (v. 2, 4). Let us remember that others will react with confusion, bewilderment, astonishment, amazement, perplexity, and even mocking (vv. 6–7,12, 13). In our preaching of Jesus, let us remember that even as He was delivered over (to be abused and killed) by the predetermined plan and foreknowledge of God (v. 25) so shall we be. And as God raised Him (v. 24), since it is impossible for God to be held in death's power, so shall we be raised on the last day. In between then and now, thank you, Lord, that because of the presence of Jesus and His standing at the right hand of the Father (v. 25), we will not be shaken. Let us like David look ahead and speak of Christ

(v. 31), but this time Christ coming in glory. When Jesus is exalted, the Holy Spirit is poured out, and when the Holy Spirit is poured out, He exalts Jesus as *Lord* and *Christ* (v. 36). When Jesus is exalted as Lord and Christ, the church is characterized by: repentance, teaching, fellowship, breaking bread, prayer, a sense of awe, signs and wonders, community and sharing, meeting daily in the temple and house to house, being glad and sincere, and praising God, having favor, and multiplying daily (vv. 41–47). Jesus, as we seek to plant the church, let us keep these essential components in mind and in praxis.

Thank you for others of like precious faith (2 Peter 1:1) that we are able to fellowship with. Thank you that *Your* divine power has granted to us everything pertaining to life and godliness *through* the knowledge of Him who called us by His own glory and excellence (vv. 2–3). Jesus, it is by knowing You that we have access to divine power, that we are granted Your precious and magnificent promises (v. 4). God, You are indeed the *majestic glory* who adores Your beloved Son, well pleased in Him (v. 17). Thank you, Father, that the pleasures we enjoy in You are shared pleasures, for You are so gloriously beautiful that You take great pleasure in Yourself and invite us into that bliss.

PURSUING CHURCH PLANTING:

Yesterday after abiding and language, I met with Thomas, the Narnian businessman who offered a partnership in a tourist company he wants to start. Narnia has a vision plan which includes the hope to have five million Christian tourists in Narnia over the next 10 years (according to one Christian brother). It may be timely to engage in the tourist sector. We had a good talk and need to investigate what a collaboration with him looks like. I also want to review again the possibility of starting our own Narnian tour company that we completely own and run. We need prayer and discernment as to what will give us the most visas, access, and gospel opportunity without demanding inordinate time that does not lead to gospel proclamation. There are many unknowns and we need the help of the Spirit.

I also looked at a large villa (a duplex) that might be suitable for us to live in if the missionary community would be served by us having a larger house that can host meetings while providing child-care. The arrangement of that house can work, but there may also be better options (in terms of space and flow). We will continue to look and pray.

PURSUING JESUS:

Thank you, Jesus, for the robust reminder from the Psalms that You are focused on all the earth singing to You (Psalm 96:1). Let me be faithful to tell of Your glory among the nations and Your wonderful deeds among all the peoples (v. 3). Jesus, I exult in Your splendor, majesty, strength, and beauty (v. 6). I join my voice to the psalmist in invitation: "Ascribe to the Lord, families of peoples… glory and strength…. Tremble before Him, all the earth" (vv. 7, 9). Lord, You command it. Let us in strength relay what the Lord commands. Let me faithfully say among the nations that *the Lord reigns* (v. 10) and that He will judge all peoples with equity and faithfulness (v. 13).

Thank you, Jesus, that You are a ruler who shepherds (Matt. 2:6). Let me lead in the same spirit. Thank you, Jesus, that You lead and warn, sometimes through dreams (vv. 12, 19, 22). Teach me, Jesus, to be sensitive to Your Holy Spirit and to ever heed Your counsel. Thank you, Father, that You have glorified Jesus (Acts 3:13) whom I deliver up and disown. Lord, I am ashamed for my many betrayals, for putting to death the Prince of life whom God raised from the dead (v. 15). Help me today to glorify You, and whatever happens point out that "it is the name of Jesus which has strengthened this man" (v. 16). Let me remember that You have decreed and announced that the Christ would suffer (v. 18); thus, let me expect it, endure it, and "enjoy" it in the sense that Your joy gives grace no matter what happens. Let me live and preach: Repent and return, that times of refreshing may come from the presence of the Lord (v. 19). Lord, how I long for times of refreshing from Your presence. I do repent of all in me that has walked away from that. I turn my heart to You, Jesus; help me run, seek, long and pursue Your presence, that You may send Jesus, appointed for the restoration of all things (vv. 20–21). Come to me, Lord Jesus, now, today with Your sweet presence. Come to us, Lord Jesus; physically come again to rule and reign in glory forever. Let me carry the sobriety daily that when You come, every soul that has not heeded You will be utterly destroyed (v. 23).

To deny Jesus is to bring swift destruction on ourselves (2 Peter 2:1). Jesus, help me not deny You in any little or private way. Thank you that You know how to rescue the godly from temptation and to keep the unrighteous under punishment for the day of judgment (v. 9). Lord, there are these twin passions that You alone can reconcile and harmonize: the sweet joy of Your presence in intimate and personal ways, and the tremble joy of Your presence in awe-filled wonder at the God of holiness who will judge and punish all the earth *because* He is love and good and true. Let me have no delusion about doing wrong and its consequences (v. 13). You cannot be mocked, and I don't fool You. Lord, save me from fooling myself. I only want to be overcome and enslaved to You (v. 19) who are holy and good. It is my only hope for good. Lord, let no other master have any power over me.

Pursuing Church Planting:

Church planting in Narnia is living the dream. And dreams tend to be unpredictable. We learned two nights ago that the way to find apartments is to drive around at night and look for the apartments that have lights on in every empty room. We found such a place and the watchman let us in. As we entered the flat, a young

Narnian woman in the flat next door poked her head out of her apartment to give the watchman some instructions. Seeing us, she insisted we come into her flat to see it and her husband, gushing that she hoped we would become neighbors. Her head was not covered, and neither was much else, as negligees don't tend to be super discreet. Jennifer was wearing the black robe and this young Narnian woman was wearing next to nothing as she ushered us into her apartment; she slipped on a robe and showed us every room of her house, including her bedroom-size closet. She and her husband were friendly, gregarious, and as warm and personable as my Greek family. A little dazed we toured their flat, said thanks to our new friends, and moved on. The husband asked what I did for work and I explained that I am a pastor, sent by the church, and that we will bring Christians and church groups to Narnia for cultural and religious education. He smiled brightly and said, "Well, Narnia is sure changing!"

It is changing indeed—and polarizing around the change. The young, modern Narnians are very different in perspective from the older generation. Many have studied abroad and have brought home a much more tolerant and open-minded worldview. Currently, the changes are rapid and disconcerting to half the population and invigorating to the other. It is a season of great opportunity, but also of great challenge. I feel the need to pray for the leaders of this country more than ever, that God would use them for His glory and give them great wisdom in how they implement change. Liberalized Muslims are not necessarily Muslims more open to the gospel. It can make conversations easier in some cases, but the devil was at work long before Islam, and materialism and secularism are as binding a tyrant as a legalistic religion. I sense we need prayer more now than ever.

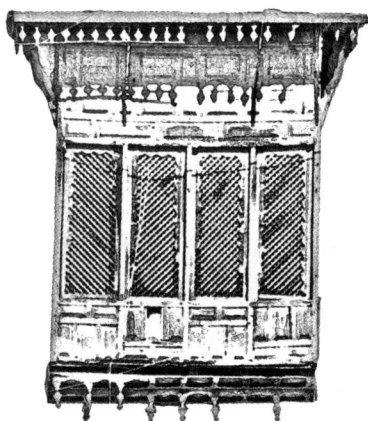

SINS OF THE SONS

David was the great king of Israel. Stunningly listed as a man after God's own heart, he bore sons who were the devil's own. How did such a good-hearted (though human and sinful) king give place to such poor-hearted seed? More importantly, what evil seeds are we planting within ourselves, seeds that, according to the inviolate laws of harvest, will one day bear fruit?

DISCONTENTED AMNON

The Fruit

"Then Amnon hated her [Tamar] with very great hatred, so *that the hatred with which he hated her was greater than the love with which he had loved her.* And Amnon said to her 'Get up! Go!'" (2 Sam. 13:15 ESV, emphasis added)

The Seed

The fulfilment for which we long can become a curse to us. In Amnon's case he longed for fulfilment through sexual possession of a beautiful woman, but we can lust for many things including position, power, influence, and title. The seed in Amnon was that he was discontent with his lot, he wanted something that was not his to have—at least not in the way he wanted it.

We recognize sexual lust as horrific and destroying. Do we have the same horror when we are discontent with our level of leadership and influence? We can long for more authority, status, responsibility, and control. When we go about getting it in sinful and inappropriate ways, we end up hating it more than we thought we loved it, and in the end it leads to our death.

The fruit of Amnon's discontentment was rape, hate, and ultimately death. Our discontent will lead us down just as damaging paths. Let us be horrified when we sense positional lust in us. Let us repent of it and choose to be thankful and content with where God has us.

THIEVING ABSALOM

The Fruit

"After this Absalom got himself a chariot and horses, and fifty men to run before him. And Absalom used to rise early and stand beside the way of the gate. And when any man had a dispute to come before the king for judgment, Absalom would call to him and say, 'From what city are you?' And when he said, 'Your servant is of such and such a tribe in Israel,' Absalom would say to him, 'See, your claims are good and right, but there is no man designated by the king to hear you.' Then Absalom would say, 'Oh that I were judge in the land! Then every man with a dispute or cause might come to me, and I would give him justice.' And whenever a man came near to pay homage to him, he would put out his hand and take hold of him and kiss him.

Thus Absalom did to all of Israel who came to the king for judgment. So ***Absalom stole the hearts of the men of Israel.***" (2 Sam. 15:1–6 ESV, emphasis added)

The Seed

We can observe many negative things about Absalom: his long burning hate for his brother that ended in scheming murder; his crafty way of dealing with Joab; and his pride and self-promotion. But what is most alarming to me is his "stealing the hearts" of good men away from their rightful king.

An orderly in the military is supposed to make the soldiers he leads *more* loyal to the authority in place—not more loyal to himself. Do we make our followers more loyal to our leaders or more loyal to ourselves? Do we make our disciples more loyal to Jesus or more loyal to us? Absalom sat at the gate, charmed and wooed the populace, and sighed and said, "If I was king, you would be happier." The reality was that when the thief becomes king, no one is better off.

We must be vigilant against our own thieving hearts. The sin within us wants to steal the authority of those that lead us by stealing the affections of their followers. The pride within us wants to steal the glory that goes to God alone by taking credit (even if in a supporting role) for the acts of heaven. There is but one fruit for the thief—grief for all, including himself. Stealing leaves you hanging with javelins through your heart.

SNEAKY ADONIJAH

The Fruit

"[Adonijah] said [to Bathsheba], 'You know that the kingdom was mine, and that all Israel fully expected me to reign. However, the kingdom has turned about and become my brother's, for it was his from the Lord. ***And now I have one request to make of you; do not refuse me.'***

She said to him, 'Speak.' And he said, 'Please ask King Solomon—he will not refuse you—to give me Abishag the Shunammite as my wife.' King Solomon answered his mother, 'And why do you ask Abishag the Shunammite for Adonijah? Ask for him the kingdom also, for he is my older brother, and on his side are Abiathar the priest and Joab the son of Zeruiah.' Then King Solomon swore by the Lord, saying, 'God do so to me and more also if this word does not cost Adonijah his life!'" (1 Kings 2:15–17; 22–23 ESV, emphasis added)

The Seed

Adonijah declared himself king, which didn't work out so well. Wise enough to see he lost the first round to Solomon, he bided his time and then sneakily asked Bathsheba to procure Abishag for him. He didn't want Abishag. He wanted the kingdom. And this was his sneaky plan to establish a claim—hollow as it was. Adonijah fooled Bathsheba, a good woman, a woman wise to the twists and turns of palace life, a woman with her own scars and secrets, but he did not fool the king.

The conniving often fool themselves first. We convince ourselves that we are innocent and harmless, but with little words, postures, actions, hesitations, nuances, smirks, and shrugs, we are actually sneakily positioning ourselves for takeover. Adonijah ended up losing his head, but first he lost his honesty—self-honesty and honesty before others. There is nothing holy about being sneaky. The fruit of sneakiness is self-deception. A web of half-truths and clever exaggerations make you first lose your sight, then your way, then ultimately your head. Next, the conniving fool good people. They play on pity. They take advantage of the goodness or kindness in others. The empathy of good people does not automatically verify a pure heart.

We all craft our image. We all try to present ourselves at times as something we are not or as better than we are. We all protest innocence and claim the moral high ground. This is not a harmless seed. It leads to deceit and death. When we connive, we speak against our own life.

INSECURE REHOBOAM

The Fruit

"Then King Rehoboam took counsel with the old men, who had stood before Solomon his father while he was yet alive, saying, 'How do you advise me to answer this people?' And they said to him, 'If you will be a servant to this people today and serve them, and speak good words to them when you answer them, then they will be your servants forever.' But **he abandoned the counsel that the old men gave him and took counsel with the young men** who had grown up with him and stood before him." (1 Kings 12:6–8 ESV, emphasis added)

The Seed

It can be unsettling to lead those smarter and more experienced than we are. It can be tempting to want to be different from our predecessors, fathers, and colleagues, and in pursuing that distinction we can cause more harm than good. It is far too easy to notice what others have done wrong and think that we will easily improve on them. In Rehoboam's case insecurity drove him to be harsher than his father when wisdom called for being gentler. Afraid of being thought weak, Rehoboam cut his own legs out from under him and lost half the kingdom. He spurned the counsel of his father's counselors because he thought he had to prove himself strong and forceful, stronger and more forceful than his notable predecessor.

Insecurity is afraid that something will be lost if we do not dramatically distinguish ourselves from those that go before us, whereas security realizes that gentleness can make us stronger, that we don't have to be different to be noticed. Security is patient, it allows our God-given uniqueness to be demonstrated by time and does not force or rush a distinctive unduly.

The fruit of insecurity is always loss. When we try to grab prestige and commendation, it eludes us. Insecurity is not harmless; it is ruthless. Insecurity makes us act strong, while security makes us act kindly. Insecure leaders cause greater damage to their followers than incompetent ones.

GREEDY, UNACCOUNTABLE SOLOMON

The Fruit

"Now *King Solomon loved many foreign women*, along with the daughter of Pharaoh: Moabite, Ammonite, Edomite, Sidonian, and Hittite women, from the nations concerning which the Lord had said to the people of Israel, '*You shall not enter into marriage with them, neither shall they with you, for surely they will turn away your heart after their gods.*' Solomon clung to these in love. He had 700 wives, who were princesses, and 300 concubines. And his wives turned away his heart. For when Solomon was old, *his wives turned away his heart after other gods, and his heart was not wholly true to the Lord his God, as was the heart of David his father.* For Solomon went after Ashtoreth the goddess of the Sidonians, and after Milcom the abomination of the Ammonites. So *Solomon did what was evil in the sight of the Lord* and did not wholly follow the Lord, as David his father had done." (1 Kings 11:1–6 ESV, emphasis added)

The Seed

There is sad irony in the man who had and knew everything (wisdom, riches, honor, and power) not being satisfied with what he possessed. The kings were warned not to import chariots or women from Egypt and beyond, but Solomon imported both in great numbers. The import of multiple wives and concubines was Solomon's undoing, for they brought with them their idols. Ultimately, these women turned not only his head but his heart.

I imagine Solomon's pursuit of knowledge included curiosity about the cultures and customs of the nations which supplied his harem. I presume that that insatiable curiosity (unbounded as it was, greedy for more) was a slippery path to improper thoughts, experiments, and ultimately worship. It was Solomon's intelligence combined with his appetite that led him to rationalize what he knew to be wrong and twist it somehow into cleverly seeming right.

What prophet or priest could argue with Solomon? Who could hold a candle to his discernment, insight, intelligence, and acumen? Who then could challenge him, hold him accountable, or push back when wisdom began to decay into sophistry, when much learning began to drive him mad? Having too many women in his life and none that he adored uniquely and cherished solely, who indeed could restrain or even caution his racing mind?

How rare and pure is the one man–one woman romance of Isaac and Rebecca, and how convoluted and painful is every record of polygamy in the Old Testament. What would Solomon's end have been if he had married one woman and that woman was simple, pure, and godly? What if Solomon had one Jehovah-fearing wife, a wife that he respected, honored, and listened to? The seed was greed and lack of accountability, and the fruit was an evil of stupidity. At the end of his life the wisest man of history made the most foolish of mistakes.

PURSUING JESUS:

The Lord reigns; let the earth rejoice (Psalm 97:1). It is good for us all that the Lord rules; but let us be clear what that means. Clouds and thick darkness surround Him; He is so wise that there are things about Him we will never understand, yet we can rest knowing that all He does is right and just (v. 2). The goodness of God to every level means that the mountains will melt like wax at the presence of the Lord and the heavens will declare His righteousness while all peoples see His glory (vv. 5–6). Judgment is a revelation of glory! For the Lord is most high over *all* the earth and light is sown like seed for the righteous (vv. 9–11).

Wrath is coming (Matt. 3:7); therefore, we must repent and reform (v. 8). The axe is laid at the root of the tree, and every tree that does not bear good fruit is cut down and thrown into the fire (v. 10). Jesus will baptize us with the Holy Spirit and fire, and He will winnow and thresh us thoroughly and He will burn up the chaff with unquenchable fire (vv. 11–12). Lord, I both desire Your cleansing flame and tremble.

Therefore, let me be faithful to teach and proclaim Jesus as God, the God who is coming to judge the heavens and the earth, and let me do so knowing it has ever been problematic (Acts 4:2). Let me be filled with the Holy Spirit and speak about Jesus as the chief cornerstone, for salvation is found in no one else (vv. 8, 11–12). Can anyone recognize that I have been with Jesus (v. 13)? Does the fire burn within me so that I cannot stop speaking about what we have seen and heard (v. 20)? What was done to Jesus was whatever God's purposes predestined (v. 28); so shall it be for me. Grant then, Jesus, that I may speak Your word with all confidence while *You* extend Your hand to heal with signs and wonders (vv. 29–30). Lord, we are desperate for our own

Pentecost. We must pray in order to be shaken and filled with the Holy Spirit, that we might speak the word of God boldly and with great power give testimony to the divinity of Jesus (vv. 31–33).

Lord, send this burning flame, this fire of the Holy Spirit, always reminding us that by Your word the heavens and earth are being reserved for fire, kept for the day of judgment and destruction of ungodly men (2 Peter 3:7). Let me not forget that the heavens will pass away with a roar and the elements destroyed with a fervent heat, and the earth and *all its works* will be burned up, all these things destroyed by fire, the heavens burning and the elements melting in the intense heat, in order that there be new heavens and a new earth (vv. 10–13). In the light of this fire, Jesus, let me not fall from steadfastness, but let me grow in grace and the knowledge of Jesus (vv. 17–18). To Him be the glory; from Him comes the fire.

PURSUING CHURCH PLANTING:

After abiding and language study yesterday, we had our first team leaders meeting. There were four TLs represented from four different organizations, and it was good to gather together. The partnership here has been sweet, and we want to add value as best we can. TLs have not been meeting as they are all busy, so we offered to help give a little more coordinating support to the partnership that is focused on planting churches among Narnians and other Arab Muslims in country. We are asking the Lord to show us how to serve the community best.

I proposed an annual rhythm with a men's meeting one month, then a ladies' meeting the next month, then an all partnership meeting the third month, then repeat this cycle four times in the year (except summers). This would give the men a chance to bond, the ladies a chance to bond, then the whole group come together for prayer and CP training, etc. Then for a weekly schedule I proposed one day a week be a partnership day: week 1 as a date night and kids club (young families drop their kids at our house and then go on a date or do EV or a visit together); week 2, a prayer meeting at our house; week 3, date night/kids club; and week 4, the TL meeting. The TLs were glad that we (empty nesters now) have the energy to host and coordinate something like this, and so now we are looking at which day of the week is the best day (many in the Arabian Peninsula have full-time jobs) and when is the best time on the calendar for the monthly events.

Following the TL meeting I met with a man who our language teacher told us about. He arrived fashionably late (45 minutes), and we shared a nice meal with his 21-year-old son. His son has lived in Ireland for the last 11 years and speaks with an impeccable Irish brogue. Our conversation was partly in Arabic, English, and Irish-English. This gentleman is quite senior in the Hashemite family; in fact, his father had 32 wives and was the uncle to King Hussein in Jordan. This new friend is in his late 60s and is very kind. He is some kind of tribal chief for Hashemite clans around the world. The family is introduced with the title "Sharif" as they are descended from the uncle of Mohammed and used to be the guardians of the two holy sites before moving to Jordan and Iraq due to the ascension of the Saud family in Arabia.

At one point the young man said to me, "When I first got your text, I thought you were a missionary!" I asked him, "And what do you think a missionary is?" He said, "You know, like St. Patrick who came to Ireland and built a church." I said, "Yes, indeed I am a missionary. But that does not mean I coerce anyone to leave their faith, or pay children to follow my faith, or deceive anyone in anyway. Being a missionary means that I love Muslims so much I tell them about how their sins can be forgiven and how they can have eternal life in heaven. I have a different view than what Islam teaches of how that must happen, but I present my view openly and respectfully because I love Muslims so much. If I really love you, I must share with you how you may receive eternal life. In fact, it is kind of like if you had AIDS and I knew the cure for AIDS, and I told you I respected you and loved you, but never shared the cure for AIDS that I had learned about. Well, that would *not* be love." We had a very interesting conversation and the father said, "You are a Christian missionary and I am a Muslim missionary. No problem. It is like we are playing a football match and the fans watching decide who they will support."

We had a most pleasant and interesting evening. I asked the older man if he had a Bible. He said he had one long ago and lost it. I asked him if he would like a Bible. He said yes. I asked if he would like an Arabic Bible and his eyes lit up. I had one in my car, nicely wrapped as a gift, so at the end of the evening, we walked to the car and I gave him the Bible and promised him that if he had any questions, I would be happy to explain. He also agreed to receive and speak to any Christian tourists we bring to the country and asked to stay in touch. His son is a scuba diver like my sons, Luke and Zack, so we agreed to go diving together when my boys visit in December. Living the dream!

DAY 39

PURSUING JESUS:

I will sing, for Jesus has done wonderful things and gained the victory (Psalm 98:1). He has made known His salvation and revealed His righteousness to the nations (v. 2). He has remembered His lovingkindness and faithfulness to the ends of the earth (v. 3). Let me shout joyfully, break forth, sing, praise, roar, and clap for the Lord is coming to judge (vv. 4–8). Let my whole being erupt in physical demonstration of the joy, hope, expectation, and longing for Jesus to come again in glory and power on that great and terrible (awesome) day.

Let me never lose sight of the deity of Jesus, nor lose awe for the majesty of His person and presence. In Matthew 4, Jesus responds to the temptations of Satan by hammering away on His own divinity. When Jesus said, "Man shall not live by bread alone, but on every word that proceeds from the mouth of God" (v. 3), He was in effect rebuking Satan: *"I am God. I give food. I don't need it!"* When Jesus said, "You shall not put the Lord your God the test" (v.7), He was in fact saying: *"Satan, I am your God! How dare you put me in the dock."* When Jesus said, "You shall worship the Lord Your God and serve Him only" (v. 10), He was thundering out to Satan, all demons, and every people everywhere: *"Worship you? Anathema! I am God! You shall worship Me! You shall serve Me!"* Jesus, let me every carry in my spirit the realty that *You* are very God of very God.

It is never appropriate to test God; when we do, the consequences are fatal (Acts 5:9). Great fear of the Lord (v. 11) keeps us from His great wrath and judgment. Fear is always a factor ("none dared associate with them," v. 13). The question is, who we will fear more? God or man? God tells us to "go, stand, speak to the people the whole message of this life" (v. 20) and to fill the city with teaching *despite* orders from the officials not to, for we must obey God (vv. 28–29). Lord, let our obedience constantly exalt Jesus, the One exalted to forgive (v. 31). Let us rejoice when our obedience counts us worthy to suffer for His name as we proclaim Jesus in public and private every day, as we keep right on teaching and preaching (vv. 41–42).

Then the life of Jesus will be manifested (1 John 1:2) as we proclaim what we have heard and seen of Him (v. 3). Nothing must be deceptive as God is light, and in Him there is no darkness at all (v. 5). If we will walk in His light, we will have both fellowship and forgiveness (v. 7). He is our guarantee.

Pursuing Church Planting:

Yesterday we enjoyed a restful morning and worship with the international house church. In the afternoon we looked at different apartments. We are trying to find something in local Narnian community with enough space to host prayer meetings (with childcare room) and partnership events. In the afternoon we did some correspondence and a conference call.

Jennifer and I have been talking through and praying through identity here in context. God has made her a peacemaker and me a fighter. This can cause tension—not in fighting one another so much as in when Jesus calls me to fight for something for Him, Jennifer has to share the repercussions. In the Narnian context, I feel the Lord has asked me to have a clearly church-related and pastoral identity. This is somewhat new, though it is actually old. As such our presence here in country is a bit of a concern to other missionaries as they feel our online presence and overt identity as church planters in the Muslim world jeopardizes them.

I feel a conviction to follow what Jesus has put on my heart (bold and open church/pastor identity and function). The danger for me as a fighter is that I do that in the flesh from wrong motives in a pugilistic manner. The danger for Jennifer is that in not wanting to offend any other worker, to please them and make peace, she asks or desires me to act in a way counter to my conscience. These are tricky waters as our personalities are different and we both can err in our own ways (me looking for a fight when I shouldn't and she wanting to avoid a fight when she shouldn't). On the positive side, we both recognize our weakness. We are talking through the challenges and are praying and asking Jesus to help us. We want to be obedient, not just in the act, but also the timing and manner of the act. Jesus, help us!

DAY 40

PURSUING JESUS:

The Lord reigns; let the peoples tremble (Psalm 99:1). Jesus, awe of You is so precious and it's what makes intimacy and friendship so sweet. Let me not lose a sense of awe. Let me ever tremble in Your presence. Let me ever see Your greatness (v. 2), that You are exalted above all, that all the peoples (including me!) would praise (v. 3). Jesus, I want to exalt You and worship at Your footstool (v. 5), trembling because You both forgive and avenge sin (v. 8). Holy are You, O Lord God of hosts.

If I am insulted, let it only be because You are insulted (Matt. 5:11), because I was faithful to You, spoke like You, thought like You, acted like You, and was rejected like You. Jesus, help me not to lose my saltiness, help me to shine in such a way that God is glorified (vv. 13, 16). My little light is very insignificant and flickering. Help me to both keep and teach the commandments (v. 19), help me to teach by keeping. Tear out and throw from me anything that makes me (or others) stumble and that does not make You glad (v. 29). Keep my words simple and far from the evil of excess or exaggeration (v. 37). Let me deeply love my enemies as I see them with Your eyes. Let me pray for those who persecute me (v. 44) as well as for those who wound me from within Your house. Make me like You, Father, never forgetting that Your standard is perfect, complete (v. 48).

Complaints are normal in the ministry (Acts 6:1). Jesus, give me the emotional fortitude to embrace the difficult situations, the conflicts large and small, so that the word of God can spread and Jesus can be magnified (v. 7). Help me to arrange my practical life so that I can devote myself to prayer and to the ministry of the Word (v. 4). Grant, Lord, wisdom by the Spirit in all my speaking and writing; grant that my face would shine (v. 15) because the fount of all my words is the reality of just having You.

Thank you, Lord, that when I fall short in all the above (I am not perfect, my face does not shine, I do not pray), I have an advocate (1 John 2:1). Let me not abuse that grace; rather, teach my love for You to be perfected in obedience by loving my brothers in Christ, abiding in the light so there is no cause for stumbling (vv. 5, 10). Thank you that all my sins are forgiven *for Jesus'* sake (v. 12). I have no merit or goodness, but the Father looks on the Son and not at me and gives me the good of the Son. Oh, what wonder! As a response, let me not love the world that passes away, but let me see that it is the last hour (vv. 15, 17–18). Thank you that the anointing of God is given to the community and we can *all* know the way forward as You teach *us* all things (vv. 20, 27). Let me not arrogantly isolate from the wisdom and anointing of God that is found in the collective body of Christ. Let me humbly learn and submit to others. Let no antichrist spirit (denying the Father and Son) infect my soul. Let me stay clear-minded about the essence of all religion that denies the trinity. I rest (in my earthly fatigue) in the knowledge that You have promised me *eternal life*; thus, let me abide in You confident of Your appearing (vv. 25, 28).

Pursuing Church Planting:

Jennifer and I are enjoying getting to know God's team here in country, and we had a lovely brunch with a young couple who have been here two years. They have two boys as we do, and their parenting stress brought back fond memories of those challenging yet marvelous years. It is our prayer to Jesus that our boys (who were born and raised in the Islamic context) would deepen and mature in Jesus, free from all besetting sins and consecrated to His glory for His purposes in the earth, first, for Him, and second to encourage other families that it can be done, that families can be brought to and into the Muslim world and survive and thrive for the glory of Jesus. The enemy uses many tricks to discourage us, including attacking the family. As part of our contribution to church planting here and to family health and joy, Jennifer and I want to host a kids' club for missionary kids two days each month. Parents can drop their kids off and then go out for a date or a visit, or to evangelize, minister, or just take a nap. Healthy church planters need a healthy family life. We are at a place (empty nest) where we have more time than young parents, and as a TCK (third culture kid) myself, plus Jennifer's great love for children, we also derive great joy from blessing TCKs. That's also why I send out children's songs by video to the young TCKs every other day or so. Many future missionaries will arise from these little ankle biters. Serving TCKs is an investment in the future of missions.

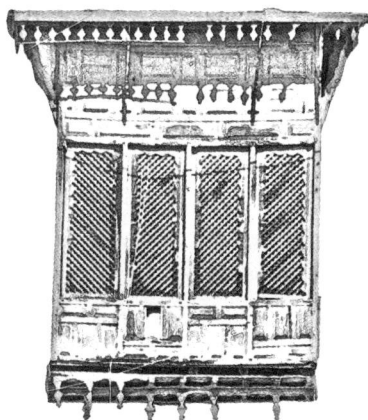

IN TIMES LIKE THESE

"For God has not given us a spirit of fear,
but of power and of love and of a sound mind."

(2 TIMOTHY 1:7)

On January 27, 2019, security police arrested a colleague in one of our challenging Live Dead locations in Africa. Per protocol his wife left the country.[9] Prayer networks were immediately activated as were advocacy efforts through different government and human/religious rights partners. AGWM leadership coordinated our response in communication with the AG General Council leaders. Events like this will likely be repeated in the days ahead—other colleagues in other contexts—and in these moments we can remember who God is, what our assignment is, and how we go forward in joy.

GOD HAS NOT GIVEN US A SPIRIT OF FEAR

We are not ashamed of the gospel. We realize that the goal is not to be loved, that we will be hated (Matt. 24:9). Likewise, we affirm that the goal is not to be hated, provocative, inflammatory, or abrasive; the goal is to be faithful messengers of the gospel. Wherever the gospel advances, it will meet both faith and fear. Some will respond in faith and others in fear of losing their place and power. The devil himself is terrified of the presence of Jesus and the losing of his long-held territory. We refuse to allow that fearful spirit into our thinking, planning, or obedience. We commit to continuing to send missionaries to difficult places. We commit to being at peace when they are imprisoned or worse. We commit to being fearless, bold, courageous, and risk-oriented. Imprison our friends and our response will be to send more just like them. Kill our colleagues and we will leap to life in sending their brothers and sisters, sons and daughters. We will not be shaken from our obedience to send God's messengers to the most difficult and dangerous places of earth. We fear Jesus most. He is worthy of all.

GOD HAS GIVEN US A SPIRIT OF POWER

When under pressure or persecution, we are not averse to appropriate diplomatic and advocacy pressure, but our hope is not in governments or earthly powers. When our colleagues suffer, we know our power is in prayer and praise. Our power is in the God who rules over the kingdoms of men. Our power is in falling on our knees and asking the omnipotent One to change the heart of kings and to manifest His glory. It is God who opens prison doors. It is God who strikes off the shackles. It is God who gives us a voice to sing out praise in prison nights. We resolutely commit ourselves to trust first in the wisdom, strength, and power of Jehovah. The weapons of our warfare are not carnal, coercive, political, or financial, but they are mighty in the Holy Ghost. God has given us the power to stand behind barred windows and sing out into the prison courtyard and into the spirit realm:

In times like these I have a Savior
In times like these I have an anchor
I'm very sure, I'm very sure
My anchor holds and grips the solid rock
This rock is Jesus, yes, He's the One
This rock is Jesus, the only One
I'm very sure, I'm very sure
My anchor holds and grips the solid rock[10]

GOD HAS GIVEN US A SPIRIT OF LOVE

The love of God compels us, not our love. Our love is finite. In times of duress we must be intentional not to demonize people or persecutors. God grants the ability to see those who harm and threaten us as frightened slaves, deceived by false religion and under the lash of demonic power. Our prayer for our colleagues in prison is that they would see the walls of their cells as reminders of love, reminders that those who resist the gospel are deceived and bound by the devil, reminders that the God of all nations and all peoples has a love that will burst through all walls of restraint and overcome all lies. Let us convict and confound those who resist us by showering on them smiles, joy, prayers, grace, compassion, and witness. Let us not depend on our love, rather let the love of God compel us. Let us receive and pass on His love, even in duress—especially in duress. In the New Testament the best sermons and proclamations were uttered from prison or before tribunals. The gospel has ever gone forth under pressure. The love of God gives us the compulsion, even in prison and persecution, to publish glad tidings. Prison magnifies proclamation; it does not silence it.

GOD HAS GIVEN US A SPIRIT OF A SOUND MIND

Fearlessness, power, and love are not to be equated with foolishness. God did not give us a spirit of power, love, *and a cavalier mind*. He did not give us a reactionary mind. He did not give us a short-term mind. God has given us the ability to have a thoughtful, disciplined missiology that does not panic and thinks long term for the good of the gospel and the indigenous church. A clear-thinking, disciplined mind does not take unnecessary risks and does not make reactionary decisions that affect long-term fruitfulness. If God's purposes are served by our people spending more time in prison, then a sound mind will make that principled decision. If God's glory is best grown by a measured, private, patient advocacy, then we will not castigate the current authorities but graciously and persistently request. If God's mission is best maintained by bold, prophetic, power encounters, then a sound mind will link with a heart of faith to be God's voice speaking truth to the halls and hounds of power. If the advance of the King is best served by a tactical pause or temporary retreat, then we will gladly obey. A sound mind neither views our personnel as cannon fodder nor as irreplaceable. A sound mind sees the end goal, holds steadily to it, and makes the difficult decisions that are best in the long run for the soul, for the mission, for the indigenous church, and most importantly for the King.

FEARLESSNESS, POWER, LOVE, SOUND MIND

*"…No one should be shaken by these afflictions;
for you yourselves know that we are appointed to this."*

(1 THESSALONIANS 3:3)

Let us not flag nor fail when we face the expected resistance from demonic powers and their human vassals. Let us be fearless. Let us depend on the power of the Spirit. Let us act and react in the love of God. Let us have the mind of Christ who for the joy set before Him endured. Let the glory of God be manifest and cover the earth. Let the nations rejoice and the heavens ring. Let the gospel go forth in power and praise from pulpits and prisons. Let Jesus be lifted up and cherished. Let no one be shaken. we were appointed to this.

DAY 41

PURSUING JESUS:

Jesus, I want to serve You with gladness (Psalm 100:2). I want to embrace every aspect of being a missionary and to do the private, tedious things with great joy. It is *You* who have made us and not we ourselves, so I can enter the gates of service, *Your* gates, *whatever* they be, with thanksgiving, praise, and blessing (vv. 3–4). For the Lord is *good*, kind, loving, and faithful eternally (v. 5). Let me not lose sight of the great privilege it is to be in the service of the King.

In that service I want to beware of doing *anything* in order to be noticed or seen by men (Matt. 6:1, 5). Let it be enough for me that the Father sees and rewards what is done in secret (v. 18). Let me focus on storing up treasures in heaven (v. 20), the treasures of being obedient and making disciples. My heart follows my treasure, so let my treasure be in You that my heart be there also (v. 21). Free me, Father, from the many worries because I know that You know (vv. 31–32). Give me energy to throw myself into making a way for the King to come back, seeking Your return with all I have through making You known among all peoples assured that when I seek the King and His rule (heavenly things) that this very King will take care of all my earthly needs (v. 33). Let me not worry about tomorrow (v. 34) as I only have room in this body, soul, and mind for the great day of the Lord, and all my energies are consumed on laboring towards that glorious and terrible moment.

In my zeal for You and Your return, let me not make the mistake of Moses who labored diligently to deliver with a plan utterly different than Yours (Acts 7:17–29). Moses failed and was shocked, shamed, shattered, and disappointed. I wonder if this leader who was at one time mighty in word and deed gained his stutter and lost his confidence because he realized he had been working his plan, not God's? The cure was 40 years in Narnia (Midian), for it takes a while to get deeply ingrained self-confidence and then deeply mortifying shame out of us. To be disowned by your own is a knockout blow. Then in time God used Moses to lead, rule, and judge (vv. 35–36, 40). Lord, I find myself in Narnia ashamed how I have often tried to deliver or minister according to my plan, realizing that there is still pride deep within me, wondering if I too need 40 years of anonymity. Help me, Jesus; I don't trust myself and I can't help looking at the sand dial of time and its inexorable march onwards. Let me trust You with my life and times.

Two things seem to anger the religious and the secular alike, and they are all the more combustible when they are combined: God's passion for missions and the deity of Jesus (vv. 51–57). When God's representatives stand up for the deity and worth of Jesus and the worth of Jesus to be worshipped by every tribe and tongue, we make more enemies than friends. Yet this is our mandate—to adore and worship Jesus Christ and to invite all nations to do the same. We should not be surprised that our assignment is hated and resisted, nor that we are hated, resisted, and stoned when we are faithful to proclaiming and living out these two primary passions of the Spirit of God: Jesus exalted and every people group evangelized.

All of our attention and our energy should be directed towards the appearing of Jesus with the hope that on that day we will be made like Him; and everyone who has this hope purifies himself (1 John 3:3). No one that abides in Jesus sins (v. 6). We can't linger in the presence of Jesus with sin lingering in us; they are mutually exclusive. And how much better to have Jesus than sin! Jesus, I thank Thee, that You appeared to destroy the works of the devil. I cast my mind to calvary again and worship. I love You, Jesus. Help me show it by loving my brothers especially as the world will hate us (vv. 11, 13). We know what love is because You laid down Your life for us; help me to lay down my life for my brothers (v. 16). Thank you, Jesus, that You are greater than my heart (v. 20), so You will lead me, nudge me, and whisper to me (or slap me when I need it) to show me the way that I should go. And when I don't know what to do, let me just focus on what I know that never changes: Let me love and believe Jesus, and let me love others (v. 23).

PURSUING CHURCH PLANTING:

This evening we (my teammate and I) have a Bible study planned with a Muslim seeker and some of his friends. His name is Michael and has many American friends. He is attracted to American culture, not realizing that it's actually Jesus people that he likes. Last week we agreed to do a Bible study with him if he would host it in his home and invite local friends.

Michael proceeded to invite his American Christian friends. I met with him yesterday and used an analogy to explain why that was problematic. Michael is a basketball player, so I used a sports analogy: "Michael, I am a Bible coach. In coaching you don't have ten coaches for every player; you have one coach for ten players or so. My one assignment from God is to coach the Bible, to help those who want to understand who Jesus is by explaining the Bible to them. If you want to gather a 'team' of friends together to understand the Bible, then I am very happy to come and be your coach. But I am not interested in a group of coaches hanging out with one or two students." It was a bit of a direct explanation, but he seemed to understand. We will see how tonight unfolds. If there is a group of sincere seekers, I am willing to help start a Bible study (and would then like to pass it to the younger missionaries who have started the journey with Michael). If Michael does not mobilize anyone, he can continue in relationship with the other younger missionaries who are his age.

I understand this is a little clinical, but I do feel a stewardship responsibility from God to spend my time with those who are interested in reading the Bible, understanding who Jesus is, and wanting to follow Him with others. If we don't focus on evangelism, discipleship, and the formation of indigenous leaders, we will spend a lot of time without church planting traction. I don't want to be busy—I want to be fruitful busy.

PURSUING JESUS:

I will set no worthless thing before my eyes (Psalm 101:3). It doesn't have to be evil to be worthless. It can just be time consuming, distracting, and not contributing to gospel advance. There is a time to rest, read, and even be entertained, but entertainment (it's sports for me) can be a time waster if not managed tightly. Worthless things can still make you fall away.

Thankfully, I am not the judge of anyone else (Matt. 7:1). What a relief! By the standard I measure others, I will be measured (v. 2), so it is in my best interest to be merciful and gracious to all. There is a parallel reality that truth and help are not always wanted, and to force it means I am being foolish and opening myself up to being torn and trampled (v. 6). This is not to discount the prophetic voice that must bear its wounds, but it is to say that we are responsible as best we can to present truth in a way and time that others can hear it. In everything (including the passing on of information, correction, rebuke, or difficult news) I must treat people the same way that I want to be treated (v. 12). As a proclaimer and teacher, I must ever bear the weight that the gate to life is narrow and small (v. 14) without ever losing the faith that God can do impossible things. Jesus, let me not be a ravenous wolf (v. 15) who unnecessarily devours the sheep, or bites them, or wounds them for some misguided sense of needing praise or affirmation or being considered edgy. Lord, keep my heart soft and Jesus-centered. You who are full of truth and grace, help me dispense them in the measure You balance and ordain.

No matter what happens, even if we are scattered, we are to go about preaching the Word, proclaiming Christ (Acts 8:4–5). Jesus, it seems so clear that there is baptism of the Holy Spirit that follows saving faith (v. 15). I don't just want to teach this; I want to experience it (v. 16). With the baptism, in any theology, missions, ministry, I feel the searing flame of Your holiness burning at the obvious confusion (to You) of my motives and desires as if the Spirit is saying to me, "Your heart is not right before God" (v. 21). Lord Jesus, have mercy on me and help me. Purge my heart. I am ashamed, not just of twisted, selfish motives, but also how I cling to them, repeat them, and struggle to let them go. Jesus, help me! Help me repent (turn from and forsake the past sins and be horrified and revolted at any future sins) and pray that the intention of my heart may be forgiven (v. 22). I fear that I could be in the gall of bitterness and the bondage of iniquity (v. 23) with some spiritual petulance (not chosen to lead) or insecurity (the shame of others seeing my arrogant heart). Jesus, help me! I am a ridiculous fool who desperately needs You to cleanse my heart and ambitions from these reoccurring fleshly cravings. Jesus, help me!

Lord, Your word is so plain. False prophets are those who deny that Jesus came in the flesh; this is the anti-Christ spirit (1 John 4:1–3). It's easy to point fingers at historical false prophets, but I'm also alarmed at my own heart and how often I deny the lordship of Jesus over every thought and action. I too deny Your deity when I don't obey everything Your Spirit asks immediately and with the right motives and means. Jesus, help me! Help me to love others (v. 7). In the same way You, Holy Father, manifested love by sending Your Son (v. 9), let me love by laying down my life for others. Let me love You back since You have loved us and crucified Your own Son to cover Your own wrath (v. 10). Oh, let me not forget the wonders and horrors of the cross. Jesus, not just for me, but for the world (v. 14). Let me not lose the magnitude of Your majesty. Thank you that in contrast to all other gods, You are love, and thus, You help me love from Your infinite supply (vv. 16, 19). Jesus, I am so ashamed of how I love my unworthy self. Help me, Jesus. Help me to love Your worthy self with all I have; and help me to love others with the measure of love with which You have loved me. Help me, Jesus. I am so far from what I need to be.

Pursuing Church Planting:

I finished writing sections on the Gospels (for the devotional book *Missionary God, Missionary Bible*) yesterday and was moved to tears at the wonder of being allowed to participate in God's great plan. I look forward to finishing the book but will miss the daily digging into the Word to be reminded of God's great heart and plan for all people.

My colleague and I went to meet our Muslim friend Michael. He was not able to mobilize others interested in Bible study, but we had a nice visit and were able to study the first nineteen verses of John 1 with him. It is not clear whether he is really interested in responding to the claims of the gospel or not. It might be that he just wants to hang out with Americans. Even if that is the case, we rejoiced that the gospel went forth, we were able to exalt Jesus in study, song, and prayer, and we trust the Spirit to call and convict. We will see where it goes from here, but I will probably step back and let the other young men (who are his peers) keep up the relationship with Michael.

Returning from the long evening at his house with his family (he openly studied the Bible in front of them, and the family generously shared their simple food with us), we rejoiced that we are able to be in Narnia, sharing the gospel with Muslims, lifting up Jesus. Who knows what God will do; we know He can do all things. There is no better place to be than in His presence and in His purpose bearing witness to His grace and truth. Our joy is in that obedience before it is in any response (which we will also delight in).

PURSUING JESUS:

Thank you, Jesus, that You will arise and have compassion on Zion, for it is a time to be gracious and the appointed time has come (Psalm 102:13), so that the nations will fear the name of the Lord and all the kings of the earth Your glory (v. 15). Jesus, arise and do great things to and through Your people that there may be consequences to the ends of the earth! Lord, do whatever must be done to me and in me (compassionately!) for Your glory to the ends of the earth! Let me not only be reconciled to, but also resolved to, the reality that I must decrease as the church grows stronger, that You will weaken my strength in the way (v. 23). Let me remember the plan is never the exaltation of man or missionary, but the glory of God alone. You must increase, and I must decrease. As God's work grows stronger, the role of God's vessel/apostle/minister/servant/ herald grows weaker. Help me, Jesus, to resist and repel the lie that as ministry grows, so must the influence, control, and direction of one person (which in the flesh I want to be me). Let me live in the biblical light that we all wear out and will be replaced (vv. 24, 26) and let me find comfort, not threat, in this, for the children of Your servant will continue (v. 28).

Jesus, help me believe, for You have promised it will be done as we believe (Matt. 8:13). You who can cast out spirits with a word and heal all who are brought to You (v. 16) teach me to rely on You for miracles, signs, wonders, healings, and power encounters in a way that naturally believes for the supernaturally and gracefully gives You all the glory. Let me be willing to follow You to nowhere (v. 20) and to learn from You how to be used by God greatly *and* hidden in Christ deeply at the same time. With twisted motives and surging pride like mine, I cannot see the way this will be done outside Your divine enabling and covering.

I take comfort in the promises to Paul, namely that he was a chosen instrument to bear Your name before the Gentiles, kings, and the sons of Israel (Acts 9:15). I take caution that to be used in this way also means to suffer many things for Your sake, and I note that I can barely suffer perceived slights without agitation. Thus, I wonder how I would hold up under even moderate duress when all the romance of suffering for Jesus flees away in the early moments of trial. For me, I see that the starting place must mimic Paul's transformation: First, I must get knocked off my high horse, then I must have my sight generously restored (not only of Your goodness, but also my badness), and then over time I must regain strength (vv. 17–22). From there I must testify to the deity of Jesus, even if others in the body are afraid to let me associate with them (v. 26). I must move about boldly and freely speaking and preaching, even when there are those who would want to put me to death (v. 29). At some point that will mean my removal and the church will grow with a season of peace, being built up in the fear of the Lord and the comfort of the Holy Spirit, continuing to increase (vv. 30–31). Lord, Thy sweet increase can only be my decrease. Let me find joy in this beautiful appointment; forgive me for kicking against the goads.

I love Jesus by obeying His non-burdensome commands (1 John 5:3). This is not a selective choice that implies some of His orders are burdensome. It's a total acceptance that none of His commands are burdensome and that I love Him by living in joyful obedience to all of them. If I do this, I experience the truth of the claim. It is when we selectively obey or disobey that we find the commands heavy. Joy is only gained when the whole heart, will, and emotions fully obey. Faith (in this goodness and promise of God) is the victory that overcomes the world (v. 4) and our flesh and the devil. I must fling myself off the unclimbable cliff of obedience. I cannot stand at its edge in worry, I cannot hang on its lip, I cannot scale it down. I must leap. This belief is centered on the deity of Jesus (v. 5). If I really believe He is God with all power and all goodness, all grace and all truth, then to jump is the most logical and wisest course of action. Life is in Jesus, and if I do not fully have Jesus, I do not fully have life (v. 11). When I have full confidence of the full leap into His sovereign love and power, then I can have full confidence that He hears whatever I ask and will answer (v. 14). When I fully have faith, I fully have Him, and He will keep me so that the evil one cannot touch me (v. 18). Thank you, Jesus, that You came so that we would know who is true (v. 20) by the Spirit of truth (v. 6) and thus be true as we are in truth—You!

PURSUING CHURCH PLANTING:

It was a delight to sit with a brother yesterday whom God is using to encourage an indigenous leader here in Narnia. This Narnian brother has suffered for Jesus, but his suffering has empowered and propelled him to witness and give leadership encouragement to other brothers. They meet in groups of six, number over sixty in total, and identify very clearly with Jesus and Christianity, rejecting the Muslim label or identity. Curiously, a missionary who did his PhD on identity—advocating for Muslims who come to Jesus to stay Muslim followers of Jesus—contacted my friend asking him to encourage these believers to retain their Muslim identity in some way. I am not privy to all the details or the conversation, so I may be misrepresenting him, but the danger is that we sometimes ask indigenous believers to act in a way that supports our theories rather than encouraging them to follow Scripture and the Spirit's leading. I as a conservative can be just as guilty as those from the "insider" perspective, pushing my opinion rather than letting the Spirit lead.

In this particular case, the local brothers are very clear that they think Islam is demonic and they pray for its downfall. Attempting to guard my own opinions from overstatement, it does seem to me in the Arab world that the majority of those who know Islam best are the most adamant in its incompatibility with biblical faith in Jesus. They want nothing to do with a Muslim identity and desire to be clearly connected to Christ, the body of Christ, and a clear identity that has nothing to do with Islam. They do not wish to be Americans, and they do not wish to be separated from their culture. They see a distinction between being Narnian and being Muslim and seek prudently to establish that middle ground without falling off the horse in either direction of missionaries: either to stay Muslim and follow Jesus or to adopt all of Western Christianity's forms and lose their Narnian identity and culture. May the Lord help us help them without injecting our prejudice. We will have to constantly and ruthlessly seek to be biblical and Spirit-led.

In the evening I sat with a delightful South Asian couple who have been in Narnia over 35 years and have seen many people come and go and many things change. They spoke with hope of the new day in Narnia, the fulfilment of prophecy, and the opportunity that all the internationals have to evangelize their Narnian friends in ways that were much more problematic in the past. It was a delight to hear how for decades they prayed, how God is answering prayers, and how God has put some lowly expatriate Christians into hands-on interaction with the very highest human powers in the land. Surely what we see now is connected to the hidden prayers of these humble saints over these many years. In Jesus' name I bless them. They have by their faithfulness opened the gates for so many of us. Jesus knows; may He reward.

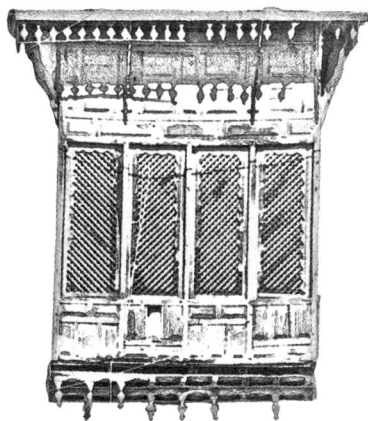

LEADERSHIP AND CHURCH PLANTING

1. The best job in missions is frontline evangelism, discipleship, and church planting.

2. We need to make the frontline disciple maker and church planter the "hero" of who we are and what we do by giving them a legitimate, empowered voice to shape us. We need to counter the sense that a position is the only way to have a legitimate voice at the table. We need to examine and probe our own systems and structures for where we unwittingly project that sense.

3. Any/every step away from personal participation in evangelism, discipleship, and church planting clouds our decision making and reduces our moral authority. When I began to consider stepping down from leadership to become a boots-on-the-ground church

planter again, I resented myself as the consequences of my decisions as a leader I did not appreciate as an implementer. In just six years I forgot what it really truly meant to be on the ground in frontline church planting on a daily basis.

4. We still need leadership, and I believe we need strong, decisive leadership, but I believe we need leadership to have one foot in the soil of daily evangelism and church planting at some level. Of necessity this will probably mean a hybrid of some kind that allows travel and influencing, but it should be done from a living, working, current model of ministry. If this means our leaders lead fewer people, so be it. More leaders (of fewer people) with greater capacity (to both make disciples and church plant and lead others in it) is a good settlement.

5. Leadership and training do not trump evangelism, disciple making, and church planting. Every missionary should be involved in evangelism, discipleship, and church planting at some grassroots level. It is the base missionary and biblical requirement. If our systems remove our leaders from this base requirement, then something is seriously wrong. Again, I am not saying this is all they should do (it would be impossible in our current world to lead broadly), but I am saying for their own good and for the visionary, strategic health of the organization it should be part of what they/we do.

6. Evangelism, discipleship, and church planting should not be sacrificed on the altar of leadership and training. At minimum there needs to be a hybrid. If we can't figure out how our leaders and trainers can have one foot in basic missionary practice, then we need to release them from leadership.

7. When leaders are responsible for the consequences of their decisions (if they have to make the changes that their followers make, if they have to process their decisions through how it affects their own evangelism, discipleship, and church planting), then they make better field level decisions.

8. If there is a systemic leadership problem at the lower levels, there is almost certainly a leadership problem all the way up the chain. Upper leadership sets the culture, and if there is something broadly wrong or unhealthy at our team level, then all of us in the chain are liable. Introspection and correction are needed. I'm not thinking in terms of character or sin, but in terms of style, personality, and culture of leadership. Whether we realize it or not, we absorb and pass on what we receive from leaders.

9. Empowered TLs build up and produce empowered team members. We all have a responsibility to empower our direct reports. The critical nuance is not whether we think we empower, but if our direct reports feel and act empowered. The digging to the real answer there is incumbent upon us and eminently tricky when we are strong leaders, for our direct reports tend to tell us what we want to hear, not necessarily the reality of their experience.

10. Leadership runs on the twin legs of influence and authority. The more authority (legitimate decision-making power and approvals) we can put in the hands of the lowest level of leadership, the better. This authority has to be legitimate in the sense that it's not revoked upon mistakes, though ongoing correction and coaching must remain a part of the mix. These empowered leaders need to be allowed the time and space to both make and fix their mistakes. If upper-level leaders step in too soon or too often to fix the mistakes, then empowerment is undermined and the leadership learning process is truncated, undermined, or even aborted. This requires us to live with some discomfort in the process.

PURSUING JESUS:

Bless the Lord, O my soul, and forget *none* of His benefits (Psalm 103:1–2): who pardons and heals, redeems and crowns, satisfies and renews, is compassionate and gracious, slow to anger and abounding in lovingkindness, who has not dealt with me according to my sins, because compassionately He knows my frame (vv. 3–5, 8, 10, 14). Thus, His lovingkindness is from everlasting to everlasting and His sovereignty over all (vv. 17, 19). How can I then *but* bless the Lord (v. 21)? Jesus, You are so wonderful. I love You.

Jesus, manifest Your wonders in such a way that Muslims are awestruck, that they glorify You (Matt. 9:8) and confess Jesus is God with the authority to forgive sins. Lord, let me be so focused on Your glory and awe that none of me gets in the way or wants any credit. Let me be lost in the shuffle as You are found. Let my faith be in You (not in faith, v. 22), and let me believe that You are able to do impossible things according to our faith (vv. 28–29). Thank you, Jesus, that You see the lost in places like Narnia as distressed and dispirited and that Your response is to call for prayer for more laborers. Help me, Jesus, be part of the answer to that prayer, not just personally, but by providing a way for many others in this country.

Let me never say "no, Lord" in the same breath (Acts 10:14). You have something for me to do that I have not thought of or imagined. When You reveal it, let my answer be "yes." Thank you for Your great heart for all peoples and let me despise no one while I deify only You (v. 29). Thank you that in Your redeeming sight no man is unclean and no person beyond saving grace, and that You do not show partiality, but those in *every nation* that fear You are welcome (vv. 34–35). Let me preach and solemnly testify that You are the judge of the living and the dead (v. 42). Let me obey the revealed will of God (preach and teach Jesus as God) and let You take care of the rest, trusting that *everyone* who *believes* will receive the forgiveness of sin (v. 43) and that the gift of the Holy Spirit will be poured out on all people (v. 45).

Along the way, let all my acts be crowned with love of others and my love marked by obedience to You (2 John 1:5–6). Let it be known that deceivers are those who say Jesus was not God and did not come in the flesh (v. 7). Let me be careful not to lose ground or cede ground that others in Christ have established (v. 8), watching myself and the flock with the sobriety of knowing we can go too far in our own ideas and stray form the teachings of Christ (v. 9). Let me not empower false teaching through my friendships, but rather let me bring joy wherever I teach (vv. 11–12).

Pursuing Church Planting:

Today is a day of fasting and prayer with others around the world. In October 2017 at the "Abide, Bear Fruit" consultation for those that work with Muslims, we committed together to fast and pray, asking God for at least 10 percent of the Muslim world to be saved in the next 10 years (by October 2027). My work is to believe that Jesus can do this, to believe Him, to pray for laborers, to teach and preach the gospel, and to heal the sick. I sometimes long for more specific instructions, or a title, role, prominence, or any other good (or vain) thing instead of just obeying the revealed will of God.

Essential to church planting is prayer and fasting, and I am so very weak in this most vital and elemental component. Jesus, teach me to pray. Jesus, help me to fast. Jesus, let these commitments be ever focused on You that my trust is in Jesus (not in faith, prayer, or people). What we have been asked to do is quite simple, and the Bible has clear injunctions to follow. At this 2017 conference, we studied and committed to the basics which follow. Jesus, let me commit to them again.

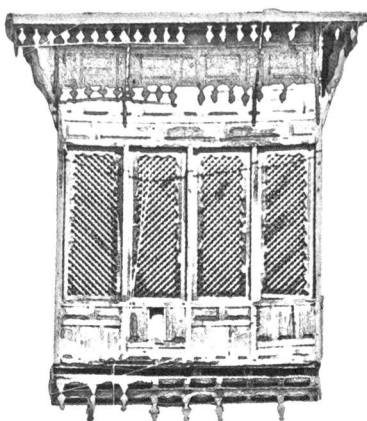

THE ABIDE, BEAR FRUIT COMMITMENT

For the glory of God and the engagement of every Muslim people group through effective church planting, we make the following commitment by God's grace.

1. ABIDE IN JESUS

Psalm 1:1–3; John 15:5; 1 John 4:16

He who abides in Me, and I in him, bears much fruit; for without Me you can do nothing.

We commit to consistently give Jesus extravagant time and to make abiding in Him our first priority and foundation of ministry.

2. BE FILLED WITH THE SPIRIT

John 1:1; Acts 1:8, 2:4, 4:8, 31; 1 Corinthians 1:17–23, 2:1–5; Ephesians 5:18

Be ye being filled with the Spirit...And they were all filled with the Holy Spirit...then Peter filled with the Holy Spirit...and they were filled with the Holy Spirit and they spoke the word of God with boldness.

We commit to seek to be continually filled with the Holy Spirit that we boldly proclaim Christ, the word of God.

3. PREACH THE WORD

Isaiah 40:8; Matthew 28:19–20; Mark 4:14; Acts 28:31; 2 Timothy 2:2, 4:2

Preach the word! Be ready in season and out of season. Convince, rebuke, exhort, with all long-suffering and teaching...the sower sows the word... the grass withers, the flower fades, but the word of our God stands forever... preach and teach...faithful men who will in turn teach others.

We commit to faithfully obey, boldly preach, and widely sow the whole word of God, making disciples among every Muslim people group by lovingly demonstrating Biblical truth.

4. INTERCEDE

Daniel 9:3; Acts 13:3; Ephesians 6:18; 1 Thessalonians 5:17

Praying always with all prayer and supplication in the Spirit, being watchful to this end with all perseverance and supplication for all the saints...As they ministered to the Lord and fasted...make request by prayer and supplications, with fasting.

We commit to regularly pray and fast with perseverance, individually and corporately, for church planting movements among every Muslim people group.

5. DIE DAILY

Luke 9:23; John 12:24; 1 Corinthians 15:31; Galatians 2:20

I have been crucified with Christ; it is no longer I who live but Christ lives in me...unless a grain of wheat falls to the ground and dies it remains alone, but if it dies, it produces much fruit...if anyone desires to come after Me, let him deny himself and take up his cross daily...I die daily.

We commit to follow Jesus, taking up our cross daily for the effective engagement of every Muslim people group.

CONCLUSION:

"In the love of God, by His grace, and for His glory, we commit to God and each other to abide in Jesus, be filled with the Spirit, preach the Word, intercede, and die daily, believing that every Muslim people group will experience a church planting movement."

Signed _____ on October 17, 2017, so help us, God.

DAY 45

PURSUING JESUS:

Thank you, Lord, for Your Spirit that both creates and renews. Let Your glory endure forever and may You be glad in Your works (v. 31). Jesus, may my compliance with what Your Spirit does in me make You happy. And when You are happy, I can sing to the Lord as long as I live; I can sing praise to my God while I have my being (v. 33). My meditation of You shall be sweet, and I will be glad in the Lord (v. 34). Bless the Lord, O my soul, and praise ye the Lord (v. 35).

The kingdom of God is not gained by passivist means, but by active (violent) pursuit (Matt. 11:12). Men and women are saved through hard work. Lord, let faith not be an excuse for me to be lazy. May trust not be a cover for fear. Let me aggressively pursue Your fame in all the earth. Teach me, Jesus, the delicate balance between not being able to do anything in my own strength and attempting great things for God. Thank you, Lord, that zeal, passion, effort, and labor do not have to be in the flesh and do not have to be complicated, even if they are hard. Thank you, Jesus, that You are well pleased to reveal Yourself to the childlike; and thank you that You do will to reveal the Father to us (vv. 26–27). Thank you, Lord, that in all of Your majesty and power You are gentle and humble and You give rest to the weary and the heavy laden (vv. 28–29).

There will always be resistance to gospel advance (Acts 11:2). Let me not become irritated or defensive if people question what I do; rather, let me be able to explain in orderly sequence what and why, being able to genuinely say, "The Spirit told me." (vv. 4, 12). Jesus, let me be so intimate with You that when I speak, the Holy Spirit descends (v. 15). Let me not stand in Your way, let those who hear me glorify God, and let me only preach the Lord Jesus (vv. 17–18, 20).

It is certainly true for Jennifer and me that we have no greater joy than hearing that our children walk in the truth (3 John 4). Lord, we ask that You preserve the heart and holiness of our sons, for Your namesake, for their own eternal souls, and for the good of the gospel in all the earth. I pray, Jesus, that we would also see many disciples from Muslim peoples and places that rise up and follow You because we were faithful to proclaim Christ. Help us, Jesus, to go out for the sake of the name of Jesus accepting, asking, and demanding nothing from the Gentiles (v. 7). Lord, please eradicate from me the love of being known or being first in the body (v. 9). That desire to be recognized is so deep in me; Jesus, give me the desire instead to be unknown and to find delight in that quiet place. Which is after all just imitating the good character of God (v. 11). You are so strong and so humble; as humans we struggle to find our strength in being lowly. Teach me, Jesus, for I know there is joy and rest there if I will but trust.

PURSUING CHURCH PLANTING:

We had supper last night with a beautiful Pakistani couple who have been leading an underground house church for over twenty years. Two years ago, he had a routine MRI and due to an accidental overdose of anesthesia passed away. After about fifteen minutes, he was resuscitated, and when he came back to life (on earth), he was so disappointed. He said that words can never express the rest he felt in that short time in heaven, nor the horror he felt at descending down to earth. As best he could describe it, heaven was perfect rest, the realm between heaven and earth demonic ("the prince of the power of the air," Eph. 2:2), and earth so disappointing and ugly compared to the sense of perfect rest he felt in heaven. He simply said that if we could sense that perfect rest and beauty, we would have no desire to remain here on earth, and that the only way to spend our few breaths on earth is in bearing witness to Jesus among all peoples.

I was reminded again how much my soul longs for heaven—not the clouds, but the restful presence of Jesus—and that the only reason we are here on earth is to see how many we can win to our heavenly home. Jesus, let me be faithful, diligent, active, and industrious. Show me how to wisely spend my time for Your glory in all the earth, not in hiding, not in selfish living, but being consumed with seeing You soon and bringing as many friends as I can with me.

DAY 46

PURSUING JESUS:

Jesus, I give You thanks, I call upon Your name, and I will make You known among the peoples (Psalm 105:1). Jesus, I will sing praises to You and I will speak of all Your wonders (v. 2). Jesus, I will glory in Your holy name and be glad in You (v. 3). Jesus, I will seek You and Your strength; I will seek Your face (v. 4). Jesus, I will remember all You have done (v. 5). Jesus, in You I can have so much confidence. In You, I am safe, and no harm can touch me (vv. 14–15). I am invulnerable until it is Your time for me to die (Acts 12:11). Let me trust Your word and Your promise and delight in any delay (Psalm 105:19), knowing that as I revel in You and relax in You, You will bring everything to pass that You desire. Whether that is positional or not (v. 21), it will be used by You for Your glory. And You will bring *all* Your people out from *all nations* with joy (vv. 42–43).

Jesus understood His mission to not just *include* the Gentiles, but to view *all* peoples as one collective and equally loved unity (Matt. 12:18). The heart of Jesus was from eternity for *all* the varieties of people and peoples He would create, for He knew that in His name the Gentiles would hope (v. 21). So then, Jesus was not focused on the Jewish people or land but on the *cross*—the redemption of *all* peoples. All peoples redeemed (those who repent, a representative of all peoples) are the result of the cross. Jesus focused on the one thing that would do all things. What a beautiful, audacious plan! What wisdom of God! The cross! The cross! The cross! Jesus did what only He could do, and because He so fiercely loved all peoples, He (seemingly) ignored them by confining Himself to one assignment. But the whole goal was the whole world. Likewise, Jesus, may I focus all my preaching on the cross and the one assignment that You have given to me. Let there be no careless words from me, whether private or public (v. 36). Let everything I do point to Jesus, the cross, eternal life, the day of the Lord—which all make room for all the nations. To speak in the flesh, to glory in self is to assure my own worm-eaten doom if I steal or envy any of Your glory (Acts 12:23). Rather, Lord, let the word of the Lord continue to grow and be multiplied (v. 24).

Because we have a common salvation, we must contend earnestly for the faith (Jude 3). Jesus, let me have a holy intolerance for anything or anyone that does not honor You (v. 4)—including myself and my words, thoughts, and actions. And let me do what seems impossible— to be a zealot for Jesus, a fire that is both humble and constrained. Let me not dare to presume, whether in spiritual warfare or any spiritual endeavor or representation (v. 9). Let me be simple and true, the right words with the right attitudes, doubly alive instead of doubly dead (v. 12), nothing false in me, just You, Jesus, shining through. Let me not be a divider, full of myself. Let me be full of the Spirit uniting men and women to *You* (v. 19), not to an organization or cause. Jesus, let me keep praying in the Spirit, let me stay in the love of God, and let me stay longing eagerly for the coming of Jesus and the issuance of eternal life (vv. 20–21), having mercy, searching and saving, hating even the garments stained by sin (v. 23). Only You, Jesus, can help me be both a merciful agent of search and rescue and a holy hater of all that disgusts You. I can't get the balance right; only Your Spirit counseling and correcting me can calibrate those two volatile, worthy spirits. Only You can keep me from stumbling and bring me blameless to the presence of the glory of Jesus (v. 24). Glory, majesty, dominion, and authority to *You* before all time, now and forever (v 25).

Pursuing Church Planting:

Fred Faroukh is an MBB who said, half in jest, "Unreached people groups don't poop." What he meant, and not unkindly, is that we can romanticize missions and fall in love with the concept of unreached peoples or pioneer church planting. The reality in making disciples anywhere (how much more among long unevangelized peoples) is that it is long, hard, slow, arduous work.

Last night Thomas asked if we could hang out. He brought over his daughter Denise who is in grade 3. She lives in a neighboring city with her mother who divorced Thomas a few years ago. We played "Sorry" and "Operation," some classic children's games. We laughed and had a nice supper that Jennifer prepared, three relaxed adults and a little young girl, just people enjoying a quiet and delightfully domestic evening. I never want to view Muslims as targets, numbers, or statistics. I want to love them simply, to love them as people made in the image of God, fearfully and wonderfully made. And I want to burn with passion to enjoy their company in heaven forever, for they are beautiful people made by a beautiful God.

As I walked Thomas and Denise to the car, I asked Thomas if I could do anything for him. He said, "Just pray for me." And I will. My prayer is that Thomas will read that Bible resting in his glove compartment, that he would come to Jesus and have his sins forgiven, that he would lead his daughter to Christ, and that we would have many more times of joy and fellowship in heaven.

On another note, the body of Christ is so beautiful when it is generous. There is an Egyptian/Syrian couple with YWAM who I first met when he was arrested for bringing Bibles into Syria. In 2011, I travelled to Benghazi to meet with his wife to see if there was anything we could do to help. Eventually he was released, and they are now missionaries in Syria. Yesterday, Turkey began to bomb their city (which is in the Kurdish north) and so he contacted me to pray. When I inquired a little deeper into their situation, he said that in the case of evacuation there is general disorder, so he asked if we could help with funds for a vehicle to help them evacuate as needed or to be used in ministry if they are able to stay. I contacted some colleagues who due to the generosity of churches in America are able to steward some funds for Syria and they were delighted to offer this assistance. What joy I felt to be able to tell this brother that others were going to stand with him and help. I am constantly amazed at the generosity of the body of Christ who continually help, bless, and resource God's missionaries (of every color and culture) around the world. I pray a blessing on every giver. Jesus, be sweet to them today.

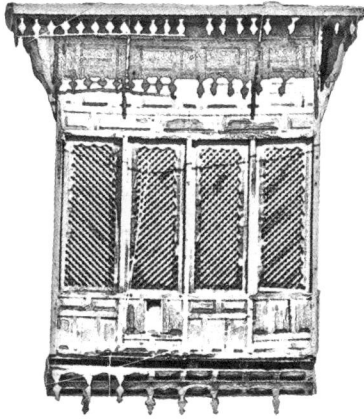

IS THERE A HOLE IN
OUR HOLISM?

As we wrestle with holism, let us avoid the unhelpful generalizations which posit that those who are engaged in compassionate ministries do not proclaim, that those who evangelize do not touch with compassion, and that compassion or evangelism are best done through programs rather than inter-personally. Arguing against straw men generates heat, but not much light.

The body is important, vitally so. There is no biblical support for a gnostic dualism that devalues the body, temporal or resurrected. It's just that the *soul* is more important. Temporally, the consequences of losing a part of your body are much less severe than losing a part of your soul. Losing your leg, tragic as that may be, cannot be equated with losing your conscience. Temporally, the body can only inevitably wear out while the soul can eternally be ever young and grow from glory to glory. Ministry to the physical body is "necessary but not sufficient." If as we feed, clothe, soothe, educate, and medicate without ever proclaiming Jesus as the only Savior, we have hated not loved.

Biblical holism values and cares for the needs of the temporal body while retaining a priority on the eternal soul. Therefore, there is an undeniable priority on preaching/verbal evangelism/conversion of the soul in biblical holism. Faith still comes by hearing, and hearing by the word of God (Rom. 10:17). The prioritization of proclamation in life and mission need not and should not diminish ordinate attention to physical needs. Prioritizing verbal proclamation is no insult to compassionate touching in the same way that prioritizing love for God in no way diminishes love for my wife and children.

A hypothesizing of a primacy/priority of proclamation in biblical holism is based on the recorded action of biblical figures. What the Bible relates about how Jesus, John the Baptist, Paul, Peter, John, and Stephen actually ministered is indicative of what the Spirit thinks is important.

JESUS

Jesus quoted Isaiah 61 in Luke 4:18–19 when He began His ministry. Sometimes this reference is used to propose that social action is equal to (or can replace) verbal proclamation. This is impossible on three fronts. First, the preponderance of proclamatory verbs in the reference ("The Spirit of the Lord is upon Me, because He has anointed me to *preach*...heal...*proclaim*...set at liberty...*proclaim*....") give a focus on proclamation, and the other verbs (heal and set free) were most often in the life of Jesus accomplished supernaturally and spiritually. Second, Jesus gave multiple clear pronouncements on why He came (see below), and taken in the collective there is a decided emphasis on verbal proclamation and the soul. Thirdly, Jesus' life and ministry clearly prioritized verbal proclamation.

Jesus left no doubt why He came. His own testimony revealed His priority on proclamation and the soul, and Jesus was undeniably holistic as demonstrated by His healing of physical and emotional brokenness. In order to start on clear biblical ground, let me state the times in the

Gospels where Jesus gave reasons for why He came. Taken together a clear priority on the soul and verbal proclamation emerges.

Matthew 10:35 – "I have come to 'set a man against his father....'"

Mark 1:38 – "Let us go into the next towns, that I may *preach* there also, because for *this purpose* I have come forth."

Mark 2:17 – "I did not come to *call* the righteous, but [*I did come to call* the] sinners to repentance."

John 6:38 – "For I have come...not to do My own will...."

John 8:42 – "...Nor have I come of Myself, but He sent me...."

John 9:39 – "For judgment I have come into this world...."

John 10:10 – "I have come that they may have life, and that they may have it more abundantly."

John 12:46 – "I have come as a light...that whoever believes in Me should not abide in darkness."

John 15:22 – "If I had not come and *spoken* to them, they would have no sin, but now they have no excuse for their sin."

John 17:13 – "But now I come to you, and these things I *speak* in the world, that they may have My joy fulfilled in themselves."

John 18:37 – "For this cause I was born, and for this cause I have come into the world, that I should *bear witness* to the truth. Everyone who is of the truth *hears* My *voice*."

Perhaps the clearest text advocating a priority on proclamation in the ministry of Jesus is the extended story found in John 6. The narrative of Jesus feeding the five thousand clearly shows His compassionate touch and care for the body while underlining the priority of proclamation in His own thinking.

After the initial feeding of the hungry, the crowd wanted to be fed again. Jesus responded to them in John 6:26–27: "Most assuredly, I say to you, you seek Me, not because you saw the signs, but because you ate of the loaves and were filled. Do not labor for the food which perishes, but for the food which endures to everlasting life, which the Son of Man will give you, because God the Father has set His seal on Him." Jesus went on to state that He is the bread of life, a different bread than the repeated manna Moses provided in the wilderness. Jesus is a bread (gives a life) that physical bread and drink cannot rival. Jesus continued on, saying that we must feed on Him (v. 57) which confused and offended those who viewed him as a free bakery.

He then dropped the hammer. He stated in no uncertain terms the priority of the soul over the body in John 6:61-63 (emphasis added): "Does this offend you? What then if you should see the Son of Man ascend where He was before? *It is the Spirit who gives life; the flesh profits nothing. The words that I speak to you are spirit, and they are life.*" Jesus in no uncertain terms declared His priority on the soul and His priority on the verbal proclamation of the gospel. Jesus' incredibly shocking explanation was given in the context of refusing to meet an ongoing physical need of the body.

There is one clear distinction between Jesus and any before or after Him. Jesus was the Living Word whose primary destiny was to die as atonement for sin and to break death's power by His resurrection from the dead. One could make an argument that Jesus' one redemptive act outweighs all His spoken words, that all Jesus' words were empty without the cross and that the cross would have been efficacious even without all of Jesus' words. While this is obviously an unnecessary and hypothetical proposition even for Jesus, it cannot be true or considered for anyone else. Our deaths cannot atone for sin. We have no inherent resurrection power. We are not the Christ. There is one Christ and His work on the cross is done. Our work is to proclaim what Christ has accomplished on the cross and in the resurrection. Because humans attribute their own meanings to the actions of others, the clearest way we have to communicate a truth is through verbal or written communication. This premise (that our primary role, the priority in biblical holism is verbal witness of what Jesus has done) is borne out in the way that all the prophets, including John the Baptist, and the apostolic figures ministered.

THE PROPHETS

What is interesting to note is that what remains of the prophetic contribution to holism *is* their spoken/recorded verbal proclamation. The holism of the prophets is generally implied, not exemplified. We have little to no record of Isaiah's, Hosea's, or any other prophet's social or compassionate action outside their exhortation of others to the same. We correctly assume that they had the integrity to live consistent with their own exhortations: justice, orphan care, provision for widows, and kindness to the captive. The prophets were primarily oracles, speaking the word of the Lord. We know nothing of how Jeremiah or Ezekiel lived out their holism; what the Spirit records as important is their speaking ministry. To build a case for compassionate ministry being valid in and of itself outside of verbal proclamation from the prophets relies somewhat ironically on the prophetic word, not the prophetic deed. Did the prophets compassionately touch the poor? Undoubtedly! Was it their priority? Absolutely not! The priority of every biblical prophet was speaking the word of God!

JOHN THE BAPTIST

Jesus declared that John the Baptist was the greatest human ever (Matt. 11:11). No one born of women was greater than John the Baptist. This is the same John who never dug a well, never held an orphan, never built a school, and never fed a widow—not at least as far as we know. What do we know about John the Baptist? He considered himself a voice (John 1:23). He preached repentance (Luke 3:3). And he offended a ton of people, and he even lost his head as a result of his words (Matt. 14:3, 10). John, best witness ever, was a proclaimer. I'm sure John loved on people—he had disciples after all. But the priority of his life was to open his mouth and preach repentance.

PAUL

Paul's priority was to preach the gospel. Paul saw his appointment in terms of being commissioned to proclaim: "I was appointed a preacher and an apostle..." (1 Tim. 2:7; 2 Tim. 1:11). Paul stated in passionate, fire-in-his-bones fashion: "Woe is me if I do not preach the gospel" (1 Cor. 9:16). He even gave the strategic "where" to his fiery passion when he declared: "I have made it my aim to preach the gospel, not where Christ was named" (Rom. 15:20). Paul told the Corinthians that he "came [to them] with the gospel" with the aim to "preach the gospel in the regions beyond" (2 Cor. 10:14, 16). Paul was eager to care for the poor (Gal. 2:10), but his undeniable priority was the verbal proclamation of the gospel. It was what he rejoiced in (Phil. 1:18) and the primacy of the eternal soul.

PETER AND JOHN

The first eight chapters of Acts give us a concise overview of the effect of the baptism of the Holy Spirit on the early apostles. Consistent with the breadth of Scripture, the baptism of the Holy Spirit always affects the tongue. The same group that was filled with the Holy Spirit in Acts 2:4, speaking in tongues, was assembled in Acts 4:31 and refilled with the Spirit, speaking the word of God with boldness.

Peter, full of the Spirit, stood up, raised his voice, and preached (Acts 2:14–39), and his culminating recorded words were an appeal for the conversion of the soul. Peter and John did not give a handout. Instead, they prayed out a healing in Jesus' name, and the healing led to extended, public proclamation (Acts 3:11–26) including the central theme "repent therefore" in verse 19. In Acts 4:20, Peter and John protested: "For we cannot but *speak* the things which we have seen and heard." Miraculous signs and healings were common (Acts 5:12–16) and the priority of the apostles' ministry (soul over body, proclamation over service) is then clearly spelled out in Acts 6: "It is not desirable that we should leave the word of God and serve tables… but we will give ourselves continually to prayer and the ministry of the word" (vv. 2, 4).

In this passage we again see the clear biblical priority. Meeting physical needs was important. Men full of the Spirit were appointed to wait on tables (v. 3), but what was more important was prayer and the preaching of the Word. There was an undeniable priority for the apostles. What is often overlooked is how Stephen fulfilled his service role.

STEPHEN

What do we know about Stephen's holism? How many widows did he serve? What kind of programs did he run? The Bible is surprisingly silent on the logistical details of Stephen's social ministry and surprisingly equally verbose on Stephen's priority of proclamation. "Stephen, full of faith and power, did great wonders and signs among the people" (v. 8). "And they were not able to resist the wisdom and the Spirit by which he *spoke*" (v. 10). His enemies criticized him: "We have heard him *speak*…" (v. 11), and then most informatively, "This man *does not cease to speak*…" (v. 13), for "we have *heard* him *say*" (v. 14). If Stephen is your model for holism, then you have no hole, for while we know little of his compassionate work (which he surely did and it was incredibly important), we have 52 verses of his sermon (Acts 7:2–53) and the testimony of his detractors regarding his constant proclamation.

A priority on proclamation is not just for apostles; it is also for the layman, the everyday believer, the volunteer at the soup kitchen, the staff at the orphanage, the engineer digging wells, and the dedicated rescuer of the trafficked.

MISSIONAL IMPLICATIONS

Muslims and secularists, Hindus, Buddhists, and pagans all love it when we meet their physical needs, and all resent it when we address their spiritual condition. I sincerely advocate the importance and the necessity of touching the lost with the love of Jesus. My wife and I have started centers for women, humanitarian organizations for refugees, schools with feeding programs for children, and adult education centers for the illiterate. We have dug wells and built bio-filters, and we encourage others to do so. We believe completely that followers of Jesus should minister in word, sign, and deed to body, soul, and spirit, *and* we believe there is biblical priority on proclamation and the saving of the soul. Whenever we have physically loved the lost (through compassionate acts), we have been embraced and lauded. Mohammed is reported to have said: "The worthiest acts are water for the thirsty and knowledge for the ignorant." Muslims love me when I help their bodies; they hate me when I help their souls. Often when we have spiritually loved the lost (by calling them to repentance), we have been vilified, rejected, and expelled. Let us not minister to the body and neglect the soul because that is how the world accepts us. Let us be careful that we do not cease proclaiming because of what it costs us. Let us never cease to speak even as we wait on tables.

Furthermore, let us be careful that we do not take up institutional compassion because we are bereft of spiritual power. The biblical blueprint for ministry to the sick is divine healing. Every follower of Jesus can pray for the sick. Jesus was not a medical doctor, nor was Peter, John, or Stephen. Their ministry to the sick was to pray for divine healing. By all means, let us start clinics, dispense medicine, and bind up wounds. But let us never stop standing in faith, praying with risk that God would demonstrate His love and power through the miraculous. Let us be used by God in divine healings, signs, and wonders.

For a Muslim to come to Jesus, it often takes an interworking of three encounters: love, truth, and power. A love encounter is a physical act, life on life, loving compassion that meets a legitimate need in the body or emotions. A truth encounter is a verbal presentation of the gospel, some precept of the Bible, and a call to repentance. A power encounter is some supernatural intervention, a miracle, a healing, or some obvious answer to prayer.

Let us be truly biblically holistic. Let our lives and ministries constantly include acts of truth, love, and power. If we lack any one of these three, there is a hole in our holism. Let us with Stephen be full of the Holy Spirit and prioritize proclaiming the gospel verbally as we seek to save eternal souls.

PURSUING JESUS:

Thank you, Jesus, that You have chosen people from every nation (Psalm 106:5). Thank you for the goodness of the reality that You save first for Your sake (v. 8) and second for ours (v. 45). Let me never slip into the idolatry of thinking I am the center of the universe or the center of God's heart. God is the center of God's heart. God is most valuable. God is most worthy. It is *good* that all things are first about God. The devil has done an excellent job at making man think he should be the center and that God is bad because God is good. For because God is the greatest good, it is only fitting that He be the center of all. Thus, in this understanding or in any other, I don't want my will at the cost of leanness to my soul or any type of barrenness (vv. 13–15). Let me wait, Lord, for Your counsel, for it is best. It is envy and lust that rush me into my own will (vv. 14, 16). Forgive me, Lord, and help me trust that You know best and that Your will and way are sweetest.

Thank you for these advance pictures of gospel truth in the Old Testament: Moses standing in the breach to turn away wrath (v. 23) and Phineas interposing to slay the plague of anger (v. 30). These are both beautiful pictures of what Jesus did on the cross to appease the wrath of God. Thank you, Jesus, for mercy, that You relent from very real and holy anger due to the greatness of Your lovingkindness and compassion (vv. 44–46). Let me ever preach the cross and the beauty of Jesus. In order to preach faithfully, let nothing evil, from the nations without or the flesh within, mingle with the holiness of God. Let me be completely consecrated to You and You alone. Let the result of me reveling in the gospel and revealing it to the world be that God is blessed and all the people (all the peoples) say, "Amen" (v. 48).

I love that Jesus preached from the normalcy of daily living (Matt. 13:1). He ambles out of the house and sits by the sea, and from this domestic normalcy preaches the gospel. Let it thus be interwoven in my life, that I am ever at rest *and* ever at evangelism. Thank you, Jesus, that Your desire is to heal (v. 15); let me not be the retardant in the equation. Let me remember that wealth is deceitful (v. 22) and that I must ever trust in You, not in mammon. I can only serve one of the two. Thank you, Jesus, that You are so considerate in Your harvest action; let me likewise be as patient and kind. You don't want the (necessary) removal of tares to destroy the true crop (v. 29), so You delay for the greater good and then ultimately burn what is evil (v. 30). Jesus, I err on both sides: first, being too hasty to correct (and harming what is good in the process), and then not being severe enough. Only in You does great mercy and great wrath combine in any fashion that is life-giving. Help me, O Spirit of God, for I cannot find the way through these great components of Your character without Your help. Let me not fret at being small or hidden, for such is how the Kingdom starts (vv. 31–33). Let me learn to blend the new and old, for this is how wisdom endures (v. 52). C. S. Lewis wrote about how the devil sends his errors into the world in pairs. It is an error to discard the experience of age, and it is an error to resist new applications and opportunities. Lord, here in Narnia where there is a difficult past and uncertain, more diverse future, help me discern from the Spirit what is the way forward in both wisdom and boldness, mercy and judgment, patience and action, partnership and obedience.

There is a blending of personal responsibility and corporate submission. Paul and Barnabas were called by God, sent out by the church, and also sent out by the Holy Spirit (Acts 13:2–4). Jesus, teach me how to work submitted to others while I am first submitted to me. In Narnia there is a history of caution and discretion; I feel the time is right for boldness and transparency. Teach me how to go forward under the governance of Your Spirit, living at peace, as much as is possible, with all men. I don't want to despise the hard-won lessons of others, nor do I want to be constrained by their opinions if and when they differ from what the Lord is saying. Neither do I want to use the Spirit as an excuse for being foolish or hasty. Jesus, let me be protected by being lowly like John, completing my course (the obedience peculiar to me) that is marked by a humility which does not have a messiah complex (v. 25). Let me remember that I am not worthy to be Christ's servant (untying His shoes), much less His equal or replacement. There is only one Christ, and His work on the cross is done. I must point to Him, to the cross, to the day of the Lord, and to eternal life with every word and every action. If I will do that, through *Jesus*, everyone who believes will be *freed* from *all* things (v. 39). For this service, Lord, I do need, along with all the disciples, to be filled with joy and the Holy Spirit (v. 52).

Jesus, unveil Yourself to me, for the time is near (Rev. 1:1). Thank you that You have released me from my sins by Your blood (v. 5) so that You can use me to point to Your coming when every eye shall see You (v. 7). From Your mouth comes, and will come, a sharp two-edged sword (1:16); let me declare that word with simple authority and tangible anointing. Let me not be afraid (v. 17), even as You reveal fearsome, terrific, terrifying aspects of Your reality. The fact that You are the First and Last, the Living One, that *died* and *rose* is…terrifying. Let me tremble in awe and joy, fearing You without being afraid.

PURSUING CHURCH PLANTING:

Yesterday, Jennifer and I went for a prayer drive, passing the outskirts of a religious center. Since Narnia has begun issuing tourist visas, they are more careful to not let non-Muslims drive through the city. There are various ring roads, but it seems they may be pushing non-Muslim traffic to the outermost ring. We were stopped today at a checkpoint and redirected on a longer route. All the same, it was a pleasant drive through the desert and then up into the beautiful mountains. We took the backway home which has a descent with even more stunning and rugged views.

What wonder there is in prayer. I still don't think I realize how important and powerful it is. I think of all the prayers that the people of God have quietly prayed through the last 50 years and more here in this land; how they must have dribbled into streams, flowed into rivers, and now gush forth in violent joy before the throne. Once prayers are prayed, the enemy can do nothing about them (which is why perhaps he works so hard at stopping prayer before it begins or distracting it once it starts). Now here in Narnia, the prayers of the saints from within and without are unleashed, and the devil must tremble, for he is powerless now that those petitions are in the ears and hands of God. Jesus, teach me to pray. It is more important now than ever that we pray. Now that the dam is breaking, the enemy surely will gather himself for a counterattack. Jesus, teach us to pray.

DAY 48

PURSUING JESUS:

Let the redeemed of the Lord whom He has gathered from every land speak up and testify (Psalm 107:2–3). Jesus, let me lift up my voice and glory in the cross, glory in Christ. Let me give thanks to the Lord in public ways for His kindness and for His wonderful works to the children of men (v. 8). Jesus, You alone satisfy my thirst (v. 9). You alone save, bring me out of darkness, break all bonds, and shatter all prison gates (vv. 13–14). You alone save me from all my distresses (vv. 19, 28). You alone send Your word to heal (v. 20), You alone calm my storms and guide me to our desired haven (vv. 29–30). You alone set me securely on high and bring me into the flock of the family of God (v. 41). Jesus, I give You thanks for Your lovingkindness and Your wonderful works to this child of men!

Let me always remember that I must merely bring the crowds to Jesus to be fed (Matt. 14:18). The pressures of ministry and missions are untenable when I think I must feed or help others; it is in bringing the crowds *to Jesus* that they are helped. Lord, I believe that Muslims all across this land will worship Jesus and declare, "You are certainly God's Son!" (v. 33). This will happen because *You* feed them, not because I do. They will be healed by touching the hem of *Your* garment (v. 36), not by touching mine. Let me be very careful not to take (or receive) *any* of Your glory (Acts 14:15). Let me simply focus on preaching the gospel and making disciples (v. 21) with the clear-eyed understanding that it is through many tribulations we must enter the kingdom of God (v. 22). Let me be faithful to seek and empower local elders through prayer and fasting (v. 23), not through natural selection. Let your "supernatural selection" weed out all those unfaithful as *You* open the door of faith (v. 27) in surprising places.

Along the way in missions and ministry, Jesus, don't let me forget my first love (Rev. 2:4). Let me remember from where I have fallen, repent, and do the deeds (simple zeal for Your presence) I did at first (v. 5). I think of all the time I spent praying in Mauritania. Jesus, let me again be a man of prayer, having only Your presence, needing only You. Don't allow a holy intolerance, godly toil, doctrinal guardianship (v. 2), and a hatred of what dishonors Jesus (v. 6), all of which are good and necessary things, to harden or calcify my spirit. Jesus, help me grow in tenderness, even as I keep to the narrow way. Help me to stay big-hearted as I walk the narrow path. Jesus, You are very clear that I should not fear what I am about to suffer (v. 10). Help me to be faithful unto death and to hold fast to Jesus even here where Satan has his throne (v. 13). Thank you that You give hidden manna to those who hold on to You faithfully. I may not be able to do much but cling to You, but cling to You I shall as You give me strength. Your eyes are like fire and they search my mind and heart (vv. 18, 23). Lord, I know and confess there are things in me that need to be burned up. Fearfully I ask for that burning, trembling I ask that You burn up mercifully. I am not strong; I am foolish and weak. But Your Spirit in me cries out for both judgment and mercy; get rid of sin and flesh in me, Jesus, tenderly. You make it very clear that You reward according to our deeds (v. 23) and my record is sullied. Lord, have mercy on me and help me do mercy; help me give out what I plead from You. I hope in the promise that You will give both authority and the morning star (vv. 27–28) if I will be faithful and overcome.

PURSUING CHURCH PLANTING:

Language learning is sanctification. Over and again our patient teacher is correcting us and accommodating our poor pronunciation and grammar. In order to improve and grow to the place where we can faithfully present the truth in the heart language, we must first be wrong over and over again. It is in speaking, making mistakes, and being corrected that we learn how to speak like a local. Learning where we are wrong is so necessary to staying right. We see this in so many practical ways: This road does not get us where we need to go; this shop is not open at these hours; this item is not available in this hardware store; this illustration is not understood by the hearer; this approach was not fruitful in evangelism; this partnership idea is not yet ripe for adoption; this business idea is impractically expensive; and this visa option is no longer available. And on and on it goes in things practical and ministerial; we are learning over and over again what does not work. There is a joy in this, for all our closed doors inevitably lead us to what will work in God's timing, strength, and wisdom. On his discovery of how to make an efficient lightbulb, Thomas Edison said: "I have not failed. I've just found 10,000 ways that don't work!" He also said: "Negative results are just what I want. They're just as valuable to me as positive results. I can never find the thing that does the job best until I find the ones that don't." Church planting requires this same joy and persistence in discovering what does not work, and the attitude that these discoveries are actually helpful wins, not setbacks. We keep working. We keep grinding. We keep smiling when we use the wrong words or verb agreement. We rejoice at every lesson, for the roadblocks of today lead us to the open roads of tomorrow.

PURSUING JESUS:

I will give thanks to You, O Lord, among the peoples (Psalm 108:3). I will stand in Narnia and lift my voice in praise and thanks. If all the nations will come here for Hajj, so will I sing praise to You among the nations (v. 3). For Your lovingkindness is great above the heavens and Your truth reaches to the skies (v. 5). *Be exalted, O God*, above the heavens, and let Your glory be over all the earth. Thank you, Jesus, that all the nations belong to You (vv. 7–9) and that You do with them as Your creator rights determine. Let me always remember that deliverance by man is vain; it is through God that we will do valiantly (vv. 12–13). It is *He* who shall tread down our adversaries.

Let me always remember that the word of the Lord always trumps tradition (Matt. 15:6). May my private heart honor you, not just my teaching/preaching/public lips (v. 8). If I honor You, some leaders (religious and otherwise) and some listeners are going to be offended (v. 12). I can't make the avoidance of offence the main goal. At the same time, I must ever remember that Jesus is compassionate (v. 32), and I can't represent Him and not be compassionate. I must preach His word, and I must partake in His loving heart.

There will always be points of contention and much to debate (Acts 15:7). Let me remember that the Spirit is given to all who turn to Him by faith through grace (vv. 8–9, 11). Thus, if I disagree with a brother, let it be in the Spirit and by the Spirit. Let me also not think I am wiser or holier than the Spirit. There is a time to stop speaking and let the Spirit (through the spiritual eldership) make a declarative decision (v. 13). Let us in all our deliberations not lose sight of God's priorities: God *first* concerned Himself with taking from among the Gentiles a people for His name; therefore, let us not trouble those who are turning to God by imposing our cultural forms and traditions, and let us all—together—flee from idolatry (v. 14, 19–20). Idol breaking is a collective exercise, for we all have them. Every culture has fallen aspects. Missionaries who call other cultures to forsake idols must constantly be cleaning our own houses and hearts from the idols we have brought in and accommodated.

Thank you, Jesus, that You open doors that no man can shut (Rev. 3:7). You have put before us an open door, even though we have little power (v. 8). Help me not to deny Your name. Help me to keep the word of Your perseverance, that no one take my crown, and so that I might be a pillar in the house of God never to go out again (vv. 10–12). What beauty! God stands humbly at the door of our hearts, offering Himself and all His fullness. God opens a door that we might go out into the world to faithfully serve Him. God allows us into His presence to luxuriate in Him, never having to leave the glory of Himself. Oh, thank you, Jesus, I just want to stand in Your presence, never having to leave, knowing You never leave me. This is my bliss and Your great gift to me, to us, to all who are born of the Spirit, redeemed by the blood.

Pursuing Church Planting:

It is interesting how national churches and missionary partnerships can reflect the culture of their host context. I met today with a brother who expressed some concern about my public identity and how that could possibly jeopardize others of God's people. He is not wrong; he has experience here and much wisdom. At the same time, I do think there must be an allowance for God's leading of individuals if and when they are submitted to Him, not confusing boldness for folly. This brother has mentioned several times that he has heard concerns "from others" about me. He is referring to other gospel workers located there and, I assume, to a discreet group of leaders who have formed a "by invitation only" partnership circle.

What is of note is that a centralized, controlling body in the capital city, which is secretive and by invitation only, is not that far off from how governance works here. It is ironic to me that people who do not know us, in a city far away, who have a private little huddle, have opinions on my identity and praxis. Again, these are people with wisdom and experience who have valid perspectives and reasons for what they have done; yet, all the same it is curious. It has been a good lesson for me to be on the other side of the "in" group. In the past I was the one "controlling" information and partnership and trying to keep the dangerous elements out. In my case that was the Sudan partnership, and I did not want high-powered donors in the meetings that would sweep in and hand out money somewhat unwisely (in my opinion). Now I am the higher profile, more public identity worker that makes others nervous. It is good for me to have to swallow some of my own medicine.

The lesson, however, is that none of us are immune to our context, and we must be vigilant that in responding to the reality of the situation, we do so with Kingdom values trumping earthly systems. To be very clear, I am not accusing this secret group of leaders of being un-Kingdom, but I am saying we should be careful to walk the narrow ridge of stewardship (informed caution) without sliding into controlling tendencies or conforming to systems that are more like the context than the Christ.

In my own leadership I need to learn this lesson, to grow in the ability to manage the tension between inclusion and stewardship. I am not able to do this without the Spirit's counsel.

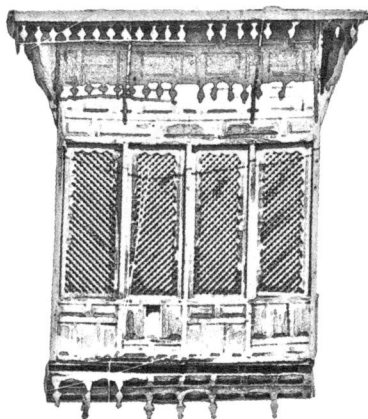

MANIFESTATIONS OF PRIDE

BY STUART SCOTT[11]

1. Complaining against or passing judgment on God

2. A lack of gratitude in general

3. Anger

4. Seeing yourself as better than others

5. Having an inflated view of your importance, gifts, abilities

6. Being focused on the lack of your gifts and abilities

7. Perfectionism

8. Talking too much

9. Talking too much about yourself

10. Seeking independence or control

11. Being consumed with what others think

12. Being devastated or angered by criticism

13. Being unteachable

14. Being sarcastic, hurtful, or degrading

15. A lack of service

16. A lack of compassion

17. Being defensive or blame-shifting

18. A lack of admitting when you are wrong

19. A lack of asking forgiveness

20. A lack of biblical prayer

21. Resisting authority or being disrespectful

22. Voicing preferences and opinions when not asked

23. Minimizing your own sin and shortcomings

24. Maximizing other's sins and shortcomings

25. Being impatient or irritable with others

26. Being jealous or envious

27. Using others

28. Being deceitful by covering up sins, faults, mistakes

29. Using attention-getting tactics

30. Not having close relationships

PURSUING JESUS:

O God of my praise, do not be silent (Psalm 109:1). It is a painful thing to be misunderstood, and it is just as painful to be understood—to have the flaws and follies of my heart seen by others. Lord, have mercy on me in both cases. Where I have had love and good intentions criticized, let me respond in prayer: "In return for my love they act as my accusers, but I am in prayer" (v. 4). What assurance! When our hearts are broken, we can take it to Jesus in prayer. Jesus, help me pray and long for the right things. We will be granted what we love and what we seek, so please help me love what is good and pure. Help me not love respect, notoriety, recognition, or vindication, for in getting them I will be dissatisfied. Help me just to seek and love *You*, for that is the only way to be satisfied. In afflictions (v. 22) and reproach (v. 25), thank you, Jesus, that you deal kindly with me (v. 21), more kindly than I deserve, for honestly it is often my folly that has brought reproach and many times I have done good things with mixed motives. So help me, Jesus. Save me according to Your lovingkindness (v. 26), not because I am worthy. Let all know that any deliverance I experience is from Your hand, and if "they" curse, You bless (vv. 27–28). And then, in the midst of many, I will give thanks abundantly and praise the Lord (v. 30), with Your help keeping my heart right, laying down any hurt, bitterness, pride, and desire for vindication. Let it be enough for me that You are loving and kind towards me, more than I deserve.

Let me not seek signs (Matt. 16:4); let Jesus and His presence be my sign. Let me be consumed with the wonder that Jesus is the Christ, the Son of the Living God (v. 16). All things, including the church (v. 18), are built on the reality that Jesus is God, and on the reality that we must see the church built through suffering God's interests.

To think otherwise is not to be mindful of the purposes of God. Suffering must, in this age, precede glory. And when we suffer, let us sing hymns and pray our way through it (Acts 16:25) bringing earthquakes and salvation wherever we so praise.

The gospel must ever be preached (v. 10); it's just a matter of where. The Holy Spirit's "no" is a loving refusal (v. 6). The Spirit of Jesus' "no" is eternally wise. Let me receive the "no" of God with as much loving thanks as His "yes." Let me ever preach, allowing Jesus to decide where, as in those holy directives and directions we will find men and women of peace whose heart God has opened to the Word (v. 14). The real opposition will come when the god of all men and women (mammon) is undermined. It was when the "hope of profit" was gone that the real god of the age manifested. Religions cloak the universally fallen heart of man which is ever about power, sex, and money.

What wonder that there is a door standing open in heaven for us and that Jesus invites us to "come up here!" (Rev. 4:1), immediately immersing us in His Spirit, with flashes of light from His throne (v. 5). Yes, Jesus, You are holy, worthy, and almighty (vv. 8–11). All I really want and need is to be in Your presence.

Pursuing Church Planting:

Yesterday, a veteran worker here told me that there is no real benefit to the work if expatriates go to prison. He commented that there is more benefit if local believers go to prison. I disagree on several counts, not with the benefit of prison for locals, but with the insinuation there is no benefit if missionaries go to prison. First, Paul and Silas were missionaries who went to prison and the result was the conversion of the Philippian jailer and his household. Second, Jesus prophesied that we would be arrested and that when we were, we would bear witness of Him. Paul told us it was granted on behalf of Christ to suffer and that all who desire to live a godly life in Christ Jesus will face persecution. Third, we can model for local believers that it is normal to suffer for Jesus, that we should not fear, and that we should not trade our liberty for our silence. I do not think we can in good conscience disciple others to endure trouble if we never model it ourselves. Fourth, God's purposes can be beyond our immediate awareness. In other words, what can seem like a setback for us could in fact be a surge forward in God's plans and sovereignty. We never know what He will use for His glory. Fifth, the assumption that prison means the missionary did something wrong (was too overt, was foolish) is suspect. That may be true, or maybe the missionary was just being obedient. Sixth, prison does not necessarily mean the end of witness, for even those in solitary confinement can pray and their example can mobilize the world to prayer and even to going. Perhaps it is a missionary confined to a Narnian prison that mobilizes a new generation to go to the darkest places of earth with gospel light. Seventh, prison can be a place for Jesus to make Himself real to the worker (it is not axiomatic, prison can destroy some) and perhaps produce some great gospel thoughts and writing (*Pilgrims Progress*, a number of New Testament epistles). Eighth, there are manifold stories of the gospel going forth in prison cells to other prisoners (Pastor Jules in Baghdad, Iraq, or Dimitri in the Siberian prison as told in *The Insanity of God*). Ninth, as with Peter in Acts, God can reveal His glory through miraculous deliverance. Tenth, prison can be a tender grace to refine the imprisoned so that on release they live completely dedicated to the glory of God and go forth to mobilize the church and evangelize the world with a new fervor and favor.

I do not think that prison should be sought, nor should our stay there be booked by arrogant hubris or sheer folly, but neither should it be feared or avoided at a cost that is detrimental to the gospel. God can work through prison: in the heart of the imprisoned, in the hearts of observing locals, in the hearts of the prison keepers, in the hearts of the church, and in the hearts of the world. God's Spirit is never chained.

DAY 51

PURSUING JESUS:

"The Lord said to my Lord: Sit at my right hand until..." (Psalm 110:1). It's staggering how much God does for God. It grants assurance that God can easily do things for man, or better yet use man to do things for God. If God is so dedicated to His own glory that He goes to great lengths to work for Himself, we can be assured that He will empower us to work for His glory. It is staggering how much God insists we listen to God: "This is my beloved Son...listen to Him" (Matt. 17:5). We are commanded by God to listen to God and then in the next breath we are told that God will suffer and be killed before being raised (vv. 12, 23). Then we are shown that God goes out of His way to pay taxes so that He doesn't offend man (v. 27). Taken together these revelations of God are so personable. God is so far from being robotic or detached, and the more we understand Him, the more we see how the divine image is so clearly imprinted in man. We understand ourselves best when we understand Him most. The God who came near and took on flesh, suffered, died, and was raised did so to atone for sins and along the way made it possible for us to understand Him. He became so imminently knowable in Christ, and that knowledge helps us know and love ourselves. We don't truly and purely know or love ourselves until we know and love God. Knowing and loving the God who makes flesh gives us great insight into humanity, who we are supposed to be and who we will be on that great and glorious day when God is through working for God and comes to judge the living and the dead through Jesus (Acts 17:31). We can stop weeping at the brokenness of man because Jesus has overcome all that has fallen and will restore all that is Him in us (Rev.5:5). We will then cry with the representatives of all cultures and peoples (for all represent Him in some unique fashion): "Worthy are You! Slain! Risen! Worthy to receive power, riches, wisdom, might, honor, glory, and blessing!"

Pursuing Church Planting:

We have a vision and prayer team (VPT) with us this week. Six prospective missionaries to Narnia who are taking a break from their Arabic learning and missions training in neighboring countries in order to pray about this context and serving in this nation.

Missions mobilization is an ongoing need and presents a tension for workers on the ground. God uses many means to call new laborers. One primary way is for them to visit the field and to interact with both local people, the lost, and the missionaries on the ground. The challenge is that when missionaries are hosting visitors, it usually means less time with the lost. If missionaries constantly host visitors, that time *not* with the lost increases and becomes a hinderance to fruitful church planting. So the good of mobilizing missionaries can become an obstacle if it no longer serves missions but replaces it. How ironic if we create a cycle where missionaries spend more time hosting future missionaries than they do in evangelizing the lost, making disciples, and planting churches.

Wisdom is needed to manage this tension and to find a way to receive visitors and to recruit future missionaries, but in such a way that those visitors do not disrupt missionary rhythms on the field, add value to them, and allow the missionary to do their primary work of making disciples. Church planting teams can work towards a healthy balance by: (1) determining to not constantly host visitors; (2) determining that when visitors come, ministry does not pause; (3) finding ways to outsource the hosting to local believers or contacts in healthy ways (fees can be added to each visitor to create a ministry service income for a local believer, freeing up the missionaries' time and empowering a local believer with dignity); (4) integrating visitors into normal patterns of team life and finding ways those visitors can do ministry in English, whether by prayer walking or even searching for lost people interested in the gospel; (5) dividing up the team's hosting responsibilities so that each team member gives a portion of their week to accommodating the visitors; (6) requiring visitors to do some of their own logistical work on the ground (booking lodging and rental cars, navigating themselves, feeding themselves, arranging their own airport transport, etc.); (7) planning the calendar so that visitors come at certain times of the year (for example, our goal is from August to April we will focus on local people and direct evangelism, and for spring break and May and June we will focus on receiving visitors); and (8) requiring visitors to be okay to share time with other visitors (rather than having unique time with the missionaries, they may overlap with other teams in the periods mentioned above, and while it is less personable, it is efficient for the missionary).

DAY 52

PURSUING JESUS:

Jesus, help me give thanks to You with *all* my heart (Psalm 111:1). Let me not praise You with a portion of my being, but with all. You have sent redemption and have ordained Your covenant forever (v. 9). Holy and awesome is Your name. Eternal life is a big deal! Let me grow in thanks constantly. Let me honor You and Your gift (*eternal life!*) with *all* my heart. Let me be passionate about those who have never known that the gift of eternal life is on offer. Let me constantly leave the ninety-nine as You have modeled to find the one that is lost (Matt. 18:12). Jesus, my urgency is blunted as my desire for comfort and rest grows. Fatigue seems to be winning the battle; renew my fire for those who have never heard. Let me have patient, sustained compassion even as You have had with me (v. 27).

Jesus, let not fear creep into my heart (Acts 18:9). Empower me to go on speaking, remembering that You have many people in this city and that You are with me and that *no man* can attack me in order to harm me outside of Your sovereign goodness (v. 10). Lord, if this is to be true, if fatigue and fear are to be overcome, I can't only functionally know the baptism of John (v. 25); rather, I need a fresh baptism of fire. Lord, I also understand that Your promises of protection are not promises of immunity, just loving timing. The number of martyrs has to be completed; more must be killed for the word of God and the testimony which they maintain (Rev. 6:11). Maybe terrorists will kill me, maybe time. You will choose, but Jesus, let me be a faithful disseminator of the word of God. Let me maintain a passionate proclamation of Jesus all the way to my end; when and how is immaterial as long as I have been a faithful witness with every breath from now until then.

Pursuing Church Planting:

Yesterday we took a prayer drive around a nearby city. There is always a twin wonder when so close to the heart of Islam. One wonder is, how normal it is, for in our minds it has been built into this mystic forbidden city, yet it hums along with normal people doing normal things. There is a sense of "that's all? this is all the giant is?" It is comforting to know that the giants we think so large are so hollow and fall so quickly when God slings His little stones. There is a growing church in this city that is bold and indigenous and slinging prayers and witness with courage. The second wonder is a caution, that though there is breakthrough, there is battle yet ahead. The devil does not surrender his fourteen-century-old trophy without a vicious fight. We cannot be lulled to sleep by a sense of normalcy or a misguided pride that the path ahead is easy. The battle is about to escalate. Jesus, have mercy on us and teach us to fight. If we are not under Your shield, we will be decimated.

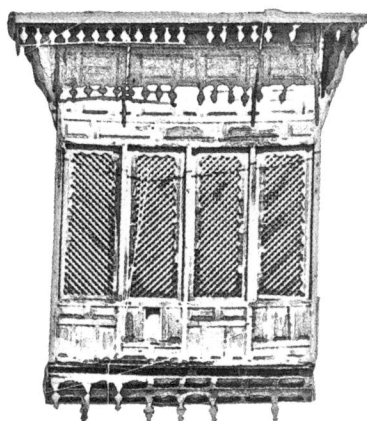

EXTRACTION: MANAGING THE COLLISION OF SCALABILITY, STRATEGY, AND PASTORAL CARE

THE SCENARIO

In a war-torn country in the Arab world, a young man (19-years-old) came to Jesus. Followed by Islamic militants he made a video; the video called for secret believers in the Muslim world to not fear and to bravely stand up for Jesus. This believer was in a discipleship relationship with some workers, and he asked the video to be released if he was captured or killed. Shortly after making the video (and the last Bible passage this believer studied with another believer before being taken was Romans 8), this young man was abducted by one of the Islamic militias. For around twenty days there was no news. The workers were on the verge of releasing the video when they heard the young believer had been released to the hospital. His ribs and clavicle were broken, and he had a punctured lung. He had "made some things up" in order to be released and communicated to the workers that he would like to leave the country.

What should the workers discipling him do? Encourage him to stay and suffer? Help him leave?

THE IDEAL

Ideally, we don't help people leave. How will an indigenous church be built among unreached peoples if the believers all leave? Should they not stay, suffer, and stand up for their faith? Is that not the historic bedrock of church planting—empowered, suffering presence over time? Should we not have the long-term missiological discipline to make tough decisions in the present so that there is a future church? Besides, we can't do this for every believer that suffers; it's not practically or financially possible. Planting indigenous churches requires indigenous people to stay, persevere, endure, and shine. Besides, Jesus never left His country; He stayed and endured trouble. Paul suffered over and over. Eleven of the twelve disciples were martyred. It's not easy and it's not pleasant to say or live, but someone has to shed their blood if the church is to be planted. Tertullian was right after all—the blood of the martyrs is indeed the seed of the church. And if we don't plant seeds, we won't reap harvest.

THE BIBLICAL MODEL

It is indeed true that Jesus set His face like a flint to go to Jerusalem and the cross. Knowing what He would suffer, Jesus for the joy set before Him endured. It is likewise true that Paul set His course for Jerusalem knowing from the prophetic warning that it did not end well. All that is true. So, too, are these events:

Matthew 12:14–15

"Then the Pharisees went out and plotted against [Jesus], how they might destroy Him. But when Jesus knew it, He withdrew from there."

Acts 17:5–14

In Thessalonica, envious Jews attacked the house of Jason and dragged him before the angry crowd. "Then the brethren immediately sent Paul and Silas away by night to Berea" (v. 10). Jews from Thessalonica followed and stirred up the crowds, and "then immediately the brethren sent Paul away..." (v. 14).

Acts 14:19–20

Paul bravely confronted idolatry at Lystra, was stoned, and dragged out of the city and left for dead. Remarkably he got up and went back into the city, and then the next day he escaped to Derbe.

The biblical and apostolic record is a wonderful blend of pursuing gospel obedience (even to death) *and* tactical withdrawals (living to fight another day). The same man who escaped from Damascus in a basket traveled determinedly to Jerusalem where he knew chains and tribulation waited. It is overly simplistic then to say the Bible teaches we must always stay in dangerous places. It is also overly simplistic to say the Bible teaches we must always leave dangerous places. Sometimes we stay and face the consequences as Jesus and Paul did. Sometimes with Jesus and Paul we make a tactical retreat, for the timing is not yet right. We will suffer and die for the gospel, but the timing must be of the Lord; otherwise we have confused faith for folly.

THE OPTIONS

In the scenario above, several options are present:

1. Publish the video anyway or make other bold ones like it. Stay in the city, preach away, and remain a public, prophetic voice to the local people, knowing he was warned by the Islamic militia that if he said anything about the gospel, they would take and kill him. He could stay and proclaim boldly, but it would likely mean a quick death.

2. Stay in the city but hide for a season. Let things calm down and perhaps in a year or two start public witnessing again. In the meantime, meet with believers and be built up in the faith. Carefully and prudently help with media evangelism and private sharing of the faith.

3. Go to a neighboring country, a country with a similar language and culture, a country replete with locals from the country from which the believer hails. Learn to minister to them in the (comparative) safety of a context that is not your home.

4. Go to a distant country in the Arab world. Grow, heal, and minister to Arab Muslims there, but with geographical space (buffer) between you, your extended family, and security forces.

5. Go to an African or Asian country and study there for some years. Be involved in ministering to Arabs or helping in media outreach remotely.

6. Go to the West and study there for some years. Be involved in ministering to Arabs or helping in media outreach remotely.

7. Deny the faith, stay home, and avoid all the transition and trouble.

Obviously 7 is not acceptable, but what about the rest? If 1 is ideal and 2 is preferred, is there any validity to 3 or 4? What about 5 and 6? Are there other options?

THE NUANCES

The God card: The God card is tricky because it is both so viable and so abused. Once you "play" the God card, the discussion is over. If God is legitimately leading you to do a certain thing, something that flies in the face of best practice (but not biblical principle), that's a valid component of the decision. Counsel and your authorities can help you discern if indeed it is God speaking to you or your emotions and pastoral heart.

Age and maturity of the believer: It is not prudent to treat all people in all seasons of life the same. Numerous factors must be considered in the equation: Is the person leader? Does the person have family? What is their maturity? Has he never suffered, or has he suffered much? Etc.

Precedent: What example does this set for others who will inevitably be in similar situations? Do the various factors legitimize you setting a precedent that you know you will have to break in the future?

Finances: Who pays for this and for how long? How does this not create dependency or the example that if you become a Christian, you get a free education in the U.S.?

Practicalities: What is actually possible? Perhaps what seems best just can't be done. So given the realities and the constraints, what can be done?

Hypocrisy: Are we demanding of local believers something we do not practice ourselves? We often leave when the context descends to a certain level of instability or danger. On what moral grounds do we ask or encourage them to stay in dangerous situations? This is not always a simplistic question. There is some biblical ground for asking believers to endure trouble that we have not yet experienced, essentially because what is true is what is God-centered, not what is our experience-centered. All the same, we must examine our own hearts. How many times have we denied our Lord (word, thought, and deed)? How many times has fear caused us to be silent or to say something clouded and evasive? The biblical reality is that we all deny Jesus multiple times. What does it mean to both give and receive grace in these situations?

Discipleship responsibility: Can we really share the gospel in good conscience, knowing it will cost the receiver all, but then modulate our response when the cost is levied? If our message demands suffering, do we not have a moral responsibility to walk through that suffering with the brother or sister in Christ? When we invite them to join the body of Christ, is that a full or partial membership? If that person were our physical son or daughter, would we do anything differently?

Near culture community: What is the role of local believers in nearby countries who are closer in culture, language, and context to the suffering friend than we are? Are our hearts completely clean when we say that near neighbor believers should receive and care for this believer rather than expatriate workers? Is there any self-preservation in us not wanting to be intimately involved in pastoral and community care?

Worker disagreement: What about when there are multiple workers who engage with this MBB and they see it differently—some wanting to keep him in country or nearby, others wanting to send him to the West? If CBBs are involved, they too might have strong opinions about when, where, and for how long.

THE RESOLUTION

In the scenario above, there is one worker who is a direct discipler of the young man. This worker is a culturally astute veteran, Arabic speaker, and TCK. He and his family live very simply and are committed to whatever price the gospel requires. They have a track record of sound, faithful missiology. They are aware of all the issues and nuances above. They are aware of indigenous principles, scalability, precedent, dependency, and reproducibility. The worker connected with a Christian organization (an organization that does not favor extraction) who specializes in advising and helping in these scenarios. The worker and his wife took counsel of their own agency leadership and talked with mentors and friends. At the end of the day, they felt the Lord speak to them simply, "Treat this very young man as if he was your own son."

The workers took into consideration this young man's plan to study abroad in the U.S. (even before his salvation). They took into consideration that he is still a teenager, his father is dead, and he needs a father figure. They took into consideration that his bold, public stance has estranged him from his family (his mother turned him into the Islamic militia). They took into consideration that the militia took him in for questioning again after his release from the hospital. They took into consideration the pros and cons of sending this young man to a neighboring country or nearby country. At the end of the day and after due diligence, prayer, and counsel, they felt that if this was their son, they would do the following:

- Disciple their son through this difficulty;
- Cast vision for God's purposes in the earth and the local nation to him;
- Help their teenage son get the best possible college education;
- Connect him with a community that can intimately embrace him; and
- Send him out of the country for a season to recover physically, emotionally, and spiritually from his trauma.

Where the above will happen is not determined, but if it means the West, they are open to it. Their hope, desire, and intention are that this young man will develop into a Paul that will lead many Arab Muslims to the Lord. They realize his extraction is a risk against that happening, but it's not a guarantee. They feel they have to obey the Lord's request of them to treat this young man as if he was physically their own. They know they can't do this to every believer

CONCLUSION

It's not wrong to be ideal, strategic, and disciplined, but it is wrong to be so without being pastoral, compassionate, and obedient. We all agree that extraction as a norm is not the way indigenous churches are planted, but we also must struggle with the reality that sometimes it is the best and most obedient thing to do for that one person in that one moment.

DAY 53

PURSUING JESUS:

Jesus, help me to fear You, live righteously, walk in the light, and
be gracious so that I will never be shaken, will not fear, and will
be trusting and steadfast with my heart upheld when evil attacks
(Psalm 112:1–8). I am so weak in my own strength, Jesus. I know
I can crumble at the least offense, smallest temptation, or weakest
attack. I am so foolish and vulnerable when I rely on myself. Jesus,
help me, for I cannot fight for Your glory in my puny, fallen self.
Fight through me, O Lord of hosts. I am a sinful coward outside of
Your cleansing, covering blood.

Let not my hardness of heart divide the body of Christ (Matt. 19:8). Let
me not be childish, but childlike (v. 14), trusting You, yet responsible.
My "one thing," my "sell what you have" is pride of missionary identity.
Our "one thing" can be a good thing twisted. Jesus, forgive me from
drawing self-worth from ministry, recognition, being a missionary,
being the son of missionaries, being different, being a leader, and from
other things that are not bad in themselves but so easily idols to me. I
am so vulnerable to wanting to be thought well of, being distinct. Lord,
forgive me and teach me the joy of "selling all" so that my identity is only
in You, and if I am small, weak, indistinct, not on the field, forgotten,
and not known, I am at peace. And if I am on the field, known, and
respected, that they are not the source of my joy (for all those things can
vanish in a moment). Let my joy be centered in You and on redemption.
Thank you, Jesus, that with God all things are possible (v. 26). Any man
can be saved, and I can certainly be delivered from bondage to my "one
thing." I look forward with hope to the regeneration of my motives and
desires, along with the regeneration of all things, and the institution of
Your glorious throne, Your eternal reign, and eternal life (vv. 28–29). Let
me not lose the wonder of *eternal life.*

Jesus, please send afresh Your Holy Spirit upon me that I may speak afresh under Your unction and authority (Acts 19:6). Teach me how to speak boldly, to reason, to persuade, to reason daily over the years, that all who live in Narnia may hear the word of the Lord (vv. 8–10). Jesus, let extraordinary miracles confirm the preaching (v. 11), ever pointing to You and never with my flesh presuming, for ministry presumption outside the knowledge of God leaves me naked and wounded (v. 16). *But Jesus will be magnified* (v. 17), no matter what foolish man or foolish me does. So, Jesus, let my wounds be only earned by lowly obedience and not by arrogant presumption. Let the words of men—including my own—be burned (v. 19), and let the word of God multiply. In this age and in this place, there is an unholy alliance between money and religion, and when it is threatened by the way of the cross, there is no small disturbance, rage, or confusion (vv. 23, 27–29). Let us be sober; as the gospel goes forth in Narnia, it will touch on money, sex, and power, and there will be a furious counterattack.

Yet, Jesus, we celebrate how it will all end: a great multitude, which no one can count, from every nation, consisting of all tribes and tongues, standing before the Lamb singing: "Salvation belongs to our God who sits on the throne, and to the Lamb! Blessing and glory and wisdom, thanksgiving and honor and power and might, be to our God forever" (Rev. 7:9–10, 12). And the Lamb who is at the center of the throne will be our Shepherd, and He will wipe every tear from our eyes (v. 17).

PURSUING CHURCH PLANTING:

We are still discerning how to wage spiritual war here in Narnia. I referenced previously that there is a spirit of bullying, a pride in Narnia being the center of Islam, a hardness and arrogance about Islam, fiercer here than in other places. The longer we stay, it appears that the core issues are the timeless human issues of money, sex, and power, exacerbated by fourteen centuries without godly Christian people praying. The human heart is the same everywhere, and other lands are rife with perversions. Yet other lands have also had Christlike salt and light to retard the decay or to push it back towards the hellhole from which it comes. But what is the effect on the spiritual climate of a land that has had so little salt and light, so little prayer for 1,400 years?

There is a veneer of purity, but the sexual perversity and abuse here are shocking—and often justified through religious allowances. The real God is mammon, and men and women revere wealth and the status and opportunities it brings. Power is held onto at any cost, and those who hold it and want to keep it make diabolical deals. Over these three idolatrous forces (money, sex, and power), Islam has spread its deceptive and demonic wings.

We must be careful then of their assault on us, for Islam is but a new and transient evil. The devil was at work long before Islam raised its ugly head. We are not immune to the allure of power, and missionaries must be careful they don't trade in their prophetic voice for access to the royal family. We are not immune to the seduction of money, and missionaries must be vigilant that the investment of time and capital put into our businesses don't make us fear being evangelists. We are not immune to sexual temptations, and missionaries must be vigilant to guard our eyes, minds, marriages, and bodies as temples of the Holy Spirit. We would be foolish to think that these idols of money, sex, and power that have ruled without local Christians to pray against them for so long will not attack and try to kill us.

Jesus, keep us vigilant; let us give no foothold to the enemy in these (or other areas) of our lives. Jesus, protect us from these temptations; let us be aware (and not afraid) of the enemy's devices and resist him in Your cruciform power, poverty of spirit, and purity.

PURSUING JESUS:

From the rising of the sun to its setting, the name of the Lord is to be praised (Psalm 113:3). Jesus, You are so beautiful and so worthy. You are all that thrills my soul. I want to praise You from the moment that I wake up to the moment I lay down, and even in my sleep I want to exalt You. Let me never stop giving You glory and from my heart being glad and thankful to You. Let me also be thankful to those who have gone ahead of us, who bore the burden and scorching heat of the day (Matt. 20:12). Let me remember that I am to be a servant, a slave who lays down my life for others (vv. 26–27). Christ, very God of very God, laid down His life as a ransom for many. I am not a redeemer, much less *the* Redeemer, but I must yield and lay down my life for the Redeemer's purposes. Lord, the one thing my soul wants is to see *You* (v. 33). Help me realize that in laying down my life, I can best take up my sight. Thank you, Jesus, that Your compassion moves You to touch my eyes, to touch my soul, to help me see You!

Let me, therefore, serve the Lord with all humility through all tears and trials (Acts 20:19). Let me not shrink back from declaring anything valuable (v. 20), whether to the lost or to the found, even if that declaration is difficult and dangerous. Let me see the declaration of who You are as a sacred trust, solemnly testifying of repentance toward God and faith in Christ (v. 21). Let me take deep joy in being bound by the Spirit, not having to know what will happen, except that in every city the Holy Spirit solemnly testifies that bonds and afflictions await (vv. 22–23). Three times in just a few verses "solemnly testifies" is mentioned. Let me not lose the sacred awe of my assignment, never considering my life of any account or as dear to myself (v. 24).

Jesus, there is so much pride in me, so much reluctance to serve, so much fear of losing control and being bound by others or even by You. Teach me the liberty of lowliness, obedience, sacrifice, and faithfulness, trusting that the reward of *You* is worth any trial, tear, insult, humility, and difficulty. Give me a holy joy anticipating difficulty, for the riches of You that I will encounter in, through, and beyond it. Along the way, please keep teaching me to pray, believing that the prayers of the saints do matter, do accumulate, and do rise up before God, that there will be a tipping point, and that the fire from the altar of God will eventually be thrown to earth (Rev. 8:4).

PURSUING CHURCH PLANTING:

Yesterday was a Sabbath day, and what I find restful is an organized desk, inbox, and mind. I spent the day first luxuriating with Jesus in my abiding time, cleaning out my inbox, and doing some editing to a paper on which I've been ruminating. I also ignored two somewhat important phone calls: one from a Narnian friend and one from an American visiting the country. I felt rest and order on this day was more important than connecting with them. Given there is such unpredictability to church planting, it behooves us to have the organizational clarity in life, work, and service that can allow for the organic variance that life and ministry always bring. A clear mind and uncluttered spirit are the basis for creativity and the unexpected opportunity. We can't sustain chaos.

In the middle of the day, I received a text from a colleague in another context as they were in the midst of an organic union between MBBs who had not met together before. There is risk and uncertainty, joy and expectation. My colleague asked for the simple guidelines that a veteran in the faith who serves as an advisor to a local leader of a movement to Jesus in another country shared about what they do. Here is the summary of his thinking and their approach:

1. Compared to the early church, we don't have it so bad.

We are adequate—if they were! We don't have it bad with resources; we have more than they did. Roman culture was perverse, immoral, violent, and prosperous. Christians were eaten, crucified, used as torches, disenfranchised (no vote or political power). Yet who did Jesus call?

The graduating class of 33, Galilee Bible College! Actually no one graduates; they all run away. They were inexperienced, cowardly, weak, fearful, unwise, uneducated.

The early church did not have much. They were disorganized. No constitution, no mission statement. No equipment, no web, no media, no newspapers. No property, no buildings, no offices. No faith promises, no Speed the Light, no BGMC, no banks. No motorized transport. No Bible schools, no correspondence classes, no online lessons, no missiology. No New Testament!

These things (including technology) are not bad—they just were not essential to the planting of the early church.

2. Conversion process

Believers must renounce Satan, Islam, and the Qur'an when they get saved. They have to make a clean cut with old religion. (1) Believers are discipled to be like Jesus. (2) Believe and practice what Jesus believed and practiced. (3) Obey what Jesus said. (4) Do what Jesus did.

3. Cell groups and fellowship

More than eight men meeting together draws attention, so they hide in the open by meeting in the mosque courtyard at non-prayer times. They baptize by using the public mosque shower. To join a cell group/house church (upper room), you must:

- *Be saved;*
- *Be baptized in the Holy Spirit or seeking it;*

- *Be baptized in water;*
- *Be witnessing to your family (or friends if family is highly hostile); and*
- *Be helping the needy.*

The approach is not complicated, but it demands full allegiance to Jesus and courageous followership that is centered on proclaiming Christ at whatever cost. To date they have had fifteen martyrs (last I heard). There is organic growth, but it is based on very clear organizational principles with high accountability. The catalytic leader used to be in Hamas and was influenced by the structure of the Muslim Brotherhood.

DAY 55

PURSUING JESUS:

"Tremble, O earth, before the Lord, before the God of Jacob" (Psalm 114:7). Jesus, I don't want to lose my tremble before You. I am so thankful for Your intimacy and condescension, but I don't want to lose a sense of awe. Help my house (my heart, my life) to be one of prayer (Matt. 21:13). Help me to grow in prayer myself and also to have a nations-oriented heart, that there is expanding room in my soul for Your passion for the nations. I don't have to fabricate it; I just need to receive and welcome it from You. Thank you for the promise that all things I ask in prayer, believing, I will receive (v. 22). You have told me to ask for the nations. You have promised me You will grant what I ask for. You give the request and the answer, and I must only believe. The stone the builders rejected became the chief stone; this came from the Lord and is marvelous in our eyes (v. 42). Jesus, You were rejected. And yet, You were God's plan, and nothing can thwart God's ambitions. Let me relish rejection whenever You ordain it, knowing that You can turn rejected stones into building blocks. It will be Your doing, marvelous in my eyes.

Let me be ready then to be rejected or bound or to die for the name of the Lord Jesus (Acts 21:13). Let my whole disposition and behavior cry out and live on in the spirit of "the will of the Lord be done" (v. 14). Let me concern myself in preaching to all men everywhere (v. 28), letting the Lord arrange and resolve the consequences. Seal my mind, O Lord (Rev. 9:4), on You and Your will, finding increasing fulfilment with increasing opposition.

PURSUING CHURCH PLANTING:

At the personal level I want to find how I can best spread the gospel to the most people and be most fruitful in making Jesus known. I would like to pursue these avenues of "wide sowing" here in the city:

1.   See if I can get the major English and Arabic newspaper to publish a daily column from me as a pastor.

2.   Produce content for YouTube on video, perhaps with subtitles for clarity. In other words, I would speak in English and add subtitles in Arabic. The videos would be evangelistic, Jesus-oriented, and Bible-based, but openly filmed in and relating to Narnia.

3.   Engage with follow-up systems to meet with all who are interested in the gospel, seekers, and potential men of peace.

4.   Pursue E. Stanley Jones open lectures on Jesus and the Kingdom in neutral venues (halls and event rooms, not churches) that are openly geared for Muslims, presenting the undiluted gospel in kind, transparent fashion.

I do not think everyone should do the above, but I do think within our personalities and giftings, we need to search for creative ways to constantly get the gospel out. Different personalities will use different mediums, but it is imperative each of us find a way to constantly preach the gospel, not being satisfied with service or activities (wonderful as they are). We have to find ways to obey our mandate to proclaim.

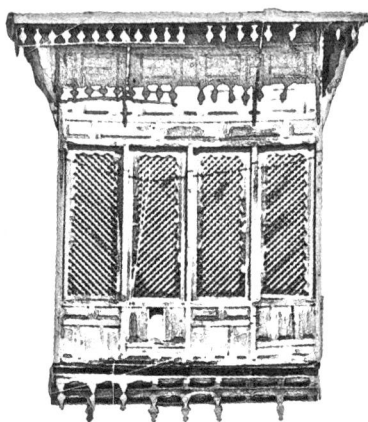

FIELD READY

For many years missions agencies required missionaries to have ministry experience before appointing them to the field. My own agency required pastoral experience of at least two years and ordination. Over the years this has changed, and for some valid reasons. I personally went right from Bible college to the field at 22 and never looked back.

The premise of this short article, however, is that whatever the age of the missionary at the time of field deployment, some basic competencies should be in place prior, and there should be intentional discipleship that grows these competencies (whether a person deploys to the field immediately after university or spends formative years in their home culture prior to deployment). What follows are qualities that would be helpful to have in place to some degree before deployment, that they can develop and mature during the course of on field training and fruitful missionary service. These qualities may be present in the very young and absent in the old or vice versa. What is critical is that they are in place and maturing. I first list some qualities more commonly absent in the young and inexperienced followed by some qualities we look for and expect in the mature and experienced. I conclude with some suggested action steps for mission senders and receivers.

QUALITIES DESIRED IN THE YOUNG AND INEXPERIENCED

Grit

In North American culture of late, everyone is "awesome" and gets a "participation award." Children are often redirected rather than disciplined, and we are repeatedly told how wonderful we are. This is not always true and it's not always bad, but a result is that our culture often doesn't always know how to deal with failure. When we leave home or university and enter the realities of a world where we are not awesome, where we don't get affirmed for mere participation, and where we have to produce and be fruitful in order to receive praise (even then praise is scarce), we don't often have the grit to keep going when no one is cheering for us. Frankly, our affluence has made us soft and our context has empowered lateral shifts while other cultures often have fewer options and thus they better teach endurance and faithfulness in the option they have, or have chosen. When a person has spent some time in the workplace, been shamed or shouted at by a driven boss, learned they can't whine/cry/complain/curl up in a ball but have to pick themselves up, square their shoulders, and go back to work, if a person has developed grit in a neutral or unfriendly workplace, they are better positioned for the harsh realities of missionary service.

Value of Money

These days in university years many students have parents paying their car insurance and phone plan, and they move right from being supported by their parents or university scholarships to raising missions support for the field. The result is, many graduates have never worked to comprehensively cover all their expenses. Bluntly, they don't know the value of the dollar; thus, they don't really understand the value of others sacrificial giving. We simply don't manage money well when we don't know how hard it is to earn enough to cover all our own bills. We spend more cavalierly. Many North Americans do not manage money well generally, living beyond their means, or choosing to live more lavishly rather than more generously when increase allows. This is a stewardship sin when our income in missions is provided by hard working supporters. There is tremendous value in the experience of paying all your own bills, in learning how much work it is to earn money. Whether during university or after, an essential missionary competency is respect for the difficulty of making money and capacity to balance a budget and live within our means.

Sober Sense of Reality

With deferred adolescence many young twenty-somethings don't yet have an accurate view of themselves or their gifts. Sometimes it takes the harsh culture of the workplace (or a church staff) for a developing minister to realize (and be told) that they are not gifted in certain areas. This helps them to both understand where they need to grow and where they need to cede that role and work to others who are more gifted. In a university setting there tends to be much more tolerance for mediocre participation. While not always true, often the workplace (market or ministry) weeds out mediocrity, ruthlessly forcing growth and a clearer view of how others see you and your gifts. This is painful but necessary, and if it can be learned in university and/or before field deployment, it will be a huge blessing to the team as well as the individual.

Love of the Church

Missions is essentially making disciples that make disciples among the unreached and growing them into churches. We cannot plant nor grow what we do not love. If we are to plant the church, we must love the church—both the organizational and organic aspects of it. We must make disciples in our own culture before we do it abroad, and these disciples need to be multi-generational. The limitation of the Bible college experience is that discipleship is naturally centered on the saved (small groups, residence directors, ministry teams), while the limitation of a Chi Alpha university experience is that it tends to be mono-generational. Marketplace service thrusts you into the domain of the lost, and church ministry experience requires multi-generational skills. Both aspects are needed for missions: living surrounded by *the lost* of *all generations*.

Both the Bible college and the Chi Alpha experiences tend to orient young ministers to thrive in the organic aspects of church; thus, we increasingly see young missionaries who either despise or neglect the organizational aspects of church. They love the community, services, worship, preaching, and prayer, but they are not so keen on the structure, administration, discipline, details, doctrine, conflict solving, routines, clean-up, and all the non-glamorous, private, and messy aspects. The best missionaries are prepared to love the church, the whole church, both the beautiful and ugly components. The best missionaries understand the church in its variegated functions in their own culture; they are then prepared to contextualize that church towards indigenous forms. Whatever the age of deployment to the field, a love of the church (organizational as well as organic) is critical.

Process of Counting the Cost

Those who give up nothing to go to the field often more easily give up in the field. If you have not given up a career, house, great church, or free childcare from grandparents, if it cost you nothing to go to the field, it costs you nothing to leave it. Often young couples and young singles who come right to missions from university have not accrued any responsibilities in the wider world or many assets to be laid down. They come gladly and relatively freely to the field, which is wonderful, but they also (having less cost to count) leave more easily. Juxtaposed to this reality is the family with great jobs and friends, a wonderful house and loving church, volunteer positions, status in society, credibility in community, nearby family, etc., and they lay all those things down to head to the field. These are massive transitions not entered into lightly, huge implications not made or unmade without resolve. This resolve then works on the field when things are rough for the family, for knowing the depth of the cost of their commitment they do not unmake that commitment easily or quickly. In our discipleship we need to continually strive to develop consistency and steadiness, calling for and training towards long-term (career) missionary commitment.

In defense of those who come to the field young, there are costs that they count. We have seen several of our young missionaries threatened, belittled or aggressively manipulated by parents who are angry at them for taking small children to the field, to dangerous and inhospitable environments. This emotional pressure can go on for years and we have seen Christian parents be some of least sympathetic and supportive. The pressure to come home is staggering at times. The fact that young parents put their children in foreign language preschools and day cares so that both husband and wife can learn language and fully engage in mission life is a further cost counted. Lastly, many of our young missionaries walk away from potential careers or potential ministry positions of excellence. They lay down high salary offers, substantial work opportunities, the potential of accrued savings, and the convenience of materialism. Many young missionaries really are exceptional leaders, intelligent thinkers, hard workers, and the cream of their generation. They lay down what they could be in their home context for what God will be among the nations.

Consequential Service

Having already mentioned the value of multi-generational service (both in the church and marketplace), there are further lessons to be learned in the home context including: theological vetting (in the church through other ministers and exposure to thoughts wider than found in a more cloistered university setting, and in the marketplace having to defend your own beliefs in hostile or intimidating settings), submission to leadership, and learning to work in a group. In both the church and the workplace, there are tighter controls regarding your use of time and higher accountability regarding work ethic. Further, you can be fired; your livelihood depends on your performance. There are fewer safety nets, less room for selfishness, and more stringent consequences for error or folly. All these realities forge maturity which is invaluable on the field. Before deployment, field workers should have a base understanding of consequences (both personal and corporate) for ineffective or unprofessional labor.

Work Ethic and Holism

New missionaries should be healthy financially (know how to budget, save, plan, pay bills, give), emotionally (deal with conflict appropriately, relate to all without being awkward), spiritually (ability to self-feed and the discipline to abide in a schedule busier than university), relationally (know how to follow, lead, be collegiate, live in mutual submission), physically (eating, exercising, sleeping, Sabbath), and administratively (managing time, projects, and assigned tasks that affect others, handling full schedules with multiple variables like chores, shopping, and banking in addition to normal work, ministry, and language.) Living holistically post-university is very different than during university, whether in a secular or evangelical college. Those who are stable (while growing) in these areas are a great blessing to the missionary teams they join. Studying language twenty hours or more a week, participating in team meetings, reaching out to the lost, navigating a new culture, and dealing with spiritual warfare in intensified ways, all of these are more demanding than even the busy schedules of the university experience. Marketplace believers have the advantage of learning how to work 40-plus hours a week, volunteer at church, reach their neighbors, and manage a household.

We want the young!

There are obviously many benefits to young missionaries coming to the field immediately after college and we welcome their presence. For example, education is easier than re-education. For example, habits and thoughts can be formed about the American church, evangelism, and discipleship in American culture that need to then be unlearned for a cross-cultural context. Life (work opportunities, children, assets, responsibilities) can suck you in and make it harder to answer God's call to the field. The younger you are, the easier it is to learn language. The less experienced you are, the more teachable you tend to be. It is also true that some who struggled the most to adjust to the humbling process of entering the field as a rookie missionary are those with the most life experience, and that some of our best missionaries were groomed on the field starting immediately after their university experience. We want the young! But we also want them to come with the above base competencies in hand, or at least knowledge that growth in these areas is inevitable and a hunger to grow and learn. The humility to want to be formed in the above and other areas is paramount.

QUALITIES DESIRED IN THE MATURE AND EXPERIENCED

Abiding

Abiding in Jesus is our core value. Through the years we have learned that some of our mature and experienced in life and ministry do not spend extravagant, intimate time with Jesus on a daily basis. Our expectation for all who come to the field is that they would prioritize time with Jesus on a daily basis, in His word and in His Spirit for extended time. We believe in obedience-based discipleship, and that obedience is only sustained in the right spirit by those who consistently abide in Jesus.

Simple Purity

Experience can unfortunately jade you, but there is no place (and no excuse for) snide remarks, off-handed comments, sexual innuendos, angry outbursts, gossip, passive aggressiveness, the refusal to confront in love, the garnering of embittered allies, verbal abuse, and the perpetuating of negative narratives about others. Some of these un-Christlike qualities are so common in the workplace, they can seep into the mature over time. When these negative attributes, born of cynicism and watered through lack of loving, corrective discipleship, make their way to the field carried within the mature, they are devastating to team and colleagues.

Cruciform Character

We need mature men and women who have learned how to forgive as Jesus commanded. Patient, dignified, gracious, restrained, mercy-praying, gossip-swallowing, Golden Rule-following, mature field workers are desperately needed. We need those who come with years of experience to not be the walking wounded who transmit their wounds, but to be the ones who know how to take wounds (theirs and others) to the Holy Spirit and have them transformed. We need the mature who truly live out the crucified life, who know what dying to self means and do it well, without show or super-spiritual drama.

Unentitled

A trap of experience is the propensity to entitlement and comparison. Those with life experience tend to think that they deserve honor or that they should make a lateral shift or that the esteem they earned in their prior workplace should be automatically transferred to them on the field. In fact, those that led previously often struggle the most as they must begin as a novice, unable to speak the language and unfamiliar with the culture. There is a season when experienced are only learners (not teachers), and few have the humility to become last and least again (especially if they hail from an executive or leadership role). Some experienced workers (especially those who have been their own boss for a time) struggle to submit to a corporate vision, resist others having input into their job description, and resist leadership by a younger colleague.

Followership

The more mature and experienced have a longer list of what they will not do, where they will not live, and what activities they will not engage in. We don't demand blind allegiance, but we do expect biblical submission. Ironically, the trend is that those who led at the higher levels previously struggle the most to follow others on the field. No matter how humble the mature start on the field, many will eventually struggle with an unspoken expectation that they will get fast tracked to leadership or to a certain title and are not always willing to do the hard (or hidden) work which is core to fruitful missionary labor.

Humility

The humility required for the mature to come to the field often feels like humiliation. Death still comes before resurrection, even for the mature. We talk on the field of the "glorious deconstruction" that Jesus puts us through when we come to the field, but the reality is that deconstruction never feels glorious. One of our workers came in their 50s and commented that transitioning to the field feels "more like decomposing than deconstructing." The death-to-self experienced on the field and in team life is very difficult; it is far more difficult for people over 30 then under. The more mature can tend to think they are God's gift to the mission because of their fruitful, public service back home. Those who were frequently praised and admired struggle most when that praise dries up and they no longer have a public platform to stand on and minister from.

Grace

As hard as it is for the mature to die to the accolades of public ministry or service, those that do it with grace and lead in this walk of humility have young people falling over themselves to serve alongside them to the end of the earth. Everyone can see through prideful, fake humility that quietly (or overtly) finagles a way to lead. Coveting a leadership position is a legitimate danger in many who come to the field with work and ministry experience. For them, as for all of us, it's easy to lose sight that the main thing we do is reaching the lost in teams. We ask the mature to truly lay down the understandable desire to lead in order to focus on reaching the unreached in teams. Cream always rises to the top. When the mature are patient and gracious, God always places them just where He wants them, just when He needs them, just as they are ready. It's a big ask, but we ask those who come to the field later in life be teachable, listen well, and truly abandon all (including their prior status and reputation), trusting that Jesus knows, sees, and rules in the kingdoms of men and missions. Resurrection is our biblical hope, but ever impossible without prior death to self.

We want the mature and experienced!

There are manifold benefits to the mature and experienced coming to the field. We want leaders, those who have navigated life, raised children, launched ministries, planted churches, and waded through the dirt and discouragement of daily service. We need warriors, battle tested men and women who indeed have much to offer from their experience, from the wisdom only acquired through wounds and war. We want the mature and experienced! But we also want them to come with the above qualities in hand and heart for their own peace and ours.

CONCLUSION

There is no magic age for missionary deployment. There are benefits to coming to the field immediately after university. There are benefits to coming with ministry and marketplace experience. There are also challenges to both demographics. Young arrivals most bless the missionary cause when they have the skills, maturity, and experiences listed above. This combination (skills/maturity/experience) is increasingly uncommon to the immediate university graduate. We desire to receive those just graduated from university (and sometimes even younger) and will do so when there is evidence that the above competencies are present and maturing in them. Mature arrivals that are entitled, unteachable, and not truly humble cause immeasurable harm, hurt, and division. We desire to receive them for all they will add to us. Their maturity is needed, but we need Christlike maturity, not a cynical spirit informed by the spirit of the age more than by the Spirit of God. Whatever the age of the field worker, senders can bless the field work by ensuring those they commission have the positives above alive and growing within.

So, the first purpose of this paper is to help senders evaluate their own (whether young or mature), that they may send those hungry to learn, humble enough to learn in uncomfortable ways, and smart enough to know themselves and others. In his book *The Ideal Team Player*, Patrick Lencioni explains "hungry" as having a great work ethic and drive, "humble" as being more interested in others than yourself, and "smart" as having emotional intelligence, common sense, and people skills. The combination of these qualities (as the chart below shows) is helpful, while the lack of one or more of these essentials leads to trouble on the field for all.

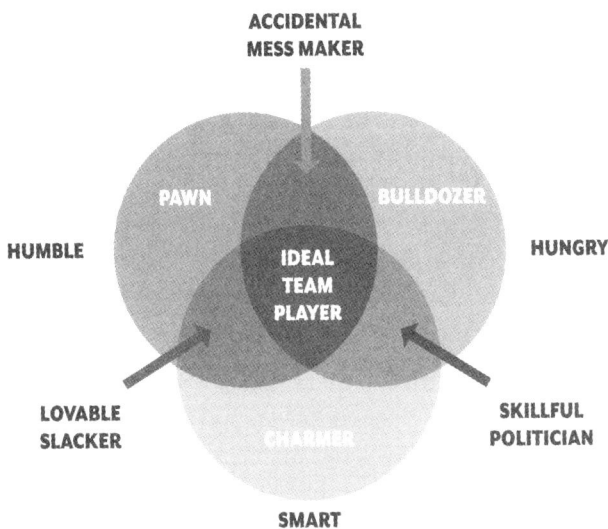

The second purpose of this paper is to suggest to mission receivers that they should not blithely receive all who apply, but that in the end an irenic screening process is good stewardship of God's time. While there are multiple ways of doing this, my recommendation is we make a shorter on-field experience part of the application process. If a prospective missionary will visit the field for an internship (ideally 6-8 weeks), the team leader will have a fairly good sense if the above qualities are in place. This internship can then open the door to longer service, ideally a 2- to 3-year first term that is training in orientation. If in that internship the team leaders see a glaring omission of some of the above qualities and sense the applicant would be better served by ministry or marketplace experience in their home context, the kindest act would be to then inform the applicant accordingly. Those who are older, more mature, and committed to the work place or ministry usually do not have 6-8 weeks available, so more discretion is required in the screening and interviewing process.

Pursuing Jesus:

Not to us, O Lord, not to us, but to Your name be glory (Psalm 115:1). Forgive me, Lord, for being a glory pirate. I want to scale Your ships and plunder what is not mine as booty. In so many ways I seek to steal credit, attention, honor, or praise. Lord Jesus Christ, King of glory, rightful owner of *all* honor, forgive my thieving heart. Let me not be so fearful that I will be dishonored. Let me trust in the Lord (vv. 9–11), that whatever His choice is for me, in it alone will I find blessing and contentment. Teach me, Lord, the folly of striving for what is not mine. Teach me the satisfaction of giving You all the glory, receiving only what You have apportioned for me, no matter if it's inglorious. Let my glory be in You alone, satisfied with Your will for me. Let me remember and revel in the fact that Your choice for me is that I am a slave sent out to call others to the King (Matt. 22:3). Don't let me lose the tremble of a King enraged when His invitation is scorned (v. 7), and don't let me lose sight of the reality that those who scorn will weep, gnash their teeth, and be thrown into outer darkness (v. 13). Only by knowing the Scripture *and* the power of God will I avoid error (v. 29). O God of the living, let me love You with *all* (vv. 32, 37).

Let me not forget who You are, King Jesus (Acts 22:8). Paul had plenty of head knowledge about the Scripture, but understanding did not descend until he encountered the power of Your person. Jesus is the Lord of glory whom we are persecuting, insulting, defying, ignoring, disobeying, wounding, and crucifying. What should we do when we realize this (v. 10)? Get up and *go*, for we are appointed to (1) know His will, (2) see the Righteous One, (3) hear an utterance from His mouth, and (4) be a witness. Jesus, let me not delay (v. 16), but whether it is to leave or to stay and pay the consequences (vv. 19–20), let me ever be obedient to share Christ. Let me have an eternal spirit of *go* (v. 21), allowing the God of all nations to determine where and how and when I must "pay." For there ever will be a cost to following Jesus. Let me have the confidence that the King ever makes a way for His messengers. The angel in Revelation 10 was a messenger of God clothed with a cloud, a rainbow on his head, a face like the sun, and feet as pillars of fire. If I am obedient to God as His angels are, I can be sure of His testimonial credibility. Let me then delay no longer, for the mystery of God is finished (vv. 6, 8). There are no more secrets and there is nothing to wait for; I must open my mouth and be a faithful prophet against all that is wicked (v. 11). This assignment seems exhilarating at first, but it has a cost—it is bitter in the mouth (v. 10). Lord, give me grace to represent You well. The reward is not earthly; the only reward sufficient to cover the pain is You forever.

PURSUING CHURCH PLANTING:

This week we are in meetings in Jordan, reviewing and praying over the Arab world. It has been a joy to pray country by country, team by team, and to remember again that prayer is not only preparation for the work, it is the work. In four days of meetings, the bulk of our time was spent praying team by team across the Arab world. Church planting goes forward on its knees. One sister shared that prophetic image with me; she had the picture of us facing great odds and fighting through them to victory, but from a posture of prayer, from kneeling to fight.

PURSUING JESUS:

I will call upon Him as long as I live (Psalm 116:2). There will never be a time when I do not need the grace, righteousness, and compassion of Jesus (v. 5). I will ever be brought low and in need of saving (v. 6), and I will ever need to return to rest in Him, for He has dealt beautifully with me (v. 7). When I die to self, He finds it beautiful and precious (v. 15), so let me daily be beautiful for You, Jesus. And when my time arrives to come home, whether by accident, age, or martyrdom, let that death merely crown a life that has ever lived to make You pleased. Let me not waste any more time, mine or Yours, in trying to exalt myself (Matt. 23:12). Forgive me for all the energy already spent in this folly, for it only leads to humbling shame. Rather let me live life with the perfectly good conscience that I have only done what You wanted (Acts 23:1). If I will do what honors You, there will be authority granted to prophesy, and fire will fall from my mouth (Rev. 11:3–6). The price of that fire is my lowliness, perfect submission to You. Thank you, Lord, that if I will truly humble myself, the breath of life from God will put me on my feet (v. 11), and You will lift me up [not in status or position but to Your presence (v. 12)], and use me to announce that "the kingdoms of this world have become the kingdoms of our Lord and of His Christ, and He shall reign forever and ever" (v. 15). The King's dominion (king-dom) will be established, and we will join the elders in falling on our face to worship with all the nations (v. 16). It does no good to be angry at God in the flesh (v. 18), for His anger will burn up ours and He will ruthlessly destroy all who have callously destroyed what He created good.

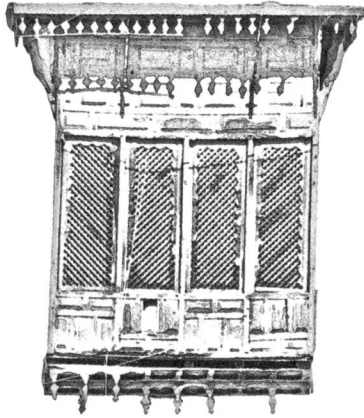

FIGHTING FOR SOULS

I don't know how it happened, but somehow I slipped into believing the lie that I was too busy leading missionaries to be winning Muslims to Jesus. Believing the lie, I accommodated it by choosing a schedule that made it virtually impossible to have time for evangelism. Chagrined, I am reminded that none of us—*none of us*—are exempted from the Great Commission. We all are to make disciples. We all must fight for souls. When it comes to fighting and winning souls, I am reminded of the following:

Souls are not easily won.

Soul winning takes time, effort, and emotional and physical energy. In post-Christian cultures, in resistant tribes, in domineering ideologies, in false religions, ground is gained ever so slowly and ever so patiently. We sow the gospel widely because so many will reject it. We search on, we ask others, we seek out—sometimes for years. In some contexts we are rebuffed and rejected hundreds (maybe thousands of times) before we find a person of peace. Souls are not easily won.

Because souls are hard to fight for, we get easily distracted into lesser fights.

The fatigue of fighting for a soul (and not winning one easily or quickly) can so easily make us turn our attention to other winnable scraps. Projects, buildings, permits, ministries, and social action all have measurable deliverables. We can see something completed; we can count assistance given out; and we can number physical bodies healed or helped. If we cannot have the satisfaction of counting converts, at least we can count convalescents. Compassionate care is measurable and within our control. Converting souls is something God alone can do, and He does it on His timetable. I am not saying any social project is without value. I am saying that projects and humanitarian assistance are not the end goal. The end goal is eternal life, souls saved, and disciples made. We must fight to win souls.

Because souls are so hard to fight for, we often turn to fighting for recognition, position, title, and honor.

A title can be tangible. A position, rejoiced in. Honor can satisfy and recognition can assure us that we are doing something of value. When we are not focused on fighting for souls, we so easily turn to defending our status, putting energy into assuring our position is not weakened or undermined. We start obsessing over petty things. We become defensive and possessive. We are more grieved that someone circumnavigated our authority than we are that men and women all around us are dying and going to hell without Jesus. Lines of authority are critical and must be honored, but I notice that when I am focused on soul winning, I care much less when my followers abandon protocol. If I am not concentrated on souls, I have more energy to make sure people treat me right. When I concentrate on souls, I don't really care how people treat me.

Because souls are so valuable, a primary tactic of the devil is to get us fighting one another, instead of fighting for souls.

Satan knows the priceless value of a soul, so in his grand battle plan he knows he wins more souls when we lose time fighting each other. Simply put, energy spent (mental, physical, emotional) in fighting one another is energy not spent (time and attention) on winning souls. We have finite amounts of daily energy, and the devil loves to see it consumed against one another. I am horrified to think how much time and energy in my life and ministry has been diverted from fighting for souls because I was defending myself or attacking my friend.

It's wartime and we were designed for battle, so we better battle for souls.

A day will come when we lay our weapons down, but night has not yet come and there are still souls to fight for. We are commissioned by the Lord of angel armies to fight for His lost ones. We are to fight through our giving (sacrificial and generous). We are to fight through our praying (constant and fervent). We are to fight through our proclamation (fearless and clear). We are to fight through our going (where the gospel has not yet gone). We are soldiers, and we fight for souls. Missionaries in difficult places have a particular calling (and affinity) for battle. We are hard heads. We wouldn't be where we are (male and female) if there wasn't a bit of feisty in us. Thus, when we don't diligently apply our battle instincts towards fighting for souls, we naturally devolve to fighting peripheral wars, and we fight for ground that strategically does not need to be taken. That's the best-case scenario—harmless distracted projects. The worst-case scenario is that we turn our weapons on our friends, colleagues, families, and leaders. When we start these civil wars and maim one another, the devil pulls up a chair to enjoy the show, cackles with glee, and swallows up lost souls like popcorn.

Summary

I love a good fight. It's in my nature to compete and battle, and if you are a missionary to the unreached, that same warrior spirit is within you. Lord, forgive us for fighting against our own people and for the wrong things. Lord, focus afresh our arsenals and our energies on fighting for souls. For those of you who never lost the vision for souls, but are weary and wounded in the fight, perhaps this stanza from an old Scottish war ballad is for you:

> *"Fight on, my men," says Sir Andrew Barton,*
> *"I am hurt, but I am not slain;*
> *I'll lay me down and bleed a-while,*
> *And then I'll rise and fight again."[12]*

Let's fight on for souls.

DAY 58

PURSUING JESUS:

All nations will praise the Lord (Psalm 117:1), and it is that praise that makes them great. God's lovingkindness is such that when we laud Him, He magnifies us. His ways are so counter to what we think and strive for. No nation can make itself great. Great nations are those who make much of Jesus, for only then is the power of God released to make something of them. This may not seem true in the short term, but it is always proved so over eternal time. History is not man-centered, for Jesus is coming in power and great glory (Matt. 24:30). He is near, even at the door, so we must be alert (vv. 33, 42). We must gather like vultures around Him, so focused that we circle Him in ever narrowing patterns, losing sight of all else.

When it is needed, let me live in such holy honesty that I can cheerfully make a defense for all my mission actions (Acts 24:10). Let me have lived with such integrity that I can admit that I have served God, believed the Bible, had hope in God, looked to the resurrection, and done my best to live in good conscience (vv. 14–16).

To focus on Jesus like a vulture on a corpse and to live in such a way that is blameless will mean that the world will not understand me. They will think me narrow, and that narrow path leads to a wilderness of sorts, a wilderness of misunderstanding and rejection, a wilderness prepared by God so that He can nourish me (Rev. 12:6). Along the way He reveals that though the devil and his minions are strong, they are not strong enough (v. 8), and we will overcome because of the blood of the Lamb and the word of our testimony and because we did not love our life, even if that kills us (v. 11). A life (or death) so trusting of Jesus that it embraces pain in the wilderness enrages the devil (v. 17), partly because it exposes his folly. The devil had the heavenly presence of

Jesus with high position and influence, and it was not enough for him. How shaming it is to him when lower beings find higher satisfaction in much more lowly assignments. I can make Jesus glad and Satan mad by being heavenly content in hellish circumstances.

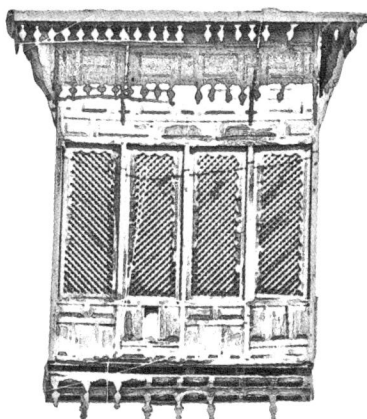

FROM SHIRE TO FIRE

There is an old chorus that says: "Oh, my precious brother, when the world's on fire, you need my Jesus to be your Savior..."[13] I sang this today while sitting in the Eden green of Malewa, Kenya. Malewa is a little haven on the Malu River outside Naivasha, nestled in forest and fauna. It's a little paradise on earth, not unlike the shire in *The Lord of the Rings* trilogy. Quaint houses are surrounded by acacia trees and indigenous foliage, friendly neighbors, peace, calm, and the imperturbable equatorial weather—never too hot, never too cold. Jennifer and I are here for a few weeks of writing and resting.

Sitting in my shire, I cannot escape the thought of a world on fire. In these last days, there are more lost than ever rushing towards hell. There are 3.15 billion in over 7,000 unreached people groups without an adequate witness of the heavenly shire. This little earthly haven has been hit by tragedy, sickness, sin, and death before, and it will be again, for it only represents our heavenly home, which, as C. S. Lewis puts it in *The Last Battle*, is "still Narnia, and more real and more beautiful than the Narnia down below…the new [Narnia] was a deeper country; every rock and flower and blade of grass looked as if it meant more." As beautiful as this lower shire is, it is just a copy of the shire above.

Which brings us to the issue: I am probably in the top one percent of the world who has the means to retreat from the fire to the shire. Most do not have this blessing. Stewardship responsibility demands that I cannot live here; I must only retreat and refresh here that I might plunge back into the fire—too many are perishing, too many burn. If you're reading this, you most likely are in that one percent of the world, too. Even the poor in the West have the opportunity to pull back from the hottest part of the flames. You, too, have the responsibility to make your shire a place of retreat and renewal, not a place of residence.

Lest this analogy is not crystal clear, let me be blunt, drawing from *The Lord of the Rings* imagery and narrative.

1.   Our world is on fire. Men, women, and children of all ages, races, and religions plunge into the eternal flame. Corruption and iniquity abound. We are in the last days, and it will only get worse. Humankind desperately needs to know of the loving Savior who has made a way to escape the eternal fire. The fires of this world pale compared to the fire to come. We can't pretend that the world is not on fire.

2.   Because the world is on fire, we cannot retreat to reside in our shire—for both practical and moral reasons. Morally, it is unjust for us to be safe while others perish when we have the means to aid them. Practically, the shire will not escape the fire. The battle is coming to us, and indeed it is the last battle. It will leave no stone of earth unturned or un-scorched. To bury our heads in the green grass of the shire, hoping the fire will pass us by, is foolish self-delusion.

3. We may be hobbits (weak and frail, silly and foolish), yet we've been chosen to leave our shires to take the battle to Mordor (the evil center of the flames). We might not feel it yet or we might know it deep down and resist it or we might have retreated, wounded from the fire and fray and reluctant to return, but we are called to battle. The times and meta-narrative demand it—even from hobbits, especially from hobbits.

I do not begrudge you your shire, and I hope you don't begrudge me mine. But neither of us can reside here. The world is on fire, and this shire is doomed. We will retreat to our shires for respite and renewal, but we must buckle on our smoke blackened armor again and return to battle. "Once more unto the breach dear friends…once more."[14]

DAY 59

PURSUING JESUS:

Jesus, let my footsteps be established in Your word, and do not let any iniquity have dominion over me (Psalm 119:133). Let me only have one King that I revere. What a wonder that You have entrusted Your possessions to us (Matt. 25:14), that here on earth You trust us to make You known and invite all people to Your eternal joy. Let me not approach this unfathomable honor cavalierly by trying to do it as I want. Not as I will, but as You will! Let me commit no offense in this stewardship (Acts 25:8), save what is fitting for Your sake. Let me evade no offense if Your honor is at stake. Let me have a single eye on the hope of the promise that You gave to our fathers (26:6-7)—all nations will be blessed in Jesus and earnestly serve God night and day in that hope, a hope made possible by the resurrection of Jesus from the dead (v. 8). Let me never lose sight of the assignment given through the heavenly vision (v. 19), for I am sent to open eyes, turn others from darkness to light, turn others from the dominion of Satan to God, and extend the offer of forgiveness of sins and an inheritance among those who have been sanctified by faith. In other words, all peoples are given the joy of joining the body of Christ; they are not to remain in their false religions.

In this world we are not unaware that evil is strong, but thankful that God has appointed limits; He gives out authority in measured months (Rev. 13:5). In the meantime, He seals who is His and the Father's (14:1), guarding their minds for His purposes and person. Jesus, seal my mind with the power of the Father, Son, and Holy Spirit. Let me do my obedient part to keep myself chaste and holy (v. 4) and to follow the Lamb wherever He goes. Let no lie be found in my mouth. Let me be blameless, fear God alone, give glory to God alone, and worship Him alone (v. 7), for God's wrath (and eternal torment for the wicked) are both real (vv. 9–11).

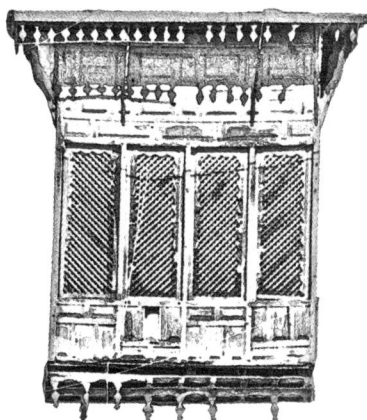

THE AGONIZING QUESTION

Who have I led to the Lord recently?

I immediately qualify my response: planting churches is hard. Others, better than I, have labored for years without seeing conversions. My role is to just pick stones out of the field. I do not have the gift of evangelism. Many have come to the Lord when I preached. Believers need discipleship, too. I have to disciple my children, and the list goes on....

But who have I led to the Lord recently?

I led Muhsin to the Lord back in Sudan. Now I travel and train others. Muslims have come to the Lord through missionaries I mentored. National leaders and local ministers I mobilized and trained are leading Muslims to Jesus. All that is well and good, God be praised...

But who have I led to the Lord recently?

I am tired. I am busy. I am not in one place long enough. An itinerant responsibility is not conducive to local evangelism. I have to spend so much time in meetings, emailing, administrating, solving people problems, mobilizing, developing others. My language fluency is not what it should be. I give out scores of Bibles. I witness in taxis. I give out evangelistic materials at feasts and to friends and neighbors. I pray for the lost multiple times a week…

But who have I led to the Lord recently?

It's too much pressure to ask the question. Who am I to judge? Only God can convert a soul, change a mind, unveil the gospel. Results can't be forced. Obedience and faithfulness is the chief required task of all laborers. Yes, 'tis all true…

But who have I led to the Lord recently?

> *O Lord Jesus, You alone the God who saves,*
> *Yet hear this anguished plea.*
> *Please use me as I am, so weak,*
> *To lead some soul to Thee.*

PURSUING JESUS:

Deliver my soul, O Lord, from lying lips, from a deceitful tongue (Psalm 120:2). Woe is me, for I dwell among the tents of Kedar (v. 5). Lord Jesus, I ask that there would be nothing false about me, that I would walk in the light, and that though I live in a place where lies abound, I would only, ever be true. Keep me from any type of deception: first before You (which is fruitless to try and deceive the all-knowing One), second before myself (which is the most insidious type of lying), third before the church (never presenting myself as other than what I am), and fourth before the lost (always being authentic with overt allegiance to Jesus).

To be in the light always leads to accusations, and when they come, let me not answer with regard to a single charge and let me not save myself when abused (Matt. 27:12, 14, 40). Every instinct of my pride wants to make a case for myself, so teach me the sweetness of silence and the joy of letting God be my fortress and my vindication. It is counterintuitive to my flesh and I can think of a dozen reasons why the record should be set straight. But let me look to Your silent absorption of abuse as You hung on the cross, and let me hang in there with You, likewise silent and defenseless.

Jesus, let me also be on guard against the ugly envy that lurks and rises in my own heart, for envy makes traitors of us all (v. 4). Let me be on guard against trying to manipulate You as Judas did because You move slower than I prefer or other than I prefer. Judas had political, earthly, temporal power goals for You, which ended in misery. Jesus, let me not think that I know at any level what You should do. Give me the humble (not rebellious) wisdom to recognize that the majority is not always right and that moderate winds are not always the way

(27:12–13). Let me have the faith that when I stand for unpopular (perhaps risky) ways forward, You will grant the safety of all who sail with me (v. 24). I do not presume that this means avoidance of all harm; it is enough to know that our safety is in Your glory, and if You are glorified, we are eternally safe. Give me the wisdom and stability not to be a deserter of my brothers and to encourage others to stay together under duress, modeling calm courage (vv. 31, 35).

Jesus, help me ever remember that Your wrath is great, marvelous, clean, bright, good, holy, and glorious (Rev. 15:1, 6, 8). Thank you also that there is a time when the wrath of God will be "finished" (v. 1); there is a limit, an end, for You are eternally merciful and kind. On that great day I look forward to singing with all the redeemed from all the nations the song of Moses and the Lamb to the King of nations (vv. 3–4). Wrath is over. Mercy forevermore.

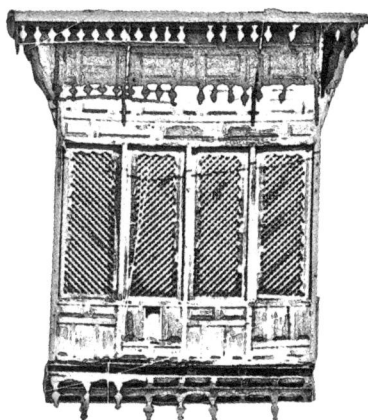

SO, HOW BADLY DO YOU WANT TO PLANT CHURCHES?

Have you ever heard of Butch Songin? Me either. Tom Yewcic? Doesn't ring a bell. Eddie Wilson? Babe Parilli? Don Trull? What about Tom Sherman, Mike Taliaferro, Neil Graff, or Tom Owen? Still nothing? Let's try Matt Cavanaugh, Bob Bleier, Tom Ramsey, Marc Wilson, Hugh Millen, Tommy Hudson, Jeff Carlson, Scott Secules, or Scott Zola? Anything? They all have one thing in common, and they share it with one final name: Tom Brady. All of these men played quarterback for the New England Patriots.

Tom Brady is widely considered the best quarterback to ever play American football. He is, in fact, called the G.O.A.T., the greatest of all time. He has been to nine championship games (Super Bowls) and won six of them. He has won more championships than any other quarterback, and when he retires he will hold every major record. He is envied and feared, respected and admired. Every other player wishes they had the success of Tom Brady, but few are willing to pay the price.

In December 2014, an article by Greg Bishop appeared in *Sports Illustrated*.[15] Bishop expounded on the disciplined life Brady espouses/practices, the discipline that makes him great and sets him apart from all others. Here are some quotes from the article with attending church planting applications:

"His career is built on, defined by and prolonged with routine."

Church planting is not built on discovering a new silver bullet or golden key. It is doing the basic things over and over again. It's more about endurance than excitement.

"...A diet that made him lighter, workouts that made him faster..."

Church planting requires lean and mean. We need to simplify, cut things from our inputs that make us spiritually or culturally fat. We need to be agile. We need to have a standard of living (location of our house, its openness to the community, the simplicity and hospitality in which we function) that empowers church planting. We must not allow our money/wealth to limit our church planting.

"Football isn't what Tom does—football is Tom. This is who he is." (Guerrero, Brady's fitness coach)

Church planting requires a single-eyed focus. We need to decide that we are going to do one thing: make disciples. Anything that does not contribute to making disciples and gathering them into churches has to go.

"Brady is a quarterback whose daily schedule, both in and out of season, is mapped clearly... Every day of it, micromanaged. Treatment. Workouts. Food. Recovery. Practice. Rest. And those

schedules aren't just for this week, this month, this season. They're for three years. That allows Brady and Guerrero to work in both the short and long terms to, say, increase muscle mass one year and focus on pliability the next. 'The whole idea is to program his body to do what we want it to do,' says Guerrero. 'We don't let the body dictate to us. We dictate.'"

Church planting requires a daily discipline: Sleep, exercise, abide, study language, BAM, evangelize, pray, disciple, time with family, mentor, sleep…repeat. We set the big rocks in place in our schedule and do them over and over again. You want to plant churches? Dictate the schedule.

"For Brady to play this well for so long isn't simply a matter of built-in aggression (although he has that) or extra film study (although he does that) or of avoiding big hits and running only when necessary. The secret to his longevity is more encompassing. 'Everything,' says Guerrero, 'is calculated.'"

Church planting requires a calculated intentionality to what we do, how we spend our time and with whom, what we read, where we go and with whom, what invitations we accept and what opportunities we deny. Church planting is about saying no to opportunities as much as it is saying yes.

"Brady…had spent the early part of his career like most athletes. He'd worried about injuries after they happened. He'd focused on rehabilitation as opposed to preventative maintenance."

Church planting requires prevention. We must think ahead and keep our soul from sin and our bodies from breakdown. We must eat right, exercise right, sleep right in the physical and in the spiritual. We must operate forward from Sabbath rest, not hold on barely surviving the week to recover on our Sabbaths.

"Brady is new age in approach but old school in composition. 'I played with a bunch of quarterbacks: Kurt Warner, Marc Bulger,' a former teammate says. 'They didn't match Tom's intensity. Not even close.'"

Church planting requires old-time grit, determination, and hard-nosed tenacity. We must have foreheads of iron willing to bash against strongholds of stone. We must have a warrior approach, willing and eager to fight, even as we must have a pastoral and gentle side towards those we lead.

"House [Brady's throwing coach] and Brady work to refine less than 2 percent of the QB's overall skill set. That's it. The upper end of the upper end."

Church planting requires that we focus down on what we are good at and let others do what they excel in. We work on our strengths, improve our strengths, and become even better in that which we are gifted by continually improving it.

"'Our method relates to being physically fit, emotionally stable and spiritually nourished,' says Guerrero. 'Emotional stability allows you to have spiritual awareness.'"

Church planting requires that we are healthy in all major categories: physical, emotional/relational, and spiritual. If any of those three legs are inadequate, we will be unstable.

"The back end of his career has been defined, in many ways, by his ability to win without continuity among his offensive personnel… and, largely, without star receivers. 'What he's been able to accomplish there is nuts,' says retired fullback Heath Evans, a former teammate turned NFL network analyst. 'There are always new linemen, new receivers, new position coaches. Change is constant.' Those who associate Brady only with the rotating cast that he throws to or that blocks for him miss and important point. His support system—his parents, his three sisters, his various personal coaches—has remained consistent."

Church planting requires accountable stability and encouragement from an inner core and the ability to thrive in the midst of constant personnel change. Church planting teams will not be composed of superstars, yet the whole will be greater than the sum of its parts. Church planters need to prioritize lifelong brothers and sisters who will be constant, though they be few.

"He has countered that fire with lighter moments that have made him more relatable to teammates who made less money. He didn't just watch pranks and laugh. He engaged in them. He won them. Evans describes Brady as the 'most humble superstars I've ever been around.' 'Since I met him, he married a supermodel, made millions of dollars and became internationally famous,' says Troy Brown, another former teammate. 'But I don't think he's changed much.'"

Church planting requires humor, joy, camaraderie, and an egalitarian approach to team members, especially the new and inexperienced. Veteran church planters need to initiate relationship and inclusion with the new. Humility and transparency encourage other church planters that we can and must do this together.

"Brady's preparation, how he works, bolsters the way his teammates view him. He was maniacal."

Church planting demands that you do not coast on your reputation or former accomplishments. Rather, you win the respect of your colleagues every day. A single-eyed focus by veterans (proven by their behavior) spreads through teams and organizations like wildfire.

"He meets with Belichick three times a week to talk over the game plan—every coverage, every hot read, every play. He summons his backups an hour before the Saturday team meetings and goes over the entire call sheet, typically between 100 and 110 plays. Twice. He asks the QBs to arrive an hour early on game day, too, then goes over everything again. Twice."

Church planting requires the intentionality of staying on the same page with your leaders—initiating and responding. Church planting requires going over and over strategies and plans and contingencies with your followers—and taking initiative that all know the plan well, that there is common ownership.

"'He has a great memory from all that,' says Bill O'Brien, once Brady's offensive coordinator, now the coach of the Texans. 'He can remember from eight years ago: left hash, toward the lighthouse, third play of the game... We'll look it up. He's always right.'"

Church planting requires we study, remember, and celebrate the past. We cannot have the hubris to think we know better than those who went before us, nor can we ignore the lessons they so painfully learned. We have one eye on the past even as we press towards the new challenges of the future.

"This is the...guy who once ate Christmas breakfast with the Evans family and quietly picked all the sausage out from his omelet."

Church planting requires fastidiousness in eliminating the little vices, the small excesses, and the minor details that in combination retard the work. Church planting requires the discipline and discernment to make a thousand small decisions that lead to breakthrough.

"Brady...had a program created to work out his brain the way he worked out his body. The various exercises help Brady to more quickly process information between plays, read defenses and make adjustments. They assist with his memory. They increase his peripheral vision and how far he can see downfield... Brady says: 'I'm building resiliency and staying sharp. I feel like that's really where my edge is.'"

Church planting is helped, not hurt, by resistance. Resiliency is a key skill for church planters, and we learn resiliency by facing opposition and enduring through it. We get stronger the more we endure, and we should have more church planting power the harder and longer the journey is.

"For years, as Brady made football his singular obsession, everyone asked what he planned to do afterward. He never really knew. He wanted only to play football, to win championships. He never considered flying airplanes or running car dealerships or whatever it is athletes do when they no longer pursue what once defined them. He thought only about football and family."

Church planting needs to be our singular obsession. Contrary to Brady, Jesus is our central obsession, but as relates our ministry and calling, we must have a single eye. We must be fixated on church planting with no other ministry or opportunity attractive to us.

"He won't need a résumé for his next endeavor, only his body of work and his actual body, how it has held up over time. 'I used to joke with Alex,' says Brady, 'one day, we have to go on the road. We have to teach people.'"

Church planting is first caught then taught. What will give us the credibility to teach others is if we do it well over time. Teaching is critical, but only powerful if we have done what we teach well over time.

Conclusion

The above applications may seem extreme even if simple. Words and phrases like "maniacal," "singular obsession," "discipline," "routine," or "focus" either scare or bore us. We must ask ourselves again: "How badly do we want to plant churches?" There is a cost to pay if we want to plant churches. We will have to be obsessed with it, maniacal about it, disciplined, focused, and relentless, and to have a little bit of Holy Spirit "nasty" that fires and guides us.

In 1 Corinthians 9:22, Paul expresses his desire that by all means he would save some. This is the context for his reminder (vv. 24–27) to run with discipline: "Do you not know that those who run in a race all run, but one receives the prize? Run in such a way that you may obtain it…. Therefore I run thus: not with uncertainty. Thus, I fight: not as one who beats the air. But I discipline my body and bring it into subjection."

Tom Brady does not have a greater intensity or focus than did Paul, the greatest church planter in history. Paul badly wanted to plant churches, and he knew what it took: Running with certainty. Fighting with focus. Disciplining our body and bringing it into subjection. Do you want to plant churches? The following is required:

- Abiding in Jesus extravagantly: your soul alive and empowered
- Eating healthy and exercising: your body in good shape
- Submission and accountability: your relationships in order
- Sabbath rest and renewal: good sleep
- Ongoing language study: gospel fluency in heart language
- Constant evangelism: never losing the heart for souls
- Steady discipleship: always pouring into someone who will reproduce
- Frequent prayer and fasting: regular times to fall on our knees before the Omnipotent
- Active faith: praying for the sick, power encounters, stepping out with no safety net
- Deep accountability: vulnerable, transparent, humble relationships
- Simple living: dying daily to comforts, preferred schedules, and luxuries
- Costly partnership: yielding to and making a way for and with others
- Risk, trouble, scorn: being thought poorly of by friends and enemies
- Dying to self: drinking the cup the Master asks of us, doing what we don't want to do
- Spiritual warfare: casting out demons, praying through, battling back darkness

And we must do all the above over and over and over and over again—until knees are calloused and bodies wrinkled, and emotions spent, and stubborn wills broken. Winning Super Bowls is easy compared to church planting. So, I ask one final time: Just how badly do you want to plant churches?

DAY 61

PURSUING JESUS:

My help comes from the Lord who will not allow my foot to slip (Psalm 121:2–3). Jesus, You are my keeper and my shade, You will protect me from all evil and keep my soul, and You will guard my going out and my coming in (vv. 5, 7–8). I think back to the warning my Arab Christian friend gave me often. He had a dream in which I was fighting off a crocodile attack against my sons and myself, when another crocodile, unseen to us, suddenly attacked with devastating consequences. Here in Narnia there are spiritual forces at war against us that we are unaware of, and I often pray that the Lord will protect me from that which I can see (understand/confront/resist) and that which I cannot see (unaware/don't understand/don't expect). Jesus, don't let my foot slip; keep and protect me from all evil. I cannot protect myself without Your sovereign help.

Jesus, You invite us to come see You and then to go quickly and tell (Matt. 28:6–7). Let me grow in the fear and joy as I run to report who You are and what You have done (v. 8). Thank you that You meet us, and we can take hold of You and worship, not being afraid of going, taking the Word (vv. 9–10). When I meet You, Lord, let there be no doubt in my worship (v. 17), so that I can be Your ambassador with *all* authority, making disciples of *all* nations, teaching *all* You have commanded, because You are with me *all* the time (vv. 18–20). Thank you, Jesus, that You will bring us safely through (Acts 28:1). Let me learn how to preach the kingdom of God and to teach concerning the Lord Jesus Christ with *all* openness, unhindered (v. 31).

Let me not lose sight of the wrath of God, not only as a reality, but also as a righteous reality (Rev. 16:1–7). You are righteous, Jesus who was and is. You have judged. You are the holy One. We sinners deserve

Your wrath. You are almighty and true; right are Your judgments. Let me ever be mindful in my own life (when You judge and discipline me) that the pain is intended to help me repent, not rebel. Let any discipline that comes from or passes through Your hands lead me back to You. Let me stay awake and clothed (v. 15) through the difficult days that come, that I may be found in You when You come in great power and glory.

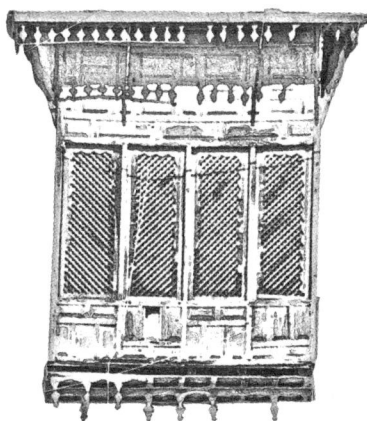

FIGHTING FORWARD FROM A PLACE OF REFUGE

The idea here is based on a kind of "superhero" illustration—not that we ourselves are super, but that we can imagine ourselves engaged in two types of fighting. One is a fight from within a fortress surrounded by walls, buttresses, and defenses with friends on either side and at our back. There is still danger, and this is a legitimate fight, but it's a defensive and protective fight with little exposure. The other is a charge out of the castle on offense. That forward, ground-taking advance puts you square in the middle of the enemy hoard. You still have colleagues around you, and they can still help, but it's chaotic. You are exposed to enemy weapons from 360 degrees.

In this scenario, and please excuse the overly militarist imagery, how do you keep mowing down the enemy even as its forces surround you?

How do you survive and advance in the midst of great danger with a "force field" around you, a force field not as obvious as castle walls and ramparts, but just as efficacious? How do we learn to both remain at rest *and* advance in the midst of a chaotic, demanding battle? What does Hebrews 4:11 mean when it says to "labor...to enter into that rest" (KJV)? Back to this hackneyed illustration, in essence we ask, "What powers up that force field?" Here are some things that come to mind.

THERE IS A PHYSICAL COMPONENT

Good exercise, good sleep (i.e. eight hours every night or whatever your minimum amount is in your current season of life, plus some boundary), and good eating habits cannot be underestimated.

Tim Enloe talks about the vulnerability of HALTS:[16] Hungry, Angry, Lonely, Tired, Sick. Some of these are physical symptoms, and when we experience any of these HALTS, our force field flickers. If we experience several or all of them at the same time, the force field becomes very weak indeed. This emphasizes the practical need for healthy rhythms of life which include (but not limited to): eating, sleeping, exercise, family play, date night (marriage health), Sabbath, holiday, and time away from ministry context (twice each year).

THERE IS A MENTAL HEALTH COMPONENT

Attitude, submission, team interaction, and leadership relationship fall under this category. When we are bitter, wounded, rebellious, or stubborn, the shield comes down.

THERE IS A SPIRITUAL COMPONENT

Daily abiding is our lifeline, but there has to be more: accountability, occasional times of solitude, fasting, corporate prayer, reading and learning (spiritual/missiological/theological), mentoring, spiritual warfare, praying through, pleading the blood, intercession for others, prophetic warning, power encounter, and miracles, signs, and wonders.

THERE IS THE INTEGRATION OF THESE IN DAILY MISSIONS

The above may be pretty obvious, but what is subtler is the integration of these in the busyness and stress of daily missions. I think the best way to describe this is anecdotally. I love routine. My best abiding days are in my own house. I have my chai tea. I have my special chair. I close all the doors. I have my pens, devotionals, journals, and guitar. I putz around and linger. It's glorious. I work through various disciplines over the course of two to three hours. I read, pray, sing, and write, and I just love it.

The reality is, the above happened *maybe* 30 times in the last year (less than 10 percent of the time). The other days I was in an airport lounge, on a plane, in someone's guest bedroom adjusting to their schedule, with jet lag and a headache or, or, or…. I have learned to live with the expectation that my abiding will not be in the castle of my home where I battle spiritually from that comfort. I have learned (and am learning) how to abide on the road with all the noise, fatigue, distraction, and challenge found there.

So, I'm tired, more tired than I've ever been. How does one retain spiritual vitality in that fatigue? I deal with more physical problems than in my younger years (sleep, shoulder, intestines), so how do I manage those and stay emotionally engaged? I face more criticism and more praise than I merit (in my opinion), so how do I ignore both and stay spiritually lowly? I'm presented leadership complexities that only get more difficult, so how do I hear the Lord's direction when the questions get harder?

What I'm trying to say is I'm not getting any younger, I'm not getting any smarter, I'm not getting any fresher, and life is not getting any simpler. The relative comfort of my office chair (and fighting from the castle) is more and more appealing but less and less available. I am learning to manage the spiritual, emotional, and physical challenges (that only increase) from a mobile position, from a position of weakness and limitation.

Life is not slowing down, and it feels like we are continually being poured out. So, the joy then must be to embrace it but to also steward it. (I think we're supposed to pour it out and spend it all on Jesus, right?) The joy then must be to find rest in the battle through faithfulness in the physical things. The joy then must be to learn to function and fight when the emotional reserves are down, the pressures high, and honestly the physical strength ebbs.

HOW DOES THAT HAPPEN

This is the heart of the question, isn't it? How do we find that joy? The reality is that we can be good stewards without being full stewards. We can be faithfully paying attention to physical health, but still be tired. We can be faithful in abiding, but not enjoying the richness for which we long. We can be emotionally healthy, but not emotionally immune. In other words, in our reality we never are driving with all the gauges at full; several or all of the gauges are at some level of depletion. Here are some steps, not necessarily sequential, to see this happen:

Step 1: Give up the illusory idea that all will be well and every gauge will always be full. I don't think it's realistic, nor do I think it's the biblical pattern. All who went before us had to figure out how to do this at some level of depletion or lack.

Step 2: Don't give up working on what can be done daily. If one error is to expect too much health and vitality, the equal and opposite error would be to give up fighting for it. Do the 7-minute app if you can't get your full run in. Do the 1-hour abiding time on the cramped airline if you can't get the 2-hour armchair version in. Do the WhatsApp accountability text if you can't get the face-to-face accountability prayer time in. Take the little 20-minute nap if you can't get eight hours of sleep. Read through your memory verse cards for five minutes even if you can't add a new verse. Take the half Sabbath or two half Sabbaths on Monday and Thursday if you can't get it on Friday. Take the once-a-month date night to eat pizza and read next to each other in bed with a quick kiss good night (rather than having sex because you're too tired to go out, cook, or undress). Don't give up on the disciplines and rhythms, even if what you *can* do is not your ideal. Be that 80-year-old man who still puts on his old white tennis shorts and jogs at a snail's pace down the sidewalk at 6 a.m. It might take him one hour to shuffle a mile, but he's shuffling. Be content with what you can do. The same goes with ministry and spiritual disciplines. So, memorize one verse if you can't memorize one chapter. Learn one word each day if you can't learn three. Spend two hours each week with the lost if you can't spend two days. Visit one neighbor in your flat if you can't visit all your friends during the Eid.

Step 3: Be really honest with Jesus. You finish an exhausting two-hour meeting and launch right into the next one. By the third hour of the day your head hurts and there is nothing left in the emotional tank. You have a five-minute break. Go to the bathroom, sit on the toilet with the lid down, close your eyes, and say, "Jesus, help me. I got nothing left. But these dear folks need help. This one, Jesus, has to be all You. Don't let me break down or do anything stupid. Jesus, help me get through this wisely, kindly, gently, purely, and strongly." There is something profoundly real about His strength being made perfect in our weakness.

Step 4: Get over yourself, and double dip without being weird about it. I complained to Dr. Jim Bradford once about not liking to preach three or four services in a day because I felt more and more fake as each service progressed. In his kind way, he said, "Get over yourself and just preach with passion each time." So, by "double dip" I mean get comfortable with using the same material in multiple locations. Learn to be passionate and engaged and to be shame-free while doing so. Get comfortable (and get good) at repetition. Don't be so proud that you think you need unique messages; learn how to share with equal passion the same story or sermon over and over with new audiences. By double dip, I also mean learn how your exercise time can be your prayer time, and your accountability time can be your evangelism time (i.e. take a young missionary out sowing, and on the way, ask the life questions). In doing so, seek a less dichotomized life and smoother integration. Let the first 20 minutes of every trip (car/train/bicycle) be prayer time. If you're with others, take turns praying out loud. Speak in tongues while you shower. This is when taxis and toilets become sanctified prayer closets.

Step 5: Be less of a perfectionist. Be content with doing several things at 70 percent quality rather than one thing at 100 percent quality. If you can find someone to do something at 70 percent or so quality of what you do well, be content to delegate and don't micromanage. Be content for some things not to get done in one day. Trust that the Lord has the important things done through you. Revel in grace. I remember my dad coming home from a busy day, a day in which he had no time to abide. He fell into bed exhausted, put his hand on his Bible on the nightstand, and said, "I love you, Jesus, good night," and fell asleep. That's awesome. He lived under grace. Legalism kills us. We can be focused, driven people without being legalistic (and of course, be diligent to give others grace).

Step 6: Lean on others where they're strong. Continually triage in your mind, and if others are good there, leave it for them to do. Be honest and transparent about your weaknesses. Bring junk into the light, for it breaks half its power in that lowly confession. Ask for help and ask for prayer.

Step 7: Compartmentalize. Exit one tough meeting and shut all its mess in its own room. Walk into the next meeting with a smile and give that new person your best without being under a cloud from the last meeting. This can feel fake at first and initially, it's exhausting. But I find it's both a muscle developed and a grace given. God helps you focus on the person in front of you and locks the person behind you from your emotions and countenance. Go to bed at night having locked *everyone* in his or her room. Don't ruminate over the day. Focus on your wife, your bedtime reading, your vespers prayers, and your children. Turn out the light and don't let those rascals from their rooms. As Omar Beiler says, "Don't give people free rent in your head." It's a "no trespassing" zone for them.

Step 8: Be goofy. Laugh and do ridiculous things every once in a while. Step out of the box. Don't be fully composed. Joke, play a prank, giggle, and enjoy irony. Charge the giant with a skip and a whistle. See the funny side of life and missions. Grin as you swing your sword. Be childlike without being childish. Most of the great lions of the faith had great joy. They could roll around on the ground with a child and then stand up and pray a prophetic prayer. In 1910 or so in Cairo, Temple Gairdner was praying an intense, intimate prayer before the church, interrupted his own prayer to tell a funny story in good taste, and then went right back into a passionately intimate prayer. Laugh at yourself. When you blow it, tell on yourself. Have self-deprecating humor. Be your own critic without self-flagellating. Admit you're an idiot to others. Laugh with them about your shortcomings all the while retaining the confidence that you do some things well and strike out on others.

Step 9: Stay engaged with the unreached. Alan Johnson says, "Don't let [Christian opportunities] wreck your life. You have a *God-given right* to be with the lost!" Fight to stay in the fight. Think of the injured football player who got hit on the head or sprained a knee. The coaches want to take him out of the game. Wave off the substitution and hobble back to the action. This can be abused, of course, but I'm talking about learning to play hurt and to fight when you're injured, to have the grit to push through and stay in the game when the wind is knocked from you. Do this in the context of "yes, I have administrative duties and leadership responsibilities, but I'm going to fight to share the gospel with at least one person today." Our "injuries" might not be conflicts or hurts, but the reality that our positions take us away from the lost regularly. Fight that. Strive to stay on the field, even if it's one day each week or one afternoon or two hours.

Step 10: Take intentional risks without fear of failure. Chalk up failure as a fun way to get experience. Try things that can't be done. Pray for miracles one hundred times in a row even if they don't happen. Put yourself in impossible situations with no parachute, situations in which either God intervenes, or you look like a fool. This is about getting out of the castle and fighting where it's risky. Know which bridges to burn. Cut off your own retreat. Plunge deeper into enemy territory where you either press forward to the victory or be overwhelmed. Set goals you can't reach, not safe goals you can reach. Set impossible goals, then watch God help you meet them. Or if you get 50 percent of the way there, send up a shout of praise for how much you got done and forget about what you didn't. Don't stop dreaming. Don't squelch others dreams. Be a "yes, let's try it" person. Be a "why not!" enthusiast. Trust the young early and watch them rise to the level of *your* faith in them. Leif Zetterlund (Swedish Pentecostal pioneer in Sudan) is someone like this. If I said, "Leif, let's drive a lorry full of Bibles overland to Saudi Arabia and hand them out at the gates of Mecca. Think that can work?" Leif would undoubtedly say with a laugh and a sparkle, "Why not! Let's give it a try!" If we're not failing, we're not trying hard enough. We're thinking too small.

Step 11: Enjoy the "slow motion" moments. Back to a superhero illustration. You know how in a battle scene everything goes into slow motion and the protagonist sees with such clarity and deals easily with the threat or attack? Everything in that moment is under control. Fiend and foe battle around him, but in that moment, there is a concentrated peace. Life and ministry are like that for us sometimes, or they can be, or we can grow into that. There in the midst of all kinds of chaos and stress, God can help slow that moment down. We see things clearly and enjoy the moment. The battle becomes manageable because it's slowed down for us to dodge the bullet flying towards us. Though it doesn't have to be about conflict. Sometimes it's just hitting the "slow motion" button to enjoy a cup of chai, the sunset, a walk, a relationship, good food, a joke, or simply the moment. In that slow-motion moment, we breathe deeply of the joy and even the restoration that God works. In that moment we touch Him, or

He touches us, and we receive life. Then the moment passes, and we plunge back into the fray.

At the end of the day, if any battle is won or if you survive the battle, take no credit and carefully give God *all* the glory. If we really fight forward, we will be intentionally placing ourselves in impossible, untenable situations, and we will only survive because God was the power in and around us and because God miraculously brought us through. The only way we get through is by the divine intervention and empowerment of the Holy Spirit.

DAY 62

PURSUING JESUS:

Let me be glad to join God's people in giving thanks to Him (Psalm 122:1–4). It is delight, not duty, that brings us together in regular fellowship with the saints. In those gatherings let us be diligent to pray for God's peace on Jerusalem (v. 6), both the lost nation and the people of God, for He indeed will use both for His purposes (v. 9).

Let me not lose sight of my basic assignment. I am a messenger (Mark 1:2); the goal is not to be liked. I am a voice crying in the wilderness (v. 3), in which the goal is to be heard and the message preached is repentance (v. 4). The Spirit still impels us into the wilderness where there are satanic enemies, dangerous beasts, and angelic helpers (v. 12). That verb "impelled" in the Greek is in the continuous tense; Jesus is still urging us on to dry places with difficult variables, and in His wisdom and power He will fill us with His Spirit for His use. We emerge from those testing times to preach the gospel of God, to teach with authority, to heal the sick and cast out demons, to pray, and to keep moving the gospel along to secluded towns (vv. 14, 22, 34– 35, 38). Jesus repeatedly went to synagogues throughout all Galilee preaching and casting out demons, healing along the way (v. 41). The blueprint is not complicated; it's just hard. Simple but hard. Doable in the power and wisdom of the Spirit. Jesus, strip from me any excuses or rationalizations and fill me with Thy Spirit that I may simply obey.

The post-resurrected Jesus was remarkably consistent to this pattern. He spent time teaching, gave orders to His chosen ones, and focused on the kingdom of God to come, giving many proofs that He is the living King who will return to judge (Acts 1:1–3). We are to wait (actively) for the promise of the Holy Spirit (v. 5), which will give us the requisite power (v. 8) to do these daunting (simple) things. We actively wait by continually devoting ourselves to prayer (v. 14), for those who will lead apostolic movements must continually be with Jesus, bearing witness to His deity and resurrection power (vv. 21–22).

The powers against us are not new and are not creative. The base of all evil seems to be typified in Babylon which is defined by immorality, violence against the saints, and wealthy greed (Rev. 17:4, 6). It's money, sex, and power, packaged differently over time, but the bane of all fallen men and cultures. Yet, the Lamb will overcome all of them (all of us) because He is the Lord of lords and the King of kings (v. 14). Those with Him are called, chosen, and faithful. God has ever used evil kings to execute His purposes "until the words of God are fulfilled" (v. 17). Remembering that the Lamb overcomes helps us endure evil, full of hope, for we anticipate we are one step closer to the return of the King.

Pursuing Church Planting:

The air conditioner in the car hummed quietly as we sat outside a Starbucks. Adam's eyes were bright as he talked of his journey out of the darkness of Islam declaring simply: "Jesus is my Savior, my Lord, and my God!" Adam is an Arab from a neighboring country who has lived in Narnia for many years and who joined the ranks of the redeemed a few years ago. Thanks to a wonderful media partnership here in country, I was put in touch with him, the first fellow follower of Jesus he had met face to face. Adam shines with the love of Jesus and is simple and sweet in his new faith. He has many fears and simple requests, such as, "Teach me to pray!"

We had a sweet time of prayer; he mimicked all I did in sincere devotion to Jesus. I helped him download a Bible app on his phone and he gladly agreed to read one chapter from John and one from Acts every day. We will meet again next week to keep learning together. We talked of his family and friends who don't know Jesus and the need for being filled with the Holy Spirit so that we have power to be witnesses. Though he is aware, sobered by, and truthfully afraid of the consequences if his faith is discovered, he also declares there is no going back and agrees that love does not hide the cure for sin no matter the cost. We talked of the balance of wisdom and courage and with a smile he said, "Though I share a room with five other men, I will pull my sheet over my head and talk to Jesus, and none of them will know what I am doing!"

Adam is so sweet, as was the simple communion in the car. In this age, media filtering plays such a critical role in helping us find those looking for Jesus. Media is a safe way to find the seeker and guide him or her to the discipler that together they may rejoice in the Savior of all people.

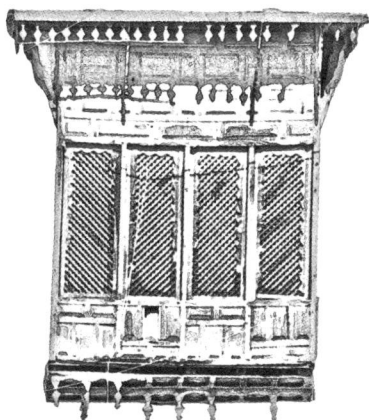

THEY CAN HAVE OURS!

O f all peoples on earth, we are most blessed. We know that we have eternal life. Through our Lord and Savior Jesus Christ we have assurance of living forever in His presence with no sin, death, night, tears, pain, sickness, or evil. Of all men and women, true followers of Jesus then are not afraid to die. Who is afraid of death when beautiful forever life with Jesus—the sum of all our hope, delight, and longing—awaits us?

This is why we can joyfully say to the world: "You can have our ventilator!"

When global plagues stalk the earth, no one is more ready to die than true followers of Jesus. We should, therefore, be last in line for medical attention. We should give up our right to be cured temporarily for those who have no assurance of salvation, for those who are not right with Jesus.

I am not saying we refuse health care at any level; I am just saying that if there is a shortage of it, we give our place to the next person in line. Having our eternal guarantee of life, we yield our place to the one who perishes both now and forever. If there is enough for all, we will gratefully be served, but if there is a shortage, we should be the ones to serve the community by dying. Why? Because we know we have eternal life, and they don't.

Think of the witness and of the impact if Christians globally laid down their lives for non-Christians by electing, wherever there is a shortage, to give their ventilator (hospital bed, medicine) to those who do not yet know Jesus! Think of the power of the gospel if millions of us died so that others could escape death now—that they might not die forever. Could there be a better testimony than "Christians so love the world that we give our one and only temporal life that our neighbor not perish, but have time to find belief, have time to be found by the Savior"?

- Do we really believe in eternal life or not?
- Is it really supremely better than anything in this current reality or not?
- Does greater love mean anything else?
- Why can't we together declare to the world that they can have ours? Our life, our ventilator?
- They can have our chance at this life that they might have further opportunity at eternal life.

And let's not be pompous about it, for the truth still is, that to live is Christ, to die is gain. We are not being heroic; we are just going home.

I envision Christians everywhere donning a simple badge or sticker that simply says, *Eternal Life*. Then when we are taken to hospital, or when long-serving and overworked physicians are doing triage, making the unimaginable choice on who to save, we do them this small kindness. Looking at our "life" and our peaceful smile, they can give our ventilator to someone else. We can die in peace and go on to our eternal joy, our last act reflecting in some small way Jesus' greatest one. Since we have the assurance that we will breath forever, the world can have our breathing machine here. They can have ours.

PURSUING JESUS:

Jesus, I look to You as a servant looks to his master (Psalm 123:2). I ask for grace, for in my own flesh, haste, envy, insecurity, folly, ambition, and every evil thing is present and every confusion possible. Jesus, for the turbulence within that is rooted in condemnation, defend me from the accuser and all accusers. For the disquiet within that is rooted in conviction, forgive me and turn me to You and Your ways, helping me forsake my own. Thank you, Jesus, that You have authority on earth to forgive sins and that You can give immediate relief (Mark 2:10, 12). I constantly need that forgiveness, and I thank You for it.

Jesus, let me spend my energy forward (not sideways or circular) speaking the mighty deeds of God (Acts 2:11), trusting that the Father has indeed made the Son to be both Lord and Christ. Let me pour energy into calling all men to repent (v. 38) living a repentant life myself. Let my words not be wasted on things (even good things) other than the gospel. With my words let me solemnly testify to Jesus and keep on exhorting all to bow before Him (v. 40).

Thank you for a vision of the church that continually devotes itself to teaching, fellowship, breaking of bread, prayer, sense of awe, sharing all things in common, meeting day by day in temple and home, living in gladness and sincerity of heart, praising God, and enjoying His favor that *You* might add daily to the number of the redeemed (vv. 42–47). Let the church be glorious, coming out of "Babylon" (Rev. 18:4), not participating in her sins (money, sex, power). Jesus, let us (as individuals and as a church) take seriously the warning that if we glorify ourselves and live sensuously, to that same degree we will have torment and mourning (v. 7), for the Lord who judges is strong (v.

8). Oh, Jesus! I am guilty of glorifying myself. I repent. Lord Jesus Christ, Son of God, have mercy on me, a sinner. Jesus, teach me to live in a way that seeks no glory of my own (or our own!) but only the glory of God.

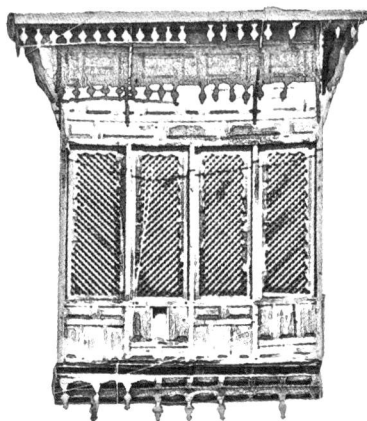

FOXHOLE COMPANIONS

I am often asked the question: "What type of churches do Live Dead teams plant?" The real question being asked of our multi-agency partnership is: What will the denominational affiliation of the churches that Live Dead teams plant be? Live Dead was started by Assemblies of God World Missions (USA) but has grown to include dozens of sending agencies and denominations. In one sector of Live Dead (Arab World), for example, we have more than twenty partner sending agencies. Assemblies of God (AG) churches want to know if we are planting Assemblies of God churches and other partners are asking if there is room for their agency/denomination to plant churches that are not Assemblies of God. Will the churches Live Dead plants be AG? Can they be another denomination? Can they be non-aligned?

Let me answer this critically important question with both a parable and some principles. First the parable. I will use a military analogy with your understanding that the application is about fighting for souls, not physically attacking any people or person.

An American infantryman in World War I became isolated from his regiment far removed from the safety of the last reinforced trench. Artillery shells burst around him, bullets whizzed by his head, and for safety he scrambled into a foxhole. The foxhole was not pleasant, there was a puddle for the floor, there was a corpse in the corner, there was the smell of blood and death all around. Alone and afraid he peeked over the foxhole rim to see an advancing hoard of the enemy firing directly at him. He ducked back down into his foxhole trembling, alone and overwhelmed.

Suddenly, two other soldiers dove head first into the foxhole. One was a French medic, the other was a British engineer, both were armed. The original soldier was so overjoyed to see colleagues that he burst into relieved tears. It did not matter that they were from different nations, it did not matter that they had different uniforms, and it did not matter that they had different weapons. It did not matter that they had trained in different camps and had different approaches to battle. All that mattered was that they were on the same side, they were fighting the same enemy. In the heat of battle, what they had in common was much more important than their differences. The immediate need was to work together against overwhelming odds.

On the parade ground and on the safety of home soil, regimental uniqueness is inspiring and celebrated. We need all the variegated skills, training, equipment, foci, and differences. But in the foxhole, surrounded by enemies, in the heat of battle, we need unity in one singular aim: defeating the enemy. And we mean, of course, winning souls. Attending this parable are some principles:

First, it is our conviction that denominations are a good thing.

Denominations emphasize different aspects of God, the Bible, the gospel, or the church. I planted an international church in Khartoum, Sudan that was part of an indigenous church denomination called the Sudan Pentecostal Churches. A self-appointed apostle visited from Germany and castigated me for belonging to a denomination; he said there should be no denominations, denominations were demonic and divisive, and there should be just one united body of Christ. Listening to him, I quickly realized that he wanted all to be united under his leadership, he wanted to rule as pope.

We believe there can and should be diversity in our unity, that denominations are good things, but here is our missionary plea to a sectarian base: Bless us to win souls. Bless us to fight in our isolated locations with whatever regimental soldier the calamity and confusion of battle plops in our foxhole. Take not from us our brothers and sisters in arms, those who are now beloved, our joy, our defense, our cherished companions in the fray.

For the second principle is this: We on the frontlines are so few and so outnumbered, that we cannot fight unless we fight together.

In 1996, the Assemblies of God had no missionaries in Sudan. My wife and I arrived alone and young at the Khartoum airport, went to a hotel, found a real estate agent, and located a humble apartment. It was a SIM couple, the Wellings, who took us under their parental wings. It was a Mennonite couple, the Koops, that befriended us. It was German couple with EMO, the Straehlers, that integrated us into the church planting fraternity. It was a Swedish couple with OM, the Neilsons, that showed us how to share our faith with Arab Muslims. It was two IMB families, the Hills and the Kellys, that became our dearest friends and closest partners in the work. We would have not made it, nor been fruitful in church planting among Muslims, if we had not been welcomed into the foxhole of Khartoum by those who were not our immediate tribe. The missionary community in Sudan was so small and so surrounded that we needed each other to survive and to thrive.

Which leads me to the third principle: All of us were loyal to our regiment. All of us were glad to belong to the agency that commissioned us.

Dear missionaries on the field, cherish our distinctives. We march with great pride on the parade ground with our particular division of this great army of God. We are not clones; we best partner with each other by being true to our own traditions and convictions. But when we move from the clean, safe parade ground to leap into battlefield foxholes, we don't fixate on the denominational badge worn proudly on our sleeves. We look at the one color of our uniform and to the immediate need of saving souls. Fighting over the peripheral points of doctrine is a luxury for those who have more disciples than they know what to do with, not for those trying to see the first person of peace in an unreached people group of millions come to faith. *Bless us, beloved mother Church, to fight for souls, shoulder to shoulder with the few, the very few, the band of missionary brothers.*

A fourth principle of pioneer mission is that the church planter does not lead with the denominational question.

When there are no believers among a people group, we do not focus on a denomination; rather, we focus on salvation. As an Assemblies of God missionary, I am not trying to bring souls into the Assemblies of God, but the kingdom of God. When I baptize my first convert, it is into the family of God. When I start my first house church, it joins the body of Christ. I will not hide my affiliation, but I don't lead with it either. My denominational belonging is not introduced early in the process of evangelism, discipleship, or church planting. In pioneer settings, we first make disciples and plant churches, and later steer those churches to our preferred organizational affiliations.

A fifth principle is that by definition indigenous churches have the right to self-identify.

David Bosch pointed out that the last verses of Acts 14 indicate that disciples and churches are synonymous. Disciples are not made in isolation. To be a true disciple of Jesus demands both community and multiplication. The commission in Mark 16 is to preach the gospel, and the commission in Matthew 28 is to make disciples; both commissions center on the *ethne*, the unreached peoples of the world, so our intention is indeed to plant churches, indigenous churches. We define indigenous churches as self-governing, self-supporting, self-propagating, self-theologizing, and self-missionizing.

If the churches we plant are truly indigenous, they must have the right to make the decision as to whether they align with a denomination, start their own, or advance organically outside an organized structure. The principle is that we plant indigenous churches, we do not plant denominations. Indigenous churches decide who they will affiliate with or who they won't affiliate with. Realistically, as indigenous churches grow, they tend to either become a denomination or affiliate with a denomination. Leadership development and training, doctrinal purity, and missions-sending capacity are all valid reasons for the more formal organization of indigenous churches.

I can anticipate the next statement or protest against this admitted idealistic stance: Just plant churches and let the churches decide how to organize. The question is if missionaries are truly neutral brokers, especially if they belong to a denominational mission agency. Of course, the answer is no; denominational missionaries are not neutral. So, let me proceed with the next principle.

Sixth, church planting missionaries reproduce who they are and how they understand the Bible.

In Live Dead we use the Lausanne Covenant as our united statement of faith and make it very clear that we are full gospel believers. By this we mean that the Bible is our inspired guide for faith and conduct. If it is in the Bible, we believe it. There is some allowance here for nuances in interpretation. If we are honest, we all cherry pick to a degree and we all bring some denominational parameters to the text.

Here is how we handle the tension in Live Dead: We give the team leader the right to interpret and apply the Bible and plant churches according to his or her convictions and denominational guidelines. If the Live Dead team leader is from a denominational mission (like AG or IMB), we are completely comfortable (and excited) if they plant AG or Baptist churches. If the Live Dead team leader is from a non-denominational mission (like Frontiers or Pioneers) and their conviction is to plant non-aligned churches, we are completely comfortable (and excited) for those churches to be planted.

I am a Pentecostal. I am going to teach, preach, disciple, train, and develop leaders from that hermeneutic. I cannot be untrue to what I believe, and I must be faithful to the doctrine of my denomination if I am going to be commissioned by them in integrity. I expect the same of my Baptist, Presbyterian, or other denominational brothers. They are going to reproduce who they are. They are going to teach biblical doctrine as they are convinced of it. They are going to plant Baptist, Presbyterian, etc. churches, or at least they are going to disciple towards Baptist, Presbyterian, etc. theology. We are fine with that; more than fine, we rejoice in it. At the end of the day, if Live Dead plants churches that belong to multiple different denominations, we will all dance jigs of joy all the way to the pearly gates. The goal is souls saved for the glory of Jesus from every tribe, tongue, people, and nation.

Anticipating one more question, and that is, if Live Dead allows the church planting team leader the liberty to plant churches according to his/her conviction, what guarantee is there that those churches (or that doctrine) is biblical?

Our seventh principle answers this valid question: Live Dead is not a sending agency; it is a partnership. In order to join Live Dead, you must first belong to an evangelical, credible missions organization.

To ensure a Live Dead team leader does not veer off the biblical rails we have three means of prevention and three means of recourse. Regarding prevention, first, you cannot join a Live Dead team as an individual. We require anyone who wants to join Live Dead to first be part of a credible, trusted evangelical missions sending structure. In a sense, we do not vet individuals; we vet mission agencies. Second, every person who joins Live Dead spends their first missionary term (usually 2–3 years) on a Live Dead church planting training/launch team. In that period, they not only learn language, but we teach missiology and church planting. No team leader can be self-appointed or go right to church planting work. They must go through the training process, apply to be a team leader, and then go through team leader training. Third, once appointed, the team leader has to frame a Memorandum of Understanding (MOU) that lays out their church planting strategy and convictions. Before they can be appointed as team leader, their team leader coach has to approve their MOU.

Regarding recourse, first, because every team leader in Live Dead is accountable to a team leader coach, there is a Matthew 18 conversation. Second, if that conversation does not resolve the concern from the Live Dead leadership perspective, we invite the sending organization into the conversation for an intervention. Third, if that intervention does not return the team leader to biblical parameters (as determined by Live Dead leadership and the sending organization in unity), then Live Dead disassociates with that team and its leader.

Summary

1. Live Dead believes denominations are good things, for they highlight different aspects of the character of God.

2. Live Dead believes that the most important thing in missions is the saving of souls, the making of disciples, and the planting of churches.

3. Live Dead works in hostile climates where missionaries are few and partnership is precious. We do not think we can survive or thrive without doing the work of pioneer church planting together across denominational lines.

4. Live Dead is not a sending agency or a denomination; it is a partnership. Membership in Live Dead presupposes the missionary has been vetted by an evangelical missions agency.

5. Live Dead empowers the trained and vetted team leader to decide what type of churches (denominational or not) they will plant and expects/empowers the team leader to teach and preach the theology of their conviction. Safeguards are in place to ensure that theology is within biblical parameters.

6. Live Dead plants indigenous churches, not denominations, understanding that indigenous churches almost invariably choose to join or form a denomination and that these nascent churches will be heavily influenced by the theology of the church planter.

7. Live Dead rejoices in every soul saved and in any and every organization/denomination that will further the work of the gospel being preached and disciples made among every unreached people.

DAY 64

PURSUING JESUS:

Had it not been for the Lord who was on our side (Psalm 124:1), we would have failed and fallen miserably. Jesus, I declare that without You I can do nothing (John 15:5). Left to my own strength and devices I make a miserable mess of everything. Jesus, I need You for every breath, every moment, every decision, every action, every thought, every encounter, every relationship, every word. Thank you, Jesus, that You are on our side!

Jesus, You are everything. When men and women touch You, they are healed (Mark 3:10). When the afflicted see You, they are delivered (v. 11). I must with all my energy seek to see and touch You, for in You is my healing and deliverance. I must with every endeavor seek to let men touch You and see You, for in You is their healing and deliverance.

What wonder that Jesus summons those whom He wants, appoints us to be with Him, and then sends us out to preach and have authority to cast out demons (vv. 13–15). Missionary life and church planting efforts can be summarized in this one verse. Jesus wants us. He wants us to labor with Him. What wonder! Jesus wants us to be with Him, to abide, to spend time in His presence. Our first appointment is to *Him*! We commit ourselves to *Him*! Jesus sends us out to preach and have authority to cast out demons. We are to open our mouths and proclaim Christ in the power of the Holy Spirit. All authority has been given to Jesus and He dispenses it by baptizing us with the Spirit, so we have dynamite power to make disciples. We must cling to, return to, focus on, and build up these essential components of life, ministry, missions, and church planting: Revel in being wanted by Jesus, remember we are appointed to be with Him, and preach with authority through the baptism of the Holy Spirit. Do this even if your family thinks you senseless (v. 21), for in so doing we show we are the true family of Christ (v. 35).

Whoever blasphemes the Holy Spirit commits an eternal sin (v. 29). That is to call Jesus evil, or even to call Jesus less than what He is: King of kings, Lord of lords, God of very God. To say (or live) that Jesus is less than Jehovah is to insult, grieve, and eternally sin against the Spirit of God. The Holy Spirit is so lowly, glorifying Jesus, and yet this Person of the Godhead is so respected in that if we sin against Him, it is considered unforgivable. Jesus, teach me to honor, worship, obey, and respect God the Spirit.

I don't have much to give in my own strength or resources. In fact, I have nothing (Acts 3:6). But what I do have I give, in the name of Jesus Christ the Nazarene, walk! Remind me, Lord, that while in me I have nothing, in You I have all the powers of the Godhead. Let me ever be in the pattern of returning, repenting, and being refreshed from the presence of the Lord (v. 19). Thank you, Jesus, for the promise of the restoration of all things (v. 21). Let me not forget that this promise is linked to the gospel going forth to all nations as all the prophets prophesied (vv. 21–24). The Kingdom comes when the King comes, and the King comes when all nations are reached through the Spirit-filled preaching of the gospel.

On that day, we will lift our voices and sing: "Hallelujah! Salvation, glory, and power to God, because His judgments are true and righteous. Hallelujah, for the Lord our God the Almighty reigns! Let us rejoice and be glad and give Him glory" (Rev. 19:1 –2, 6–7). For He is faithful, the righteous judge, and the war wager (v. 11). He has eyes aflame and many crowns, and a mysterious name (He is so far above and beyond us); His robe is dipped in blood; He is called the Word of God; He is the Lord of angel armies; His sharp sword is in His mouth; and He will strike, rule, and vent His wrath, for He is the *King of Kings*, and *Lord of Lords* (vv. 12–16). Maranatha. Even so. Just like this, come, Lord Jesus!

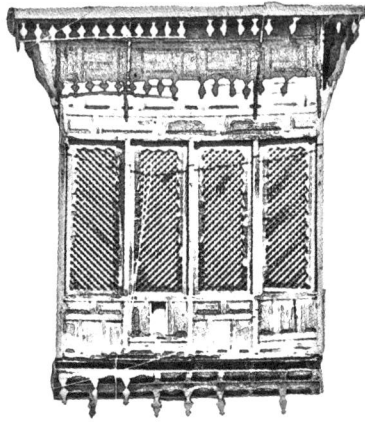

GOOD TO ONE ANOTHER

The great need of the hour is for men and women with life and ministry experience to leave their homes, extended families, and churches in order to make disciples where there are no churches, to glorify Jesus in some of the most challenging places one earth. The painful reality is that those with enough life under their belt to be wise and mature in making disciples are also those whose children now enter college and whose parents enter the last act of life. On one hand mature ministers are pulled by God's call to make disciples of all nations; on the other there are legitimate concerns about the life transitions of loved ones at home.

In *The Magician's Nephew* by C. S. Lewis, a new world, Narnia, is being created by Aslan, the Christ figure central to the story. In the first flush of the new creation, miracle is in the air and trees bear fruit with healing power. A young man named Digory has unfortunately brought evil into this new world by trying to remove a witch from earth. Just as unfortunately back home on earth, Digory's mother is ill and lays dying. Digory stutteringly, asks Aslan for help: "*Please—Mr. Lion—Aslan—Sir....could you—may I—please, will you give me some magic fruit of this country to make Mother well?*"

Aslan seems to ignore the request and instead assigns Digory the mission of collecting a miracle fruit whose seed will produce a tree that will protect Narnia from the evil witch for centuries to come. Aslan asks Digory if he is ready to help.

"Yes", said Digory. He had for a second time some wild idea of saying "I'll try to help you if you'll promise to help my Mother", but he realized in time that the Lion was not at all the sort of person one could try to make bargains with. But when he had said "Yes" he thought of his Mother, and he thought of the great hopes he had had, and how they were all dying away, and a lump came in his throat and tears in his eyes, and he blurted out:

"But please, please—won't you—can't you give me something that will cure Mother?"

Up till then he had been looking at the Lion's great feet and the huge claws on them; now in his despair, he looked up at its face. What he saw surprised him as much as anything in his whole life. For the tawny face was bent down near his own and (wonder of wonders) great shining tears stood in the Lion's eyes. They were such big, bright tears compared with Digory's own that for a moment he felt as if the Lion must really be sorrier about his Mother than he was himself.

"My son, my son", said Aslan, "I know. Grief is great. Only you and I in this land know that yet. Let us be good to one another. *But I have to think of hundreds...you must get the seed from which that tree is to grow.*

Digory completes his mission and resists the temptation to run home with the miracle fruit rather than return it to Aslan. He approaches Aslan and says:

"I've brought you the apple you wanted, sir."

"Well done", said Aslan in a voice that made the earth shake. This time [Digory] found he could look straight into the lion's eyes. He had forgotten his troubles and felt absolutely content...

"Well done, son of Adam", said the Lion again. "For this fruit you have hungered and thirsted and wept. No hand but yours shall sow the seed of the Tree that is to be the protection of Narnia..."

Aslan goes on to explain to Digory that if he had yielded to the temptation to use the fruit to heal his mother (and not return it to Aslan who would use it to help others), it would have worked. His mother would have been healed, for:

"Things always work according to their nature...All get what they want; they do not always like it. Understand, then, that [the fruit] would have healed her; but not to your joy or hers. The day would have come when both you and she would have looked back and said it would have been better to die in that illness."

And Digory could say nothing, for tears choked him and he gave up all hopes of saving his Mother's life; but at the same time he knew that the Lion knew what would have happened, and that there might be things more terrible even than losing someone you love by death. But now Aslan was speaking again, almost in a whisper:

"That is what WOULD have happened, child, with a stolen apple. It is not what will happen now. What I give you now will bring joy."

Aslan sends Digory to harvest fruit from the tree he helped plant. Digory takes that fruit back home and it heals his mother. The story concludes:

For a second Digory could hardly understand. It was as if the whole world had turned inside out and upside down. And then, like someone in a dream, he was walking across to the Tree, and the King and Queen were cheering him and all the creatures were cheering too. He plucked the apple and put it in his pocket. Then he came back to Aslan.

"Please", he said, "may we go home now?" He had forgotten to say "Thank you", but he meant it, and Aslan understood.

For those who sense God is calling them into frontier missions and are counting the cost that immediate family will bear, and for those whose loved ones God is calling to frontier missions and find it a struggle to release them with joy, this fictional tale has ten realities for us.

1. "The Lion was not at all the sort of person one could try to make bargains with..."

When God calls us, it is not a negotiation. When God calls us, He has a plan for our parents and our children. When God calls us, we have but one holy answer: "Yes, Lord!" When God calls us, our natural reasoning mind spins into overdrive and examines every scenario that is problematic. God doesn't ask us to vacate common sense, but He's not bargaining or inquiring politely about our interest and availability. He is commanding, He is giving an order. If God has called you, you must simply say, "Yes."

2. "The Lion must really be sorrier about his Mother than he was himself."

The sacred heart of Jesus abounds with compassion. Sometimes His call surprises us, and in our stunned or even anxious state, we question if He truly cares for the vulnerable ones that His calling will directly affect. If God has called you and you have loved ones who are sick, frail, or vulnerable, remember that God loves them more than you do. God is more perturbed at the cruelty of sickness, the frailty of age, or the deception of evil than you are. He has this. He loves and cares more than you do. He loved and cared before you did. He will love and care when you are gone.

3. "'My son, my son', said Aslan, 'I know. Grief is great. Only you and I in this land know that yet. Let us be good to one another.'"

"Jesus knows all about our struggles. He will guide 'till the day is done. There's not a friend like the lowly Jesus. No, not one, no, not one."[17] The Father does not ask us to do something He has not done. There was sorrow when the Son was sent to earth. There was grief when the Son was nailed to a cross. God knows what it feels like to both send and be sent; in fact, He is the only one who really knows the range of pain and joy. God does not deny that His call is laced with some agony, but He has the moral authority to call anyway, because He has been there and done that. When God's call implies some grief, there is One who understands and sympathizes more than any other.

4. "But I have to think of hundreds."

We easily become myopic, seeing only the needs and griefs, tensions and dangers of our own immediate family. The heavenly Father sees our needs, but He also sees the needs of the world. We are not the only family on earth. There are millions of other families, billions of other persons whom the Father loves, and most of them are far less privileged than our family both spiritually and physically. We can get so consumed with considering the cost to our loved ones if we go that we forget to consider the cost to His loved ones if we don't go. Our families are important to Jesus, and He weeps with us. But we are not more important to Him than other families globally, whole families and nations that have never heard He loves them.

5. "'Well done', said Aslan in a voice that made the earth shake."

There is one approval that outshouts all others. There is one approval that makes us forget the "slings and arrows of outrageous fortune." There is one approval that will life us, give us straight internal posture forever, and surge through us in healing fire. There is one approval that we long for, that we need, that will overwhelm all disapprovals and all criticisms. The "well done" at the end of it all will more than cover the cost of obedience. In that moment we will wonder why we ever struggled to surrender, and we will be so glad that we did. That "well done" is whispered into our souls now when we initially whisper back, "Here I am; send me," but it will be shouted in *that* day before heaven and earth, and matter itself will shake in support of the roared approval.

6. "This time [Digory] found he could look straight into the lion's eyes. He had forgotten his troubles and felt absolutely content…"

When we do say "yes" to God's call, we experience His peace and contentment. This does not mean ease or even healing and all things going smoothly; it just means we forget our trouble as we look into His face. When we say "yes," we do not forget our loved ones and their needs, but we do not fret over them either, for looking into Jesus' face, we trust that He cares and He will take care of those we love. When anxiety rises and returns as we process the call of God, as departure draws near, or after we have deployed and the miles between seem endless, we must look again into His eyes. Fixating on the very real problems doesn't solve them. And looking into His eyes might not solve them either, but it does bring contented peace and trust that He will solve them in His way and time.

7. "All get what they want; they do not always like it. Understand, then, that [the fruit] would have healed her; but not to your joy or hers."

It is somewhat staggering that Almighty God does not coerce us into His service. God doesn't believe in the military draft. He knows the battle is so intense the soldiers must want to fight it. This allowance and expectation of will opens the door for us to refuse His call. We can say "no" when Jesus asks us to leave home and family for the sake of the billions who perish. We have a legitimate choice. We can stay near our children and parents. We can achieve the stability we long for financially. We can provide the security our vulnerable ones want, and there can be joy, laughter, and satisfaction there in the short term. And there can be soul-stifling, spirit-emptying cost in the long term.

8. "There might be things more terrible even than losing someone you love by death."

Goers are not guaranteed return. Every battle has casualties, and this battle is coming to a climax where casualties will only increase. The slow deaths of selfishness, cowardice, sloth, and indulgence when others go to war are far worse than battlefield mortality. As a goer, it will be worse to disobey by staying and chronically live knowing you said "no" to God than to go and suffer those consequences. As a sender, there might be some private joy in keeping your security at home, but that joy shrivels over the years as you watch your loved one shrivel because they could not fulfil what God had called them to do. Watching someone else shrivel because your heart was small or fearful is a special kind of agony.

9. "What I give you now will bring joy."

If we will but trust that God is good (even when He sends to war) and that His plan is wise (even when it seems unimaginably costly), we will experience joy unmatched by our current happiness. In our limited insight, we struggle to see how the joy we have now can be greater when we are separated from the ones we love, especially when it seems so evident that they need us. There is joy in obedience. There is unique joy in costly obedience. And there is unimaginable joy set before us on the other side of endurance. Those who have walked the path before us (saying "yes" to Jesus and paying the cost of separation from family that needs us or think they do) testify from the other side. They beam at us and sing: *"But we never can prove the delights of His love until all on the altar we lay; for the favor He shows, and the joy He bestows, are for them who will trust and obey."*[18]

10. "'Please', he said, 'may we go home now?'"

There is a time to go home. It was true for Digory, and his mother was healed by the fruit he brought when he returned. And it was true for Jesus. He, too, had a glorious return home. Jesus in His goodness asks some missionaries to die on the field and others to serve for a season and return home to care for family. Whatever He chooses for you, embrace. Say "yes" to Jesus, fulfill your assignment faithfully, and then go gladly home. One day, we will all go "home." What a day, glorious day that will be!

COVID, CHURCH PLANTING, AND ENDURING PRESENCE

It is a most interesting phenomenon. Here in Narnia we are seeing more Muslims come to Jesus during the COVID-19 season than at any prior time. This is true in our personal and team experience, *and* it's true across the entire country. Those who elected to endure, despite limitations, have been inundated with the elect who have chosen to seek the Christ of the cross. Those who elected to endure have been reminded that the purposes and passions of God are irrepressible. God promised that representatives of every nation will be gathered in praise around His throne and that His promises shall stand. From March 2020 to present, we have seen more seekers, salvations, baptisms, and fellowships started than in the time we had full liberty of movement. To Christ be the glory in the church and in the world and to all ages.

There are many factors to this harvest. Certainly, Narnians had more time to stay home and search the internet. Certainly, missionaries had more time to pray and intercede. Certainly, Narnians wrestled with mortality and the consequences of death. Certainly, the population is younger, the context liberalized, the religious radicals neutralized, and the spirit of fear broken in general. Certainly, there is an element of both mystery and sovereignty at work. In addition to all these and others, I am encouraged to point out three more.

ACQUISITIVE PRESCRIPTION

In an unusual ruling[19] in April 2017, the Canadian Supreme Court agreed with the old adage that possession is nine-tenths of the law stating that it is "acquisitive prescription that grants the right, not the judgment." Simply put, the court meant that if you park in one place long enough, that parking place becomes yours by the fact of elongated presence, no matter the municipal codes.

I am increasingly convinced that the basic mechanics for church planting among unreached peoples can be simplified down to abiding in Jesus (both personally and corporately), learning language and culture, and faithful long-term presence. God uses so many different people and so many different methods and does so much that in my hubris I disagree with, that I am forced to recognize all over again that the Holy Spirit is indeed the executive of mission and that He speaks through all kinds of donkeys, of whom I am chief. I'm not saying we should act foolishly; neither am I saying that we should do nothing. I *am* saying that God does the work and gets the glory, but for the work to be done the workers must be in the field and remain there, even when the sun burns hot and the storms blow fierce.

When we are intimate with Jesus and pray believing, when we are fluent in language and culture, when we are present despite the challenges and limitations, we are positioned to be used when and how the Master decides. If COVID taught us anything, it was to hold steady at our station, for the Lord of angel armies is not limited and His winds of revival can blow at any time on anybody through any present representative. Acquisitive prescription, possession as nine-tenths of the law. Missionaries remaining in context, come hell or high water, and heaven comes down and glory fills our souls. We possess the people by possessing the land. We are used because we are present and willing. Not present in our own flimsy strength and foolish wisdom, but present with His mighty power (Acts 1:8) as a consequence of being present in His presence (John 15:5).

COMMANDER'S INTENT

There is a military principle called "Commander's Intent" that combines both strategy and tactics in fluid harmony. Those on the ground closest to the action must know what the overall vision is (the strategy) *and* be free to deal with the reality they face when their hands are in the dirt (the tactics). Missionaries tend to be hardheaded, and rightly so. Who else endures in places like Somalia, the Democratic Republic of Congo, Mauritania, Libya, Chad, the Comoros, or Pemba when days are long and fruit is scarce! But those with hard heads are not exempt from submission and collaboration, nor are they excused from working in unity with those that differ from them in personality and approach. The integrity of a diverse workforce can only be maintained by adherence to the uniting vision mixed with freedom to pursue that intent uniquely at the ground/field level.

COVID taught us that there are ways to obey the commission and the intent of Jesus that all nations be included in His family that we had not yet explored. In the Narnian context this meant starting an online service that we ran 84 times each week even though we had no parishioners and no permissions. We also launched short Facebook and Instagram videos that were viewed by about 40,000 viewers every five days. We connected to media partnerships. We did what we could from the confines of curfew and were amazed at what God did from His infinite riches in Jesus. When we started using these means to look for seekers, we found a multitude of seekers looking for us. And because we were present and they were ripe, we held out our hands and they fell into our community. We did nothing other than abide in Jesus, use our Arabic and cultural skills (limited as they are), and stay present. Then God did what God does best.

And then ideas began to flow. What can we do using artificial intelligence? How do we access the surge in gaming? What other creative means can God use to accelerate His mission while the rest of the world slams on the brakes? What out-of-the-box methods are timely for this land? Wouldn't it be ironic if women lead the Saudi revival (even as it appears that's the direction it's heading)? How do we align with that surprise? Commander's Intent is received in the briefing room but refined on the battlefield, but in order to take advantage of the breakthrough, you have to remain in the battle. Things are the clearest where the fighting is the fiercest.

SURVIVING THE FIRST ASSAULT

Another military truism is that no battlefield plan survives the first assault. We attend our trainings and conferences, we listen to missions sermons, we kneel at altars in air-conditioned tabernacles and receive our orders. Then we transition to the fields where the enemy is relentless and the setbacks are innumerable, and we face the reality that constant adjustment to the whispering of the Spirit is the only way we can be nimble enough to counterattack and prevail. These insights are purchased with blood and cannot be borrowed or even learned from others. They must be won with wounds and tears. They must be won by remaining in the war, by being shot at, by being face to face on a daily basis with those who are lost.

A few years ago, my wife and I transitioned back to field work after a seven-year period of a leadership role. During that seven years, in our ivory tower, which was mostly an airplane cabin traveling somewhere to coach, teach, train, or visit someone, we didn't lose our vision—we just lost our nuance. I realized one day what I really wanted to do was be with lost people, work on heart language fluency, make local disciples, and plant indigenous churches. What I didn't want to do was what all my leaders were asking me to do—fill out this report, read this book, go to this training, attend this conference, participate in this phone call, etc. Chastened, I had an epiphany: If I am not face to face on a daily basis with unreached persons, I don't lose my heart; I lose my head. I forget what it actually means to make disciples and plant churches on a daily, non-idealistic basis. I forgot the work isn't complicated; it's just hard.

If we don't endure the first assault by staying in context when the enemy attacks or the situations restrict or the people frustrate, we don't give ourselves enough time to make the necessary field level adjustments that pivot us to victory. In other words, we will be assaulted, but that very assault will reveal how we must respond if we will have the holy stubbornness to endure the attack and the humble sense to adjust our course of action as needed. Remaining on our fields when all is difficult is essential, for it clears our head, trims our excesses, and guides us to where we must focus and attack. We can't attack if we're retreating. We can't attack if we're not present.

COVID is teaching us to attack, and how best we should attack is made clear by being assaulted. What amazing opportunities we miss when we don't stick around to absorb the attacks and then exploit them.

CONCLUSION

Church planting is not complicated; it's just hard. At the end of the day let us abide in Jesus, let us learn language and culture, and let us be present, faithfully enduring no matter the tide. COVID-19 has taught us that on these simple stones, Christ the great Rock will build His church and the gates of hell shall not prevail against us.

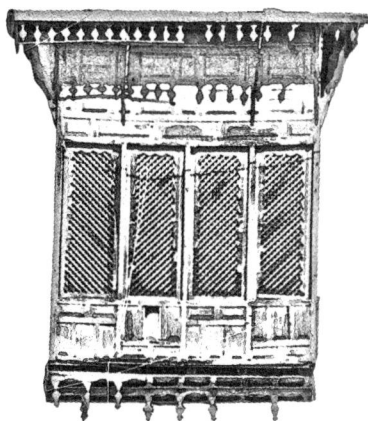

AFTERWORD: TWO YEARS LATER

Two years have passed since I wrote all you have read to this point, and in that time, God has done great things and glorified Himself. We have seen a local church planted and we rejoice that it's growing. We have had multiple wonderful baptism events. Local leaders are being developed, and the body is learning to love one another. Men and women have been saved and baptized of Narnian and a range of other Arab nationalities.

We have seen growth in both aggregate and affinity models. In the aggregate approach a church consisting of believers with no prior relationship with one another before they were saved now meets weekly. On the affinity side, there is another group of believers that largely consists of one family (twenty-five members saved as of August 2021). The family has also reached out beyond their extended family so that we are now seeing third spiritual generation believers.

A church being planted in such a (relatively) short time I attribute to the following factors

1. God's sovereignty

God does what He chooses when He chooses, and He is choosing in this moment of time to do unprecedented things in this land. There are no accidents with Him. Others around the country are seeing similar fruit—fruit that has not been seen in this land for 1,400 years. God is working in such a way that it's clear no credit goes to any strategy, person, tool, agency, or idea. God is saving Muslims to Himself. God is moving by His Spirit.

2. "Others have done the hard work."

Whether the pioneers of old or the faithful workers who labored in Narnia for the last few decades when the pressure was much more intense than it is today, we recognize that we have merely entered the race long after others gained great ground by blood, sweat, and tears (John 4:38). We honor those who have gone before us, both in the distant and recent past. We honor those who work tirelessly now in the present, gliding under the radar in Christlike humility. There is no harvest outside of someone somewhere having labored. We honor these quiet, noble, and faithful others who have gone before us.

3. Abiding in Jesus

Jesus really does honor His promise in John 15:5. When we abide in Him, when we spend extravagant time in His presence reading the Bible and praying, He does indeed help us bear the fruit of disciples. The COVID-19 virus forced us into isolation and empowered long, lingering times of abiding in Jesus. A forty-day time of prayer and fasting furthered the opportunity to look to Him believing. When in simple faith we trust Him, He does magnificent things. Abiding in Jesus is indeed the first priority and the main methodology of missions. And it so sweet.

4. Language and culture fluency

While we are not fluent, we did have twenty-seven years of Arabic learning and ministry experience. We could immediately talk, witness, disciple, and teach. We could read and write the many text messages back and forth and listen to audio messages and send them. The ability to communicate and comprehend the local heart language and to be culturally aware in context has been of immeasurable value and a critical contributor to ministry fruitfulness.

5. Presence and endurance

We were here and we stayed here during challenging times. The endurance part is more theoretical as we have only been here one year, and the challenges have not yet been stringent, but the point remains. We did nothing special, yet we were available and willing to meet, teach, disciple, gather, and baptize (taking some risks others did not want to take). We were here and willing. God did the work.

6. Partnership and teamwork

There is a great spirit of unity in this land. Our team members are the most incredible we have ever had. They speak Arabic, serve tirelessly, pray faithfully, love loyally, and rejoice always. The wider fellowship of God's team cheers each other on, rejoices in others' success, and has a learning, humble spirit.

7. Media

God has used the internet age to penetrate every secret place with His gospel. Follow-up systems are in place. We started online evangelistic videos and an online service that runs eighty-four times each week. We were trained to do face-to-face follow-up through a partner missions agency. Practically every person we have led to the Lord and are currently discipling came through these media contacts. Others did the hard work of filtering these seekers through the early stages and then we received them when they were ready and eager to follow

Jesus and join His community. Almost weekly there is a new brother or sister coming to Christ.

8. Prayer

Prayer partners have adopted one-hour prayer vigils during the online services. Other entities and prayer ministries have been praying faithfully over this land for decades. God's people globally are praying for this land and the Muslim world with an intensity and faith not seen before. God is answering all these prayers.

9. The stronghold of fear has been broken.

The God-ordained leaders of this land have made courageous, historic decisions to open up the country and liberalize society. This freedom has led to evil things (homosexuality, atheism, license, etc.) as well as good. But all the same, the land and people are emerging from centuries of crippling fear and restrictive laws. This has led to searching, questions, open minds, and open hearts. Believers are growing in courage, sharing their faith, suffering for Jesus, and declaring He is worth it.

10. Risk

With full respect to the obedience of others, we felt led to try some things that were risky, that were a little different than the common and historic approach in Narnia. I am not saying that the others were wrong; we just sensed that our obedience to Jesus was to be bold in our church identity and wide open in our approaches and testimony. We took risks and operated outside some conventional norms knowing that it might mean expulsion or other consequences. In the necessary tension between proclamation and longevity, we felt our obedience was to err on the side of bold, frequent, and even public proclamation, allegiance, and identity.

By no means do I want to imply that there is a formula to follow. I merely want to extend hope. God will indeed plant His church.

He has done so here in this most challenging of contexts in the last couple years. God can and will plant His church wherever you plant yourself, faithfully committed to the glory of God, the power of the Holy Spirit, biblical principles, and sound missiology. Merciful to work through us, He yet reserves the right to work despite us. Even when we do dumb things, He is faithful to glorify Himself. Glory to His name!

DICK BROGDEN

FEBRUARY 2022

ENDNOTES

[1] Tim Throckmorton. "But If Not." *Circleville Herald.* https://www.circlevilleherald.com/comment/columns/but-if-not/article_9501e7de-5131-5f24-b78e-69e48586969f.html (accessed March 31, 2020).

[2] Excerpt from *Missionary God, Missionary Bible.* Dick Brogden. Springfield, MO: Abide Publishers, 2020.

[3] Herbert A. Simon. "Models of My Life Quotes." https://www.goodreads.com/work/quotes/382850-models-of-my-life (accessed June 30, 2020).

[4] Jack Weatherford. *Genghis Khan and the Making of the Modern World.* New York City: Broadway Books, 2005. 86–96.

[5] John Owen. *The Holy Spirit: Works of John Owen, Volume 3.* London: William H. Goold, 1764.

[6] Hymns With a Message. "So Send I You." https://barryshymns.blogspot.com/2016/05/so-send-i-you.html (accessed April 26, 2020).

[7] Ibid.

[8] Used by permission of the author. Roland Muller. *The Message, The Messenger, and The Community: Three Critical Issues for the Cross-Cultural Church Planter.* Fourth Edition. Independent Scholars Press, 2016. 210–211.

[9] This protocol is in place so that the husband knows his family is safe and he can focus on his situation without worry about others or being susceptible to threats and lies about them.

[10] "In Times Like These." Copyright 1944. Renewal 1972 by Ruth Caye Jones. Assigned to Singspiration, Division of Zondervan Corporation.

[11] Stuart Scott. *From Pride to Humility: A Biblical Perspective.* Bemidji, MN: Focus Publishing, 2002.

[12] "Sir Andrew Barton." https://www.theotherpages.org/poems/poem-z4.html (accessed on May 5, 2020).

[13] "Jesus Is a Wonderful Saviour." https://www.recisydney.org/2013/05/jesus-is-a-wonderful-saviour/ (accessed June 30, 2020).

[14] From Shakespeare's *Henry V*: "Once more unto the breach, dear friends, once more;.... In peace there's nothing so becomes a man as modest stillness and humility: But when the blast of war blows in our ears, then imitate the action of the tiger;.... Fathers that, like so many Alexanders, have in these parts from morn till even fought and sheathed their swords for lack of argument: Dishonour not your mothers; now attest that those whom you call'd fathers did beget you. Be copy now to men of grosser blood, and teach them how to war.... For there is none of you so mean and base, that hath

not noble lustre in your eyes. I see you stand like greyhounds in the slips straining upon the start. The game's afoot...."

[15] "Given the way he prepares, Tom Brady won't be slowing down anytime soon." Greg Bishop. *Sports Illustrated.* December 10, 2014. https://www.si.com/nfl/2014/12/10/tom-brady-new-england-patriots-age-fitness (accessed May 5, 2020).

[16] Live Dead Arab World Retreat. Tim Enloe sermon. Malaga, Spain. January 2017.

[17] "There's Not a Friend Like the Lowly Jesus." Hymn by Johnson Oatman, Jr. https://hymnary.org/text/theres_not_a_friend_like_the_lowly_jesus (accessed June 30, 2020).

[18] "Trust and Obey." Hymn by John Henry Sammis. https://library.timelesstruths.org/music/Trust_and_Obey/ (accessed June 30, 2020).

[19] "Supreme Court ruling: Possession is 9/10 of law -- even for parking spots." CTV News. https://montreal.ctvnews.ca/supreme-court-ruling-possession-is-9-10-of-law-even-for-parking-spots-1.3357430 (accessed October 25, 2020).

Also available from

LIVE | DEAD

The Live Dead Journal

Live Dead The Journey

Live Dead The Story

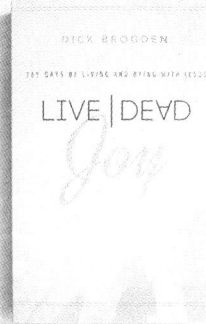

Live Dead Joy

The Live Dead Journal:
Her Heart Speaks

Diario: Vivir Muerto

Live Dead Life

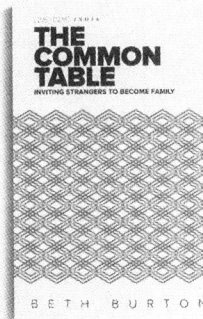

Live Dead India:
The Common Table

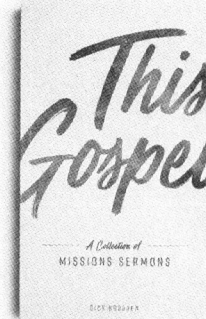

This Gospel

Leading Muslims to Jesus

Live Dead Together

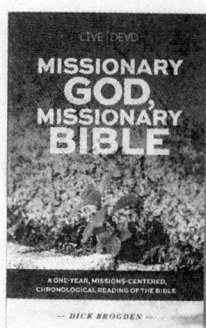

Missionary God, Missionary Bible

Cannibal Island

Hunter and Hunted

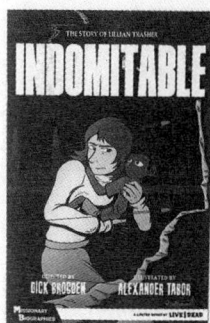

Indomitable

Check out our full line of Live Dead books at
www.abidepublishers.com which include:

Individual and group devotionals
Graphic novel biographies of missionaries
Challenging and inspiring stories from work among unreached people